WHAT MATTERS NOW

WHAT MATTERS NOW

HOW TO WIN IN A WORLD OF RELENTLESS CHANGE, FEROCIOUS COMPETITION, AND UNSTOPPABLE INNOVATION

Gary Hamel

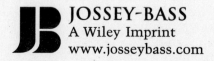
JOSSEY-BASS
A Wiley Imprint
www.josseybass.com

Published by Jossey-Bass
A Wiley Imprint

One Montgomery Street, Suite 1200, San Francisco, CA 94104-4594—www.josseybass.com

Jossey-Bass books and products are available through most bookstores. To contact Jossey-Bass directly call our Customer Care Department within the U.S. at 800-956-7739, outside the U.S. at 317-572-3986, or fax 317-572-4002.

Wiley publishes in a variety of print and electronic formats and by print-on-demand. Some material included with standard print versions of this book may not be included in e-books or in print-on-demand. If this book refers to media such as a CD or DVD that is not included in the version you purchased, you may download this material at http://booksupport.wiley.com. For more information about Wiley products, visit www.wiley.com.

Library of Congress Cataloging-in-Publication Data

Hamel, Gary.
 What matters now : how to win in a world of relentless change, ferocious competition, and unstoppable innovation / Gary Hamel. – 1st ed.
  p. cm.
  Includes index.
 ISBN 978-1-118-12082-8 (cloth), 978-1-118-21915-7 (ebk), 978-1-118-21916-4 (ebk), 978-1-118-21908-9 (ebk)
 1. Management. 2. Organizational change. 3. Organizational effectiveness. 4. Strategic planning. I. Title.
 HD31.H253 2012
 658.4'012–dc23

2011042387

Printed in the United States of America
FIRST EDITION

HB Printing 10 9 8 7 6 5 4 3 2 1

CONTENTS

To my brothers,
Dr. Loren Hamel and Dr. Lowell Hamel,
for reasons they know well.

PREFACE

This is not a book about one thing. It's not a 288-page dissertation on leadership, teams, or motivation. Instead, its a multi-faceted agenda for building organizations that can win in a world of relentless change, ferocious competition, and unstoppable innovation.

This is not a book about doing better. It's not a manual for people who want to tinker at the margins of their organization. Instead, it's an impassioned plea to reinvent management as we know it—to rethink the fundamental assumptions we have about capitalism, institutions, and life at work.

This is not a book that fetes today's winners. It's not a celebration of companies that have been doing great *so far*. Instead, it's a blueprint for creating organizations that are fit for the future and fit for human beings.

Obviously, there are lots of things that matter now, including social media, "big data," emerging markets, virtual collaboration, risk management, open innovation, and sustainability. But in a world of fractured certainties and battered trust, some things matter more than others. While the challenges facing organizations are limitless, leadership bandwidth isn't. That's why you have to be clear about what *really* matters now. So ask yourself: what are the fundamental, make-or-break challenges that will determine whether your organization thrives or dives in the years ahead? For me, five issues are paramount: values, innovation, adaptability, passion, and ideology. Here's my logic for putting these topics front and center . . .

- **Values:** In a free market economy, there will always be excesses, but in recent years, rapacious bankers and unprincipled CEOs have seemed hell-bent on setting new records for egocentric irresponsibility. In a just world, they would be sued for slandering capitalism. Not surprisingly, large corporations are now among society's least trusted institutions. As trust has waned, the regulatory burden on business has grown. Reversing these trends will require nothing less than a moral renaissance in business. The interests of stakeholders are not always aligned, but on one point they seem unanimous: values matter now more than ever.
- **Innovation:** In a densely connected global economy, successful products and strategies are quickly copied. Without relentless innovation, success is fleeting. Nevertheless, there's not one company in a hundred that has made innovation everyone's job, every day. In most organizations, innovation still happens "despite the system" rather than because of it. That's a problem, because innovation is the *only* sustainable strategy for creating long-term value. After a decade of *talking* about innovation, it's time to close the gap between rhetoric and reality. To do so, we'll need to recalibrate priorities and retool mindsets. That won't be easy, but we have no choice, since innovation matters now more than ever.
- **Adaptability:** As change accelerates, so must the pace of strategic renewal. Problem is, deep change is almost always crisis-driven; it's tardy, traumatic and expensive. In most organizations, there are too many things that perpetuate the past and too few that encourage proactive change. The "party of the past" is usually more powerful than the "party of the future." That's why incumbents typically lose out to upstarts who are unencumbered by the past. In a world where industry leaders can

become laggards overnight, the only way to sustain success is to reinvent it. That's why adaptability matters now more than ever.

• **Passion:** Innovation and the will to change are the products of passion. They are the fruits of a righteous discontent with the status quo. Sadly, the average workplace is a buzz killer. Petty rules, pedestrian goals, and pyramidal structures drain the emotional vitality out of work. Maybe that didn't matter in the knowledge economy, but it matters enormously in the creative economy. Customers today expect the exceptional, but few organizations deliver it. The problem is not a lack of competence, but a lack of ardor. In business as in life, the difference between "insipid" and "inspired" is passion. With returns to mediocrity rapidly declining, passion matters now more than ever.

• **Ideology:** Why do our organizations seem less adaptable, less innovative, less spirited, and less noble than the people who work within them? What is it that makes them *in*human? The answer: a management ideology that deifies control. Whatever the rhetoric to the contrary, control is the principal preoccupation of most managers and management systems. While conformance (to budgets, performance targets, operating policies, and work rules) creates economic value, it creates less than it used to. What creates value today is the unexpectedly brilliant product, the wonderfully weird media campaign, and the entirely novel customer experience. Trouble is, in a regime where control reigns supreme, the unique gets hammered out. The choice is stark: we can resign ourselves to the fact that our organizations will never be more adaptable, innovative, or inspiring than they are right now, or we can search for an alternative to the creed of control. Better business processes and better business models are not enough—we need better business principles. That's why ideology matters now more than ever.

These are big, thorny issues. To tackle them, we have to venture beyond the familiar precincts of "management-as-usual." These issues are also nuanced and variegated. So rather than reduce them to a few, trivial heuristics ("get everyone in the boat rowing in the same direction"), I've teed up a quintet of complementary perspectives on each of these crucial topics. If you're following the math, that means twenty-five chapters. Don't worry—they're (mostly) short and modular. You don't have to slog through all 288 pages. You can dip in and out as you like, depending on your interests. It's not a seven-course banquet; it's a tapas bar. Enjoy.

WHAT MATTERS NOW

SECTION 1

Values Matter Now

PUTTING FIRST THINGS FIRST 1.1

If you are a leader at any level in any organization, you are a steward—
of careers, capabilities, resources, the environment, and organizational
values. Unfortunately, not every manager is a wise steward. Some
behave like mercenaries—by mortgaging the future to inflate short-term
earnings, by putting career ahead of company, by exploiting vulnerable
employees, by preying on customer ignorance, or by manipulating
the political system in ways that reduce competition. What matters
now, more than ever, is that managers embrace the responsibilities of
stewardship.

To my mind, stewardship implies five things:

1. *Fealty:* A propensity to view the talents and treasure at one's command
   as a trust rather than as the means for personal gain.

2. *Charity:* A willingness to put the interests of others ahead of one's own.

3. *Prudence:* A commitment to safeguard the future even as one takes advantage of the present.

4. *Accountability:* A sense of responsibility for the systemic consequences of one's actions.

5. *Equity:* A desire to ensure that rewards are distributed in a way that corresponds to contribution rather than power.

These virtues seem to have been particularly scarce in recent years, as we've careened from Enron's devious accounting to the financial chicanery at Parmalat, from Shell's overstated reserves to BP's derelict safety standards, from Bernie Madoff's epic scam to Hewlett-Packard's spying scandal, from the predatory loan practices at Countrywide Financial to the disastrous excesses at Lehman Brothers, and from India's corruption-marred sale of wireless spectrum to the firestorm ignited by News Corp's phone hacking. Despite these and other dirty deeds, I doubt that today's tycoons are any less principled than their counterparts in earlier decades. The German word *raubritter,* or "robber baron," dates back to the Middle Ages, and was first applied to grasping toll collectors along the Rhine River. In the nineteenth century, the term was revived as a fitting epithet for America's buccaneering and occasionally rapacious industrialists.

If twenty-first-century leaders seem especially amoral, it's because a globally matrixed economy magnifies the effects of executive malfeasance. Consider the sovereign debt crisis that engulfed Europe in 2011. In a world of nationally constrained institutions, the credit problems of a country like Greece would be a small-scale catastrophe. Not so in an interconnected world where avaricious strategies are quickly aped and imprudent risks spread like a virus. It was these dynamics that led French and German banks to dump more than $900 billion into the barely solvent economies of the "PIGS"—Portugal, Ireland, Greece, and Spain. Turns out American bankers aren't the only ones who are susceptible to moral hazard. But it's not just bankers we need to worry about. In a networked world, lax security standards can imperil the confidential information of a hundred million consumers or more. A failure to exercise due diligence over a vendor can result in a worldwide food contamination scare. And a decision that puts quality at risk can provoke a global recall.

The critical point is this: because the decisions of global actors are uniquely consequential, their ethical standards must be uniquely exemplary. It's easy to feel sorry for Mark Hurd, the former Hewlett-Packard CEO who was pushed from his perch over what seemed to be a relatively minor infraction of HP's ethics rules. I don't know whether justice was done in that particular case, but I do know it's a good thing when influential leaders are held to high standards.

If the global economy amplifies the impact of ethical choices, so, too, does the Web. Word-of-mouse can quickly turn a local misdemeanor into a global cause célèbre. Nike, Apple, and Dell are just a few of the companies that have been castigated for turning a blind eye to the subpar employment practices of their Asian suppliers. There are no dark corners on the Web—miscreants will be outed.

The Web is also producing a new sort of global consciousness, a heightened sense of our interconnectedness. Increasingly we understand that we live on the same planet, breathe the same air, and share the same oceans. In civic and commercial life, we expect the same high standards of equity and fair play to apply everywhere, and are offended when they don't. And thanks to the Web, that displeasure can quickly congeal into a global chorus of indignation. Around the world, ethical expectations, if not behaviors, are leveling up.

The intermeshing of big business and big government is another force bringing values to the fore. As citizens and consumers, we're smart enough to know that when lobbyists and legislators sit down to a lavish meal, our interests won't be on the menu. Instinctively, we know that democracy and the economy do better when power isn't concentrated, but since it often is, we must do whatever we can to ensure that those occupying positions of trust are, in fact, trustworthy.

For all these reasons, we need a values revolution in business—and it can't come soon enough. In a 2010 Gallup study, only 15% of respondents rated the ethical standards of executives as "high" or "very high." (Nurses came in first at 81%, corporate lobbyists last at 7%.)[1]

This lack of trust poses an existential threat to capitalism. Companies do *not* have inalienable rights granted to them by a Creator; their rights are socially constructed, and can be *re*constructed any time society feels so inclined. (A fact made abundantly clear with the passage of the Sarbanes-Oxley Act of 2002 and the Dodd-Frank Act of 2010—two U.S. statutes designed to dramatically curtail corporate prerogatives.)

The good news is that the values revolution has already started. No one's waiting for executives to have an epiphany. One telling statistic: Between 2005 and 2010, U.S. assets invested in "socially responsible" funds (as defined by the Social Investment Forum Foundation) grew by 34%, whereas total assets under management grew by only 3%. Today, of the more than $25 trillion under management in the United States, one dollar in eight is invested in socially oriented funds.[2] And there are other harbingers. A decade ago, no car magazine would have noted a vehicle's CO_2 emissions, but now most do—at least in Europe. A decade ago, "Fair Trade" wouldn't have been a marketing pitch, now it is. A decade ago, few would have paid attention to executive pay, now millions do.

Given all that, the question for you and your organization is simple: Are you going to be a values leader or a values laggard? It's easy to excoriate fraudster CEOs and greedy bankers, but what about *you*? (And what about *me*?) We can't expect others to be good stewards if we're not. Though some executives cast a bigger moral shadow than others, we must all shoulder the responsibility for protecting capitalism from ethical vandals.

From Adam Smith to Ayn Rand, the defenders of capitalism have argued that the common good is maximized when every individual is free to pursue his or her own self-interest. I believe this to be true, with one essential caveat. Like nuclear fission, self-interest works only as long as there's a containment vessel—a set of ethical principles that ensures enlightened self-interest doesn't melt down into unbridled selfishness. Unfortunately, the groundwater of business is now heavily contaminated with the runoff from morally blinkered egomania.

As parents, we expend enormous energy in socializing our children. While a rebellious teenage son might believe his interests are best served by dropping out of school and moving in with his girlfriend, his parents are likely to have a different view. That's what parents do—they teach their children to become stewards of their own lives.

Problem is, if you're a manager or an executive, your stewardship obligations extend far beyond yourself and your family. Yet in recent years many business leaders have blithely dodged those responsibilities. That's why executives languish near the bottom of the trust table.

So before you go any further in this book, ask yourself, am I really a *steward*?

1. What about *fealty*? Like the executor of an estate, do I see myself as a fiduciary?
2. What about *charity*? Like a self-sacrificing parent, am I willing to put the needs of others first?
3. What about *prudence*? Like a committed conservationist, do I feel responsible for protecting and improving the legacy I have inherited?
4. What about *accountability*? Like the captain of a vessel, do I understand I am responsible for my wake—for the distant ripples created by my decisions?
5. What about *equity*? Like a conscientious mediator, am I truly committed to finding the most equitable outcome for all?

If you're struggling to think through what this means in practice, here's something that might help. For years I taught a second-year MBA course at the London Business School. In the final session, I typically offered my students some parting advice.

When you take your first post-MBA job, I'd tell them, assume that the following things are true:

First, your widowed mother has invested her life's savings in your company. She's the only shareholder and that investment is her only asset. Obviously, you'll do everything you can to make sure she has a secure and happy retirement. That's why the idea of sacrificing the long-term for a quick payout will never occur to you.

Second, your boss is an older sibling. You'll always be respectful, but you won't hesitate to offer frank advice when you think it's warranted—and you'll never suck up.

Third, your employees are childhood chums. You'll always give them the benefit of the doubt and will do whatever you can to smooth their path. When needed, though, you'll remind them that friendship is a reciprocal responsibility. You'll never treat them as human "resources."

Fourth, your children are the company's primary customers. You want to please and delight them. That means you'll go to the mat with anyone who suggests you should deceive or take advantage of them. You'll never exploit a customer.

Fifth, you're independently wealthy. You work because you want to, not because you have to—so you will never sacrifice your integrity for a promotion or a glowing performance review. You'll quit before you compromise.

These assumptions, if acted upon, will help nourish the seeds of stewardship in your business life and, by example, in the lives of others.

As we struggle with the uniquely complex challenges of the twenty-first century, it is good to remind ourselves that what matters most now is what's always mattered: *our bedrock values*.

LEARNING FROM THE CRUCIBLE OF CRISIS

As I write this, the U.S. economy is sputtering. Though the Great Recession technically ended two years ago, unemployment remains stubbornly high and economic growth is distressingly feeble. The percentage of the U.S. population working is at a 25-year low and with 125,000 new job seekers entering the workforce each month, it may take a decade for the United States to get back to prerecession employment levels. A number of European states are in similar straits: property prices have tumbled, unemployment has soared, and growth has stalled.

What we are witnessing is the mother of all hangovers—the inevitable and entirely predictable outcome of an epically irresponsible borrowing binge. Unfortunately, in this case, the boozers weren't hard-drinking college kids on a Fort Lauderdale beach. They were the captains of capitalism. Federal Reserve policymakers were the distillers, congressional legislators the rumrunners, and big bank CEOs the bartenders. Sure, a lot of ordinary folks bellied up to the bar of cheap debt, but they were egged on by the "adults." If you're looking for an analogy, picture a high school dance where parents and teachers are pouring shots at an open bar.

It's difficult to imagine grown-ups doing anything so reckless, but then, a decade ago, it would have been difficult to imagine the world's smartest financiers and policymakers abetting financial idiocy on a global scale.

The worst economic downturn since the 1930s wasn't a banking crisis, a credit crisis, or a mortgage crisis—it was a moral crisis, willful negligence *in extremis*. Few of us are surprised when we witness base behaviors in lofty places (like a "sexting" congressman), but the implosion of America's investment banking industry revealed Biblical scale transgressions. One is reminded of the Exodus account in which the entire Jewish nation abandons Yahweh to bow before a golden calf.

Every institution rests on moral footings, and there is no force that can erode those foundations more rapidly than a cataract of self-interest. In *The Radicalism of the American Revolution*, Gordon Wood notes repeatedly that the country's founders regarded "disinterest" as a noble virtue. As they set about inventing the United States of America, that first crop of patriots endeavored to detach themselves from selfish concerns over personal gain and loss. One would struggle in vain, I think, to find evidence of "disinterest" in the behavior of Lehman Brothers' Dick Fuld, Merrill Lynch's Stan O'Neal, or any of the other banking chieftains who pillaged the U.S. economy for personal gain.

While much has been written about the antecedents of the banking debacle (much of it opaque and tedious), it is worth taking a few moments to perform a quick moral autopsy. This will necessitate a brief rehearsal of the facts. The goal here is not to heap more blame on the bankers (well, it's not the *only* goal), but rather to understand what happens when self-interest slips the knot of its ethical moorings. It is easy to be contemptuous of the bankers and regulators who precipitated the crisis, but I am not so sure that you and I would have behaved much differently if we had been faced with the same temptations. By all means let's hold the bankers responsible (Someone? Please?), but let's also use their calamitous misadventure to do a little moral reflection of our own.

So, what happened? Let's focus first on the proximate causes of the disaster.

EASY MONEY

After the dotcom bust in 2000, the U.S. Federal Reserve, under the leadership of first Alan Greenspan and then Ben Bernanke, drove borrowing costs down to disastrously low levels. Dirt-cheap money encouraged U.S. consumers to gorge on debt, dramatically increasing the risk of widespread mortgage defaults.

Asian savings also played a role. By pegging the yuan to the U.S. dollar, Chinese authorities kept exports high and internal consumption low, thus building up huge reserves. These had to be recycled, and a lot of that money went into buying mortgage-backed securities.

SECURITIZATION

By bundling mortgages into "collateralized debt obligations" and selling those CDOs to third parties, bankers were able to move dodgy loans off their books. Between 2005 and 2007, more than 85% of all U.S. mortgages were securitized.

Historically, lending had been tied to deposit taking. By taking the brakes off fund-raising, securitization led to an unprecedented boom in mortgage lending. The net result: a serious decline in lending standards. As banks competed their way to the bottom, they handed out loans to just about anyone with a pulse.

As it turned out, securitization didn't inoculate banks from the risks of subprime lending, since many banks built up large CDO holdings via off-balance sheet "Special Investment Vehicles." Commercial banks also lent billions of dollars to the biggest buyers of CDOs, investment banks and hedge funds.

INSURANCE

Credit default swaps (CDS) made it possible for CDO investors to protect themselves from a housing collapse—in theory. As with all insurance products, underwriting prudence requires a rich seam of historical data, but given the unprecedented growth of the subprime market, and the concomitant decline in lending standards, past default rates had no predictive value. As a result, CDO insurers like AIG severely underpriced the risks of a default debacle. This error was multiplied when speculators dramatically upped the demand for CDS contracts. Amazingly, the world ended up with $62 trillion of credit default swaps and no organized trading exchange.

COMPLEXITY

The new financial instruments cooked up by the banks were mind-bendingly complex. Mortgages were packaged together, partitioned into tranches, and then sold. Many CDOs were bundles of other CDOs. These convolutions made it hard for investors and ratings agencies to decipher the real risks.

It should be noted that all this complexity didn't happen by accident. Bankers love complexity, as it creates the illusion of value-added and provides a veil behind which they can hide their porcine fees. It's even better when a financial product isn't publicly traded, as that makes it harder for a buyer to discern its real value. Unfortunately, as the world came to realize, complexity can also obscure risk.

LEVERAGE

In a bull market, the greater the leverage, the better the returns. That's why the biggest buyers of mortgage-backed securities borrowed heavily to bulk up their portfolios. With leverage ratios of 30-to-1 and higher, most of the major investment banks made massive bets on a continued rise in U.S. home prices. While this unprecedented leverage amped their returns on the upside, it obscenely compounded risks on the downside. In their rush to profit from the subprime bonanza, many bankers seemed to forget that leverage is always a double-edged sword—sooner or later it cuts both ways.

Unfortunately, much of that leverage came from loans made by commercial banks. When defaults began to accelerate, those banks started calling in their loans, forcing investment banks and hedge funds to deleverage in a down market. To do so, these institutions had to dump other assets, which sent the stock market tumbling.

ILLIQUIDITY

Because of their complexity and novelty, there was no real secondary market for many CDOs, so when things started to go south, it was hard for cash-strapped institutions to reduce their exposures.

Without a well-functioning secondary market, buyers had no way of discovering the true value of the exotic instruments they held, nor was it easy for investors and regulators to gauge the real threat to bank balance sheets. In the absence of reliable pricing data, bankers had no choice but to take punishing write-downs on their mortgage-backed securities.

Many senior bankers claimed that the subprime crisis could not have been anticipated—that it was, as the chairman of the Financial Crisis Inquiry Commission scathingly put it, an "immaculate calamity."[1] I disagree. Anyone who was watching the unprecedented run up in U.S. house prices (see Figure 1.2.1) had to know that a crisis was looming. Indeed, in 2005 I bought a financial derivative from my broker that was, in effect, a bet against the housing market. The instrument was linked to a stock index that tracked the performance of America's largest home builders. For every 1 percent decline in the value of the index, the value of my investment rose by 3 percent. The instrument expired in 2008 and paid off handsomely. My only regret is that I didn't bet bigger.

Figure 1.2.1 S&P/Case-Shiller Index of U.S. House Prices[*]

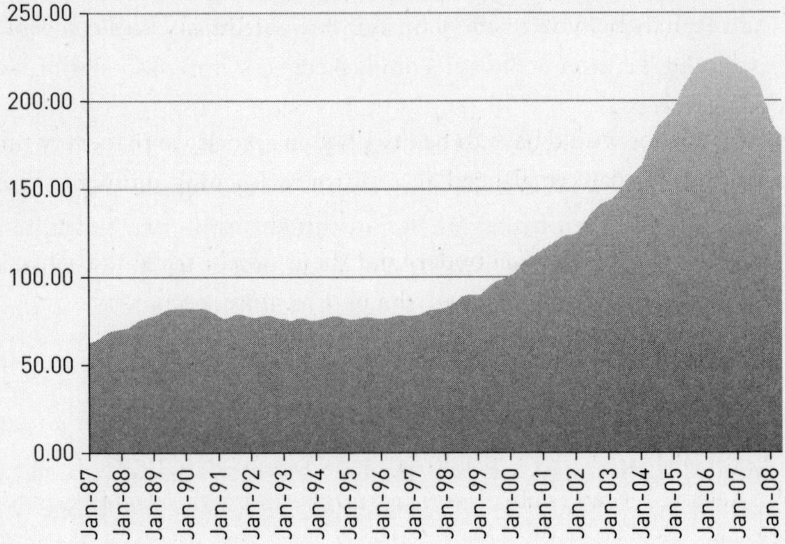

*January 2000 prices are indexed to 100.

As I watched the crisis unfold, my initial reaction was disbelief. How could so many super-smart people be so wrong? Once the poop hit the fan, pundits of every stripe came forward with their preferred remedy (turn the Fed into a super-regulator, create living wills for the biggest banks, dramatically raise capital reserves, limit banker bonuses, and so on). At the time, I wondered if the solution might not be simpler. What about tattooing a few carefully chosen lines onto the forehead of every banker who had received bailout money:

Alchemy doesn't work. What was true for Isaac Newton all those centuries ago is still true: you can't turn dross (garbage loans) into gold (triple A–rated securities) no matter how clever you are.

Things that can't go on forever usually don't. If an extrapolated trend produces ludicrous results (like million-dollar starter homes), it will soon reverse itself—so don't bet it won't.

Risks and returns are always correlated. Maybe there's someone out there who can produce a positive "alpha" year after year, but it probably isn't you or anyone you know.

Stupidity is contagious. Reflect on the mad obsession with leverage and complexity that consumed you and your banking buddies. Smart as you may be, you're every bit as vulnerable to silly fads as Japanese schoolgirls.

The tattoos would have to be inscribed in reverse, so that every time a self-admiring banker glanced at a mirror, a teaching moment would occur.

Tats or no, bankers *do* understand these simple truths, so why did Wall Street's finest fail to heed them? Or more pointedly, why did they so completely abandon their responsibilities as the guardians of capitalism's most important citadels?

As it unfolded, the subprime banking crisis revealed a Shakespearian catalog of moral turpitude. It was a perfect storm of human delinquency. Deceit, hubris, myopia, greed, and denial were all luridly displayed.

DECEIT

We now know that a good many mortgage bankers, the folks who made those subprime loans, conspired with first-time borrowers to overstate incomes and understate debts. In addition, deceptive sales tactics and a lack of disclosure encouraged many borrowers to take on loans they'd never be able to pay off. In 2009, the FBI investigated 2,794 cases of suspected mortgage fraud, up from 721 cases in 2005.[2] The simple lesson: any financial instrument that is built atop lies and misrepresentations will be flimsy at its core.

HUBRIS

The Wall Street rocket scientists who were charged with packaging subprime offal into marketable securities dramatically overestimated their ability to parse and partition risk. They would learn to their sorrow that distributing risk is not the same thing as eliminating it, particularly when that risk is compounded by nose-bleed leverage. Convinced of their own genius, they failed to distinguish between genuine sophistication and mere sophistry.

MYOPIA

In creating and pricing all those brave, new "structured products," Wall Street's whiz kids relied on complicated financial models to estimate potential risks. Because the models were based on recent trend data, covering a time frame when asset values had arced ever higher, they failed to anticipate the possibility of a major slump in asset values. Lenders and investment bankers could argue that the U.S. housing market had never been through a steep and prolonged nationwide slump, but then again, neither had there ever been a run-up in house values like the one that occurred between 2000 and 2007. Again, there's a lesson here: just because you can't remember the last hundred-year storm doesn't mean one isn't headed your way.

GREED

It goes without saying that everyone on the subprime ship of folly was earning big fees: the mortgage originators who approved all those "ninja" loans (no income, no job, no assets), the Wall Street bankers who bundled them into securities, the hedge funds who bought the new-fangled instruments and charged their clients big bucks for delivering above-average returns, and the rating agencies whose thirst for new business compromised their once-hallowed objectivity. The lure of multimillion dollar bonuses turned sober-suited bankers into frenzied speculators. As ever, greed proved to be a tireless cheerleader of human folly.

DENIAL

Organizations are occasionally overtaken by truly unpredictable events. This was the case for the U.S. airline industry in the aftermath of the 9/11 terrorist attacks. Usually, however, stupefaction is the product of denial. Companies get caught out by the future not because it's unpredictable, but because it's unpalatable. Unwilling to face facts, just about everyone who was financially vested in the housing boom chose to ignore the inevitable. To a degree, the future is always opaque, but it's a lot more so when you shut your eyes.

The subprime debacle revealed that America had a financial system of the bankers, by the bankers, and for the bankers—consumers and shareholders be damned. To a large extent this is *still* true. No high-ranking banker is in jail, the biggest banks have grown even bigger, bonuses are once again setting records, and at this moment, more than 3,000 banking lobbyists are hard at work in Washington trying to water down the reforms that were enacted in the wake of the crisis.[3]

This lack of accountability is baffling until one realizes that many of the watchdogs who were supposed to guard the economy from bankerly excesses—individuals like former SEC Chairman Christopher Cox and U.S. Representative Barney Frank, chair of the House Financial Services Committee from 2007 to 2011—were ardent coconspirators.

Here, too, one witnesses Faustian sell-outs and a feckless dereliction of duty.

As taxpayers and citizens, we expected the government to protect the economy from unsustainable booms and busts. Instead, it provided the monetary fuel for an unprecedented housing boom.

As taxpayers and citizens, we expected the government to avoid creating economically perverse incentives. Instead, it aggressively subsidized subprime mortgages. In the years leading up to the bust, Fannie Mae and Freddie Mac, government-sponsored entities that answered to congressional masters, bought billions of dollars of subprime mortgage loans from originators like New Century Financial Corp. and First Franklin Financial Corp. With the implicit backing of the U.S. government, Fannie and Freddie were able to borrow at preferential rates and ultimately assembled a $1.4 trillion portfolio of mortgage-backed securities.

We expected the government to enforce prudent banking practices. Instead, it allowed investment banks to dangerously overextend themselves. In 2004, with the housing boom well under way, America's big investment banks were chafing under SEC restrictions that limited their debt levels. Eager to boost their returns by taking on more debt, Wall

Street's leading banks joined forces to lobby for regulatory relief. Up against the united front of the nation's biggest investment banks, the SEC caved. Neutered by a belief in the omniscience of billionaire bankers, and blinded by their faith in industry self-regulation, the regulators failed to exercise the due diligence that would have prevented a financial Katrina.

As taxpayers and citizen, we expected the government to ensure transparent and orderly markets. Instead, it abdicated its responsibility to create a regulatory framework for credit default swaps and other derivatives. Thanks to derelict legislators, the world ended up with a globe-spanning bazaar for mortgage-backed securities that was less well-organized than eBay's market for snowglobes.

As taxpayers and citizens, we expected the government to indemnify taxpayers against bank failures. Instead, it stood idly by while a merger boom created banks that were "too big to fail." In the 1990s, the banking industry led all others in terms of merger activity, and by 2004, 74% of U.S. bank deposits were controlled by just 1% of America's banks.

The truth is, America's regulators had all the powers they needed to curb the "irrational exuberance" that precipitated the banking crisis— but they didn't. Again, this was a moral washout. Some of the most egregious lapses included these:

Blind indifference to the human costs of ideological zeal. In the years leading up to the crisis, there was a naive belief among many regulators that banks could be trusted to police themselves. These free market zealots failed to distinguish between the freedom to trade (generally a good thing) and freedom from oversight (generally a bad thing). In October 2008, Christopher Cox ruefully remarked that "The last six months have made it abundantly clear that voluntary regulation does not work." Duh. With the exception of Nazism and communism, it's hard to think of another ideological infatuation that has cost the world so dearly.

Public responsibilities abandoned for political gain. Wall Street used its colossal profits to buy heavyweight political leverage, and few legislators had the guts stand up to their Wall Street benefactors. Consider this: between 1990 and 2008, AIG provided more than $9.3 million in campaign contributions and spent more than

$70 million in lobbying efforts designed to batter down regulatory obstacles, according to *Time* magazine.[4] Virtually all of the game wardens on Capitol Hill were taking the poachers' money.

Milquetoast regulators more inclined to protect their backsides than raise an alarm. Undoubtedly there were officials in Washington (at the SEC, the Fed, the Office of the Comptroller, the Department of Justice, the Office of Thrift Supervision, and the FDIC) who were alert to the subprime contagion and who noticed the rapidly multiplying pathogens in the regulatory crevices. Yet rather than bark an alarm, the watchdogs rolled over and let the bankers scratch their tummies. Yes, there were gaps in regulatory coverage—but when you've been charged with protecting America's economy, your responsibility is to find and fill those gaps, not to take refuge in the sanctuary of a narrow regulatory remit. In the league table of execrable excuses, "it's not my job" ranks near the top.

Fact is, America's legislators and regulators were just as culpable as its bankers. The bomb that blew up the U.S. economy may have been detonated on Wall Street, but it was manufactured in Washington, DC.

As with the bankers, we are still waiting for a mea culpa from the regulators. None is likely to be forthcoming. (Among the powerful, blame deflection is a core competence.) What we have gotten instead is a barrage of proposals for increasing the powers of those who were either too cowardly or too compromised to exercise the authority they already had.

We need to be clear: in the banking crisis it wasn't capitalism that failed us, but capitalism's custodians. Those who should have been fighting to protect the moral high ground laid down their arms and auctioned off their integrity to the barbarian bankers.

We are left, then, with two critical questions: What is it that produces such a disastrous lapse in collective moral judgment? And what lessons are there for those of us who aren't bankers or policymakers? Let's take each question each in turn.

It seems to me that moral corrosion has its roots in the low-grade egomania that afflicts us all. For each of us, on any particular day, the battle between shameless self-interest and principled disinterest can be a close-run thing. Our better angels don't always win. If it were otherwise, the notion of "sin" would have never gained currency.

Another contributing factor is the incremental nature of moral decay. Standards seldom tumble all at once; instead, they ratchet down gradually through a series of small, nearly innocuous compromises. That's why the deterioration is easy to miss, or *dis*miss. As with a slowly rusting bridge, no alarms sound until after the structure has collapsed. Faced with the carnage, people scratch their heads and wonder, how the hell did this happen? The answer: bit by bit.

Finally, there is a social dynamic which, if not challenged, levels standards down. As human beings, we often look to others for our moral benchmarks. When we're presented with a choice between self-serving expediency and self-denying duty, we are typically relieved to find that someone else has already lowered the bar for us. In other words, we are inclined to look for, and overweight, precedents that help us to normalize our own ethical concessions. We're scavengers for excuses; that's why moral equivocation is infectious.

An example: In July 2007, just weeks before the debt bomb exploded, Chuck Price, Citigroup's chief executive, defended his bank's gung-ho risk-taking in an interview with the *Financial Times*: "When the music stops, in terms of liquidity, it will get complicated. But as long as the music is playing, you have got to get up and dance. We're still dancing." The last time I heard an excuse that lame it came from a 13-year-old: "But Dad, everyone's doing it."

The freedom of every human being to pursue his or her self-interest is an essential prerequisite for an open economy, but it is not an adequate moral foundation for capitalism. In *The Wealth of Nations*, Adam Smith, the patron saint of capitalism, made a compelling, if slightly depressing, case for self-interest:

> **It is not from the benevolence of the butcher, the brewer, or the baker that we expect our dinner, but from their regard to their own interest. We address ourselves, not to their humanity, but to their self-love, and never talk to them of our own necessities, but of their advantages.**

The moral superiority of capitalism rests on the fact that in a free market the only way to do well is to do well for others. Critically, though, the grocer doesn't feed us because he is concerned about our hunger—he feeds us because there is a profit in doing so. Capitalism is animated by self-interest, but when it's not tamed by moral self-discipline, it can easily become mendacious. When that happens, the powerless get abused and the ignorant get duped, legislators get bought and safeguards get trampled. The "invisible hand" of the market is a wonderful thing, but when not guided by a deep sense of moral duty, it can wreak all sorts of havoc.

Though his acolytes seldom acknowledge it, Adam Smith's philosophy was more nuanced than the previous quotation suggests. In *The Theory of Moral Sentiments*, Smith begins thusly:

How selfish soever man may be supposed, there are evidently some principles in his nature which interest him in the fortunes of others, and render their happiness necessary to him, though he derives nothing from it, except the pleasure of seeing it.

Thankfully, there is benevolence in each of us. Compassion, though, can shrivel. For leaders, this happens in two ways. First, compassion gets lost in the *pursuit* of success. In our strivings, we start to see colleagues, employees, shareholders, and customers as accessories to personal ambition, as instruments to be used and abused as necessary. Second, we lose our compassion in the *achievement* of success. A position of power, once attained, insulates us from the human consequences of our actions. As a twenty-first-century leader, you must be alert to these risks and consciously cultivate your compassion.

I don't have a grand plan for a moral renewal of capitalism, though I will offer a few medium-scale ideas in later chapters. Because renewal happens one soul at a time, a grand plan is, in any case, beside the point.

Nevertheless, we must face up squarely to capitalism's shortcomings. To free market zealots I would say the following: One doesn't have to disown an economic philosophy to recognize its shortcomings. So stop being so defensive! There are things about capitalism as currently practiced that are by any standards *in*defensible. As a champion of capitalism, I'm worried when I see:

- An ever bigger share of the world's wealth going to an ever smaller global elite.[5]
- Companies spending millions of dollars to tilt the regulatory playing field in their favor.
- Three-hundred-to-one pay differentials between CEOs and first-level employees.
- Governance structures that are expressly designed to deflect shareholder concerns.
- Companies that treat employees as mere factors of production.
- Executives who reap outsized rewards for mediocre performance.
- Companies that award 90% of their share options to a handful of senior executives.
- Companies that resist calls for greater transparency and consumer protection.
- Corporations that compromise their values to do business with repressive regimes.
- Corporate PR campaigns that fudge the facts and demonize critics.
- Executives who feel that society's interests are somehow distinct from their own.

If you can't find within yourself a little righteous anger about the way your company fulfills its responsibilities, then you're not going to be very effective in helping to repair the moral fabric of capitalism.

All of us who have a stake in the future of capitalism have a non-delegable responsibility to make it better—and we must start by raising our own ethical standards and by challenging others to do the same.

The rehabilitation of capitalism won't come from top-down programs of "corporate social responsibility." While welcome, clever new strategies for producing private and social gains in tandem are not enough. It's great, for example, that in 2008, Coca-Cola's then CEO, Neville Isdell, committed his company to becoming "water neutral" by

2020—this after activists challenged the company to improve its steward-ship of scarce water supplies. But a grand top-down initiative, however admirable or even profitable, will never be a substitute for a bottom-up sense of moral responsibility that informs every decision. Corporate morality needs to be proactive and pervasive—too often it is neither.

Most of us don't dump our trash out the car window, kick our pets, cheat on our taxes, lie on our CVs, or swear at telemarketers (well, four out of five isn't bad). It can be tough, though, to draw a line in the sand at work, particularly if those lines are regularly crossed by those at the top. On the other hand, if being human means anything, it means being ethically accountable—in the way that a shoe-chewing canine will never be. It was that sense of accountability that led Deitrich Bonhoeffer, the German theologian, to join the Nazi resistance, a decision that cost him his life. It was that sense of accountability that propelled civil rights marchers along the highway toward Selma, despite the tear gas and police batons. It was that sense of accountability that emboldened Aung San Suu Kyi to challenge the dictatorship in Burma.

Does the betterment of capitalism warrant the same sort of moral courage? Perhaps not, but with the exception of democracy, there's no other ideology that has done so much for so many. The ability to buy and sell freely, to raise capital, to take a risk and get a return, to start a new company, to invest where one wills, to expand or contract your business, to import or export, to innovate or cut costs, to buy another company or sell your own—these are extraordinary economic privileges—and when they're abridged, everyone loses.

But what, you ask, can one person do? Perhaps you've been told that a company's values have to emanate from the top. That's tosh. Just as turpitude compounds, so does virtue. E-mail, blogs and Twitter—these are powerful amplifiers of moral conscience, as Egypt's former president Hosni Mubarak learned to his sorrow. In a networked world, when one brave soul speaks up, it emboldens others. Yes, moral backsliding is contagious, but so is moral courage—so exercise yours!

There are risks, of course. You might piss off a few people, be labeled a malcontent, or get passed over for a promotion, but no one's going to put you under house arrest. So ask yourself, within my sphere of leadership, what standards do I regard as inviolable? Where am I unwilling to sacrifice my own integrity? What is my "moral signature"? What values do I want others to infer from my actions? And, conversely, where have I fallen victim to greed, hubris, or power lust? When have I shut up when I should have spoken up? Moral failings on a grand scale, of the sort observed in the banking scandal, are impossible without an epidemic of moral dereliction—so if you're incensed by what Wall Street did to Main Street, and you should be, stand tall for the moral standards *you* believe in.

And you know what? I think there's even hope for the banking elite. Redemption is possible. I think of Mikhail Gorbachev's embrace of *glasnost* and *perestroika* in 1984, shortly before he was appointed the general secretary of the communist party, or of F.W. de Klerk's speech in February 1990 when, against all expectations, he announced the dismantling of apartheid. Anyone can reclaim their compassion.

My friend John Ortberg, a pastor, psychologist, and author, argues that if we're going to have a world worth inhabiting, each one of us must have the courage to do a "fearless moral inventory." If you're a leader of any sort, in any organization, now would be a good time to start.

REDISCOVERING FARMER VALUES

1.3

In the midst of the banking crisis, my mother-in-law passed away. She had spent most of her 85 years working with her husband on their family farm. Starting with a single, leased tractor and a rented parcel of land, the pair ultimately grew their ranch into a 1,000-acre spread of debt-free farmland in California's fertile San Joaquin Valley. How did they accomplish this feat? By working 14-hour days, six days out of seven. By taking few vacations and forgoing most luxuries. By building up cash reserves in good years so they could survive bad ones. By diversifying their crops to reduce their exposure to fluctuating prices. And by paying themselves modestly while investing everything they could in land and equipment.

Like many of their generation, Ferne and Eldon Findley hated being in hock. To them, being in debt was being indentured. While working capital loans were unavoidable given farming's lumpy cash flow, the couple worked tirelessly to reduce their long-term debt and gain title to their land. A goal they achieved after 30 years of marriage.

My in-laws were happiest when they were elbow-deep in the muck of farming—a joy they shared with all those who subscribe to the "Farmer's Creed":

I believe a man's greatest possession is his dignity and that no calling bestows this more abundantly than farming. I believe hard work and honest sweat are the building blocks of a person's character. I believe that farming, despite its hardships and disappointments, is the most honest and honorable way a man can spend his days on this earth . . .

The Findleys' pay-as-you-go approach to life enabled them to buy a starter house for my wife and me, to fund church-building projects around the world, and to pass on a thriving business to their son.

More leverage might have allowed them to grow their business faster, or live higher on the hog, but the lessons learned in Depression-era childhoods inoculated them, and millions more of their generation, against those temptations.

The virtues that built the Findley farm—prudence, thrift, self-discipline, and sacrifice—are the same virtues that built America, and Britain, and Germany, and Japan. But in recent decades, these virtues have been conspicuously absent, as millions of consumers abandoned frugality for extravagance. As a marketing proposition, cake-on-the-plate-while-you-wait is a lot more enticing than pie-in-the-sky-bye-and-bye. So the bankers encouraged us to gorge on debt and we did.

Although I've searched for it, I can find no documentary evidence of a "Banker's Creed," no pithy celebration of bankerly virtues. Yet recent events suggest that many bankers (though not a majority, I'm sure) did in fact subscribe to a few common tenets:

I will buy out my competitors and build a "systemically important" bank, thus enabling me to privatize gains and socialize losses.

I will prey on customers at every opportunity and defend my right to profit from their misplaced trust.

*I will take unprecedented risks with my bank's balance sheet and ignore the inter-
     ests of my shareholders in hopes of achieving a seven- or eight-figure payday.*
*I will blame the consequences of my recklessness on defects in the "global financial
     system" and thereby absolve myself of any responsibility for having duped
     investors, customers, and regulators.*
*I will continue to demand the compensation to which I've become accustomed,
     even after a public bailout.*
*I will band together with my banking compatriots to ensure that any attempts at
     real reform get defanged.*

Today's bankers are not the first of their breed to embrace this merce-
nary creed. Nearly seventy years ago, in the depths of the Great Depres-
sion, President Roosevelt used his first inaugural address[1] to proclaim:

**... Practices of the unscrupulous money changers stand
indicted in the court of public opinion, rejected by the hearts
and minds of men....**

**The money changers have fled from their high seats in the
temple of our civilization. We may now restore that temple to
the ancient truths. The measure of the restoration lies in the
extent to which we apply social values more noble than mere
monetary profit.**

**Happiness lies not in the mere possession of money; it lies in
the joy of achievement, in the thrill of creative effort. The joy
and moral stimulation of work must no longer be forgotten in
the mad chase of evanescent profits....**

**...there must be an end to conduct in banking and in business
which too often has given to a sacred trust the likeness of
callous and selfish wrongdoing. Small wonder that confidence
languishes, for it thrives only on honesty, on honor, on the
sacredness of obligations, on faithful protection, and unselfish
performance; without them it cannot live.**

Today, as in 1933, bankers are easy targets. But it wasn't just bankers
who greedily overreached. Consider this: in the early 1950s, when the

Baby Boomers were still toddlers (and their parents were working hard to pay down their mortgages), the ratio of debt-to-income for the average American household was less than .4. From the mid-1960s to the mid-1980s the ratio hovered around .7. Yet by 2008, this crucial barometer had zoomed up to 1.4. Over this time span, the income-adjusted indebtedness of the average American household ballooned by more than 350%. Indeed, it increased more in the years between 2001 and 2008 than in the previous 39 years. Before being forced by the recession to scrimp and save, the typical American family was spending more money servicing its debt than buying food.

We're all grown-ups. How did we expect this debt binge to end, if not with mass foreclosures, multibillion-dollar write-downs, and a devastating economic pull-back? Even with the Chinese bankrolling us, we should have known that at some point we'd have to pay the piper.

Over the past few years, policymakers around the world have been working feverishly to reflate the global economy—with little to show for their efforts. Deleveraging always hurts. Millions of us were addicted to debt and have now been sent off to rehab, not the celebrity sort with organic salads, comfy pillows, and cooing counselors, but the court-ordered sort, with institutional food, cold showers, and surly staff.

Can any good come of this? Sure. The first benefit should be a renewed appreciation for the timeless virtues that engender *real* wealth creation and spawn *lasting* prosperity. As farmer values wax and banker values wane, we'll all be better off—and so will the economy.

A second plus: our kids may avoid becoming debtoholics. Having watched their parents overextend themselves and pay the price, one can only hope that they'll resolve to live financially prudent lives. (My son's suggestion: require every high school senior to take a course in personal financial management.) If the Millennials learn some essential lessons about thrift, hard work, and fiscal discipline, then this seemingly interminable crisis will not have been in vain. And all the hard-working Grandma Fernes who've left this world for the next will be able to look down and smile.

RENOUNCING CAPITALISM'S DANGEROUS CONCEITS

1.4

As you can probably tell, I'm a capitalist by conviction and profession. I believe the best economic system is one that rewards entrepreneurship and risk taking, maximizes customer choice, relies on markets to allocate scarce resources, and minimizes the regulatory burden on business. If there's a better recipe for creating prosperity I haven't seen it.

So why do fewer than four out of ten consumers in the developed world believe that large corporations make a "somewhat" or "generally" positive contribution to society? (This according to a 2007 study by McKinsey & Company.[1]) Why is it, in a 2010 Gallup survey, that only 19% of Americans told pollsters that they had "quite a lot" or a "great deal" of confidence in big business? (Only Congress scored worse.)[2] It seems that a majority of us *expect* big companies to behave badly—to ravish the environment, mistreat employees, and mislead customers. As ethical truants, big business seems to rank alongside Charlie Sheen and Lindsay Lohan.

Obviously, many blame Wall Street for this state of affairs. In March 2009, the *Financial Times* claimed that the "credit crisis had destroyed faith in the free market ideology that has dominated Western thinking for a decade." In the wake of the subprime disaster, hyperventilating journalists and self-righteous politicians argued that the world needed a new model of capitalism, one in which the capitalists were far more beholden to the state.

While one should never underestimate the ability of risk-besotted financiers to booby-trap the global economy, the real threat to capitalism isn't unfettered financial cunning. Indeed, in the Gallup survey mentioned earlier, banks scored higher than big business. Yes, greedy bankers are a menace, but there is a bigger hazard: imperious CEOs who are unwilling to confront the changing expectations of their stakeholders. In recent years, consumers and citizens have become increasingly disgruntled with the implicit contract that governs the rights and obligations of society's most powerful economic actors—large corporations. To many, the bargain has seemed one-sided—it works really well for CEOs, pretty well for shareholders, and not so well for everyone else.

You don't have to read *Adbusters* to wonder whose interests big business really serves. When it comes to "free markets," there's plenty to be cynical about: the food industry's long and illicit love affair with trans fats, Merck's dissembling about the risks of Vioxx, Facebook's occasionally cavalier attitude toward consumer privacy, the seldom-kept promises of airline executives to improve customer service, and the everyday reality of hidden banking fees, overinflated product claims, and buck-passing customer service agents.

If individuals around the world have lost faith in business, it's because business has misused that faith. In this sense, the threat to capitalism is both more prosaic and more profound than that posed by marauding bankers—more prosaic in that the danger comes not from predatory Wall Street financiers, but from the minor corporate misdemeanors that every day fuel the frustrations of "ordinary" folk; and more profound in that the problem is expansive—it threatens to burden every large company with the sort of regulatory constraints that were once reserved for nuclear power plants.

Some may bemoan the fact that capitalism (broadly defined) has no credible challengers, but it doesn't. Like democracy, it's the worst sort of system except for all the others. But if we fail to acknowledge its failings, the growing discontent with business will embolden all those who believe CEOs should answer first, second, and last to civil servants—to those who are ever eager to enlarge the power of the state.

This is not an outcome most of us would welcome. While cinching the regulatory straitjacket even tighter would protect us from capitalism's worst excesses, it would also rob us of its bounties. So we must hope that managers everywhere will face up to the fact that an irreversible revolution in expectations has occurred.

Millions of consumers and citizens are already convinced of a fact that many corporate chieftains are still reluctant to admit: the legacy model of economic production that has driven the "modern" economy over the last hundred years is on its last legs. Like a clapped-out engine, it's held together with bailing wire and duct tape, belches out noxious fumes, and regularly breaks down.

Though we're grateful someone invented this clattering, savage machine a century ago, we'll also be happy when it's finally carted off to the scrap yard and replaced with something a bit less menacing.

In our hearts, we know the future cannot be an extrapolation of the past. As the great-grandchildren of the industrial revolution, we have learned, at long last, that the heedless pursuit of more is unsustainable and ultimately unfulfilling. Our planet, our security, our sense of equanimity, and our very souls demand something better, something different.

We long for a kinder, gentler sort of capitalism—one that views us as more than mere "consumers," one that understands the distinction between maximizing consumption and maximizing happiness, one that doesn't sacrifice the future for the present, and one that doesn't regard the earth as an inexhaustible source of natural resources.

So what stands in the way of creating a conscientious, accountable, and sustainable sort of capitalism—a system that in the long term is actually habitable?

It is, I think, a matrix of deeply held beliefs about what business is for, whose interests it serves, and how it creates value. Many of these beliefs are near canonical (at least among CEOs of a particular generation and ideological bent). They are also narcissistic and archaic. Among the most toxic assumptions are the following:

1. The paramount objective of a business is to make money (rather than to enhance human well-being in economically efficient ways).
2. Corporate leaders should only be held accountable for the immediate effects of their actions (and not for the second- and third-order consequences of their single-minded pursuit of growth and profits).
3. Executives should be evaluated and compensated on the basis of short-term earnings (rather than on the basis of long-term value creation, both financial and social).
4. The way to establish a business' social credentials is through high-minded mission statements, green-tinged products, and a fat CSR budget (rather than through an unshakeable and sacrificial commitment to doing the right thing in every circumstance).
5. The primary justification for "doing good" is that it helps a company to "do well." (The implication: do good only when there's an upside.)
6. Customers care a lot more about value for money than they do about the values that were honored or defiled in the making and selling of a product.
7. A firm's customers are the folks who buy its services (rather than all those whose lives are affected by its actions).
8. It's legitimate for a company to make money by exploiting customer lock-in, exaggerating product benefits, or restricting customer choice. (I mean, jeez, should it really take an act of Congress to force airlines to treat tarmac-bound passengers humanely?)
9. Market power and political leverage are acceptable ways of countering a disruptive technology or thwarting an unconventional competitor.
10. A company's "brand" is a marketing concoction built with ad dollars (rather than a socially constructed portrait of its *real* values).

Perhaps these conceits were less problematic 58 years ago when General Motors' then-chairman Charles Wilson proclaimed that "what is good for GM is good for America." But today, these beliefs are discordant and dangerous. It is no good pretending that perceptions haven't changed or that capitalism's critics are simply misguided. There is a growing consensus that rampant consumerism debases human values; that pell-mell growth imperils the planet; that unchecked corporate power subverts democracy; and that myopic, option-incented CEOs are as likely to destroy value as create it.

Of course, as consumers and citizens, we must acknowledge that companies can't remedy every social ill or deliver every social benefit. We must face up to our own schizophrenia. We can't expect companies to behave responsibly if we blithely abandon our own principles to save a buck.

As for executives: if you feel your industry is still too lightly regulated, then just keep on doing what you're doing. If, on the other hand, you've had your fill of sanctimonious politicians and meddling bureaucrats, then you must face up to a simple fact: in the years to come, a company will be able to preserve its freedoms only if it embraces a new and more enlightened view of its responsibilities. Google's executive chairman Eric Schmidt is one of a handful of executives who seem to get this.

In 2010, Google formed a new social innovation unit that it describes as a think/do tank. Housed in the company's operational core rather than in its philanthropic foundation, Google Ideas is aimed at harnessing the company's innovation prowess and convening power in order to tackle some of society's most pressing problems—such as nuclear proliferation and failed states. One of the first efforts launched by Google Ideas was the Summit Against Violent Extremism (SAVE), held in the Dublin Convention Centre in June 2011. The event brought together a cross-section of former jihadists, white supremacists, and gang leaders, as well as some of their victims and a slew of academic experts. A representative participant, T. J. Leyden, was once a skinhead leader and is now executive director of Hate2Hope. Google hopes that forums such as this one will help to surface radical new approaches to seemingly intractable problems. Though it's too early to assess the success of the program, it is worth noting the principles upon which Google Ideas seems to be based:

1. In the long run, the interests of shareholders and society at large are convergent. Making the planet a "better" place serves the interests of business, and making businesses "better" serves the interests of every human being.
2. A company's social legitimacy can never be taken for granted—it can and will be challenged, so live with it.
3. Citizens and consumers expect companies to be not only socially accountable, but socially entrepreneurial.
4. Systemic problems can't be solved by a single institution or by people sitting around conference tables. Businesses are uniquely equipped to help mobilize the relevant parties and get "boots on the ground." They need to be energetic partners of public institutions and NGOs.
5. "Don't be evil" (Google's famous mantra) is a *de minimis* standard. Today, a company needs a proactive strategy for buttressing its social balance sheet. Here, as everywhere else, the only option is to *lead!*

Visit the website of just about any company and you'll find lots of platitudinous statements about "doing good," and a long list of do-gooder commitments. Maybe it will be the same with Google Ideas; maybe it will turn out to be more PR ploy than paradigm shift. In any case, there are still plenty of companies where the old conceits still hold sway. What matters now is that we change that.

RECLAIMING THE NOBLE

1.5

I'm a big fan of *New Yorker* cartoons. There's usually at least one in every issue that provokes a wry smile or a wince of self-recognition. While I've never actually participated in the magazine's weekly caption competition, I occasionally gin up a prospective entry. Last week, the contest featured a drawing of a couple lounging in a living room. The husband (perhaps?) was perusing a newspaper on the sofa while his wife lounged in a nearby armchair. She was a mermaid—naked from the waist up, her large flipper tucked demurely beneath her. With her head angled toward her companion and her mouth open in mid-sentence, I imagined her to be saying: "After ten years, I think you could have learned to scuba dive," or "Hiking in the Alps again? I thought we'd take a beach holiday this year."

One of my favorite *New Yorker* cartoons shows an office worker slumped against a wall, clutching his chest. As worried colleagues rush to his aid, the stricken employee mumbles, "Don't worry, it was just a fleeting sense of purpose."

These sardonic portraits of the human condition resonate with us because they capture something deep and true. The mermaid-out-of-water speaks to the challenges of mutual accommodation that confronts any couple in a long-term relationship, while the temporarily (and implausibly) fervent employee reminds us that the typical corporate office is an emotional vacuum. I can't offer you any insights if you're trying to get in sync with your partner, but I do have a few observations about the paucity of purpose in the average, porridge-gray cubicle.

In a later chapter, we'll dig into some survey data on employee engagement. For now, it's enough to note that a recent global survey found that only 1 in 5 employees is truly engaged, heart and soul, in their work. As a student of management, I'm depressed by the fact that so many people find the workplace depressing.

In the study, respondents laid much of the blame for their lassitude on uncommunicative and egocentric managers, but I wonder if there's not some deeper organizational reality that bleeds the vitality and enthusiasm out of people at work.

Here's an experiment for you. Pull together your company's latest annual report, its mission statement, or the transcript of a recent CEO speech. Read these documents and make a list of oft-repeated words or phrases. Now do a little content analysis. What are the ideas that get a lot of airtime in your company? They're probably captured in words like superiority, advantage, leadership, differentiation, value, focus, discipline, accountability, and efficiency. Nothing wrong with this, but do these goals quicken your pulse? Do they speak to your heart? Are they "good" in any cosmic sense?

Now think about Michelangelo, Galileo, Jefferson, Gandhi, William Wilberforce, Martin Luther King Jr., Mother Theresa, and Sir Edmund Hillary. What were the ideals that inspired these individuals to acts of greatness? Was it anything on your list of commercial values? Probably not. Remarkable contributions are spawned by a passionate commitment to timeless human values, such as beauty, truth, wisdom, justice, charity, fidelity, joy, courage, and honor.

I talk to a lot of CEOs, and every one professes a commitment to building a "high performance" organization—but is this really possible when the core values of the corporation are venal rather than transcendent? I don't think so. That's why humanizing the language and practice of management is a business imperative (and an ethical one).

A noble purpose inspires sacrifice, stimulates innovation, and encourages perseverance. In so doing, it transforms great talent into exceptional accomplishment. That's a fact, and it leaves me wondering: Why are words like "love," "devotion," and "honor" so seldom heard within the halls of corporate-dom? Why are the ideals that matter most to human beings the ones most notably absent in managerial discourse?

John Mackey, the cofounder of Whole Foods Markets, once remarked that his goal was to build a company based on love instead of fear. Mackey's not a utopian idealist, and his unflinching libertarian views are off-putting to some. Yet few would argue with the goal of creating an organization that embodies the values of trust, generosity, and forbearance. Yet a gut-level commitment to building an organization infused with the spirit of charity is far more radical and weird than it might appear.

If you doubt that, here's an experiment to try. The next time you're stuck in a staff meeting, wait until everyone's eyes have glazed over from PowerPoint fatigue and then announce that what your company really needs is a lot more *luuuuuv*. When addressing a large group of managers, I often challenge them to stand up for love (or beauty or justice or truth) in just that way. "When you get back to work, tell your boss you think the company has a love deficit." This suggestion invariably provokes a spasm of nervous laughter, which has always struck me as strange.

Why is it that as managers we are perfectly willing to accept the *idea* of a company dedicated to timeless human values, but are, in general, unwilling to become practical advocates for those values within our own organizations? I have a hunch. I think corporate life is so manifestly profane, so mechanical, mundane, and materialistic, that any attempt to inject a spiritual note feels wildly out of place—the workplace equivalent of reading the Bible in a brothel.

Again, there's nothing wrong with utilitarian values like profit, advantage, and efficiency, but they lack nobility. And, as we've seen so often in recent years, when corporate leaders and their followers are not slaves to some meritorious purpose, they run the risk of being enslaved by their own ignoble appetites. An uplifting sense of purpose is more than an impetus for individual accomplishment, it's a necessary insurance policy against expediency and impropriety. By definition, every organization is "values driven." The only question is, what values are in the driver's seat?

There was a time when Disney was in the joy business. Animators, theme park employees, and executives were united in their quest to create enchanting experiences for children of all ages. Apple, I believe, is in the beauty business. It uses its prodigious talents to produce products and services that are aesthetic stand-outs. There are many within Google who believe their company is in the wisdom business, who believe their job is to raise the world's IQ, democratize knowledge, and empower people with information. Sadly, though, this kind of dedication to big-hearted goals and high-minded ideals is all too rare in business. Nevertheless, I believe that long-lasting success, both personal and corporate, stems from an allegiance to the sublime and the majestic.

Viktor Frankl, the Austrian neurologist and psychologist, held a similar view, which he expressed forcefully in *Man's Search for Meaning*: "For success, like happiness, cannot be pursued; it must ensue, and it only does so as the unintended consequence of one's personal dedication to a cause greater than oneself."

Which brings me back to my worry. Given all this, why is the language of business so sterile, so uninspiring, and so relentlessly banal? Is it because business is the province of engineers and economists rather than artists and theologians? Is it because the emphasis on rationality and pragmatism squashes idealism? I'm not sure. But I do know this—customers, investors, taxpayers, and policymakers believe there's a hole in the soul of business, and the only way for managers to change this fact, and regain the moral high ground, is to embrace what Socrates called the good, the just, and the beautiful.

SECTION 2

Innovation Matters Now

DEFENDING INNOVATION

2.1

Hunkered down is the new normal. This is hardly surprising given that thousands of companies around the world are facing stagnant economies, hyper-efficient competitors, and tight-fisted customers. When you seem to be caught in a cycle of endless retrenchment, it can be hard to be optimistic—even if you believe the world is filled with more promise than peril. And if you're a champion of innovation, it's even harder to put on a happy face. If you're a mid-level VP, you've probably had a pet project gutted by some newly empowered bean counter. If you're a struggling entrepreneur, you may have had to lay off some key talent and cut expenses to the bone. And if you're a consultant who helps other folks to innovate, you may be one "spending freeze" away from posting yourself at a busy intersection with a hand-lettered sign that reads, "Will brainstorm for food."

In recent years, left-brain types have had the upper hand while starry-eyed innovators have struggled to get a hearing. Nevertheless, before innovation slips any further down the list of corporate priorities, we need to remind ourselves that we owe *everything* to innovation.

WE OWE OUR EXISTENCE TO INNOVATION

Our species exists thanks to four billion years of genetic innovation. Since time immemorial life has been experimenting with new genetic combinations, through sexual recombination and random mutation. As human beings, we are the genetic elite, the sentient, contemplating, and innovating sum of countless genetic accidents and transcription errors. Thank God for screw-ups. If life had adhered to Six Sigma rules, we'd still be slime. Whatever the future holds for us bipeds, we can be sure that happy accidents will always be essential to breakthrough innovation.

WE OWE OUR PROSPERITY TO INNOVATION

Most of us do more than subsist. From the vantage point of our ancestors, we live lives of almost unimaginable ease. Here again we have innovation to thank. A thousand years of *social innovation* gave millions of us the right to self-determination. We are no longer vassals and conscripts. We live in democratic societies where we are free to think and do as we wish—essential prerequisites for innovation. Repeated bouts of *institutional innovation*—including the invention of capital markets, company law, and patent protection—paved the way for economic progress by facilitating trade, capital formation, and entrepreneurship. And a hundred-plus years of frenzied *technological innovation* blessed us with personal mobility, instant communications, an arsenal of disease-fighting drugs, unprecedented computational power, and TiVo. As technologies multiplied, incomes soared. Between 1000 and 1820, global per capita income rose by a scant 50%. Over the next 12 decades, it grew by 800%.[1] Put simply, innovation rescued humanity from privation.

WE OWE OUR HAPPINESS TO INNOVATION

Humans are the only beings who create for the sheer pleasure of doing so. Whether it's laying out a garden, plinking out a new tune on a piano, writing a bit of poetry, manipulating a digital photo, redecorating a room, or inventing a new chili recipe—we are happiest when we are creating. Yes, we innovate to solve problems, to make money, and to get ahead. But for most of us, innovation is an end, not a means. We don't need a practical justification to innovate. We create because we were born to; we have no choice. From Mihaly Csikszentmihalyi[2] to Tal Ben-Shahar,[3] the experts agree: human beings are happiest when they're exercising their ingenuity. Throughout history, millions of human beings were denied the chance to exercise their creative gifts—because they lived at a time when the tools of creativity were prohibitively expensive or in a society where creative freedoms were abridged. Our generation, by contrast, is blessed. We have access to dirt-cheap tools (like a $100 video editing program), can connect with our creative fellows around the world, and are able to share our innovations with any and all (thanks to the Web). Forget the Renaissance, the Enlightenment, and the Industrial Revolution—ours is the golden age of innovation, and we should take delight in that fact.

WE OWE OUR FUTURE TO INNOVATION

Today, human beings confront a daunting array of problems that demand radical new solutions. Climate change, global pandemics, failed states, narco-crime, terrorism, nuclear proliferation, environmental degradation—meeting these challenges will require us to invent new innovation *systems*. (The idea behind Google Ideas.) We have to learn how to solve problems that are multidimensional and multijurisdictional. In the early years of the twentieth century, Thomas Edison and General Electric invented the modern R&D lab, and with it a set of much-imitated protocols that would help to generate a century's worth of technological progress. Today, humanity's most pressing problems aren't merely technological; they're social, cultural, and political, and global in scope. That's why, like Edison, we must innovate around innovation. Luckily, there are new meta-innovations (like idea markets, crowdsourcing, and folksonomies) that can help us innovate across disciplines, borders, institutions, and ideologies. This is the only way we'll solve the make-or-break challenges now facing our species. Our future, no less than our past, depends on innovation.

So don't give up. Innovation isn't a fad—it's the real deal, the only deal. Right now, not everyone believes that, but they will—even all those corporate cost-cutters with shriveled right hemispheres.

CATALOGING THE WORLD'S GREATEST INNOVATORS

2.2

If you were compiling a list of the world's most innovative companies, which businesses would top your list? No one would be surprised if you picked Google, Apple, or Amazon, but what about Wal-Mart? (What? Did they find a new way of crushing little retailers?) Or PG&E? (A utility? Are you kidding me?) Or how about the Chinese data equipment maker Huawei? (No way!) While these companies might not have made it onto *your* top ten list, all of them were featured in a recent *Fast Company* ranking[1] of innovation all-stars.

The list toppers:

1. Facebook	6. First Solar
2. Amazon	7. PG&E
3. Apple	8. Novartis
4. Google	9. Wal-Mart
5. Huawei	10. Hewlett-Packard

As you might expect, *Business Week* has its own list[2] of innovation standouts:

1. Apple	6. Amazon
2. Google	7. LG Electronics
3. Microsoft	8. BYD
4. IBM	9. General Electric
5. Toyota	10. Sony

Apple, Google, and Amazon are the only companies that appear on both top ten lists. Three of *Business Week*'s picks (Toyota, LG Electronics, and Sony) don't make it into *Fast Company*'s top 25, and Facebook, #1 on *Fast Company*'s list, ranks a lowly 48th on *Business Week*'s roster. That's five places behind Fiat, if you can believe it. Conversely, three of *Fast Company*'s top ten—Huawei, First Solar, and Novartis—don't show up anywhere on *Business Week*'s top 50 list.

What gives? Is the definition of innovation so murky that even business editors can't agree on which companies are truly inspired and which are not? Apparently so.

There's a reason for the befuddlement. Trying to rank the planet's most creative companies is a bit like trying to rank the world's most accomplished athletes. How can one possibly compare the hard-charging physicality of Sidney Crosby, a hockey player, with the explosive speed of Usain Bolt, an Olympic sprinter, with the strength and balance of Yang Wei, a world champion gymnast, with the extraordinary conditioning of Petter Northug, who won the 50-kilometer cross-country skiing event at the 2010 Winter Olympics? The answer is you can't—but that doesn't prevent list-aholics from trying. A couple of years back, a five-person panel selected by the *Wall Street Journal* named Roman Sebrle as the world's preeminent athlete.[3] (Yes, *that* Roman Sebrle). Though always entertaining, lists of this sort are more likely to start arguments than end them.

So it is with innovation rankings. They're not much help to anyone who is actually trying to *learn* something about innovation—because they fail to distinguish between five types of innovators.

ROCKETS

First, there are the *rockets*, young companies that have been boosted aloft by wacky new business models. Recent examples (from *Fast Company*'s extended list) include Gilt Groupe, the online luxury retailer; Hulu, which delivers TV shows via the Web; and Spotify, a music streaming service. Like other newbies, most of these fast-growing companies are still ramping up their initial strategies. None of these upstarts has yet been challenged to reinvent its business model—a test that history suggests many of them will fail. Like a child star whose fame dims as the years advance, many innovative companies will become less so as they mature.

Fact is, stumbling upon an innovative business model is often more luck than genius. Despite that, a fortuitously fortunate founder often ends up being venerated as a perpetually prescient prophet. As a result, the adolescent company becomes overly dependent on the vision of one or two key individuals and never develops a capacity for bottom-up business model innovation. When the founder's vision fades, the pace of innovation slows and the company tumbles down the innovation league table.

In 2006, Starbucks, Southwest, IKEA, and eBay all ranked among *BusinessWeek*'s top 25. Yet four years later, none of these companies were that highly ranked. As bambinos, they were industry revolutionaries, but as they aged, they fell out of the innovation vanguard (though all remain well-run companies).

If you want a measure of just how difficult it is to *stay* innovative, consider this: two-thirds of the businesses on *Fast Company*'s 2009 list of the 50 most innovative companies didn't make into the 2010 edition. When it comes to innovation, few companies remain on the winner's podium for long.

Nevertheless, it is worth paying attention to the tyros. While they don't have much to teach us about how to build systematically innovative companies, their game-changing strategies often illuminate important new categories of business model innovation. For example, although innovation at Starbucks may have gone from steaming to tepid, there's still much that can be learned from the company's success at turning a low-value product into a high-value experience.

LAUREATES

Next are the *laureates*. These companies innovate year after year, albeit in narrow, technologically oriented domains. They spend billions of dollars on research and development and employ thousands of super-smart boffins. Perennial benchmarks include General Electronics, Intel, LG Electronics, Samsung, Novartis, Microsoft, and Cisco.

The laureates show up regularly on "most innovative" lists, and also dominate the rankings of most patents won. This is a testament not just to their prolific inventiveness, but to the barriers to entry that newcomers face in building a world-class research organization. IBM, for example, has been the top U.S. patent recipient for 18 consecutive years.[4]

Fundamental advances in physics, biochemistry, and computer science are hard to come by; you need dozens of PhDs, lots of patience, and deep pockets. It's easier to invent a new model of online retailing, for example, than to master the intricacies of atomic scale manufacturing—that's why Intel, Samsung, and Toshiba recently joined forces to produce 10-nanometer computer chips.

Inventive as they are, the laureates are a bit one-dimensional—they're great at pushing out the frontiers of science, but are not always so good at innovation in other areas. Intel, for example, has struggled to move into adjacent markets. While its chips dominate in servers and PCs, the company has so far failed to gain a foothold in smartphones and tablets, despite years of trying.[5] Turns out the skills needed to design ultra-powerful processors aren't the ones needed to develop ultra-low power chips.

Or take Samsung. Despite having been awarded 4,551 U.S. patents in 2010,[6] Samsung isn't the #1 LCD-TV brand in the United States. That honor belongs to Vizio—a company founded in 2002 that has fewer than 200 employees and more than $2.5 billion in sales. Unlike its

R&D-centric, vertically integrated competitors, Vizio buys its flat screens from independent Asian suppliers. Following Dell's playbook, Vizio has "deverticalized" its corner of the consumer electronics industry. Occasionally, a brilliant business model can trump a multibillion-dollar research budget.

Nevertheless, if you want to learn something about maximizing R&D productivity or managing a patent portfolio, the laureates have plenty to teach.

ARTISTES

The *artistes* comprise a third and much smaller category of innovation heroes. These companies are in the creativity business—innovation is their primary product. Among the most feted are IDEO, BMW Design-Works, and Grey New York (an ad firm)—all of which are among *Fast Company*'s top 50.

Artistes are filled with tastemakers who wear black jeans, own $1,000 espresso machines, and know how to produce viral videos (like the ones where a talking baby shills for an online brokerage company). Though the artistes deserve all of the awards they win each year, they do have something of a built-in advantage. After all, everything about them—the way they hire, develop talent, and organize their work spaces—has been designed to provoke lateral leaps of genius. Everything about *your* company has been designed, well, for something else. So artistes sell the fruits of their right-brain thinking to clients who are, shall we say, hemispherically challenged.

Make no mistake, coming up with an out-of-the-box design, such as a $25 dollar latrine for impoverished villagers, the work of IDEO's Jeff Chapin, is a challenge—but it's a whole lot easier when you're sitting in a buzzy, energetic design firm like IDEO than when you're crouched in a colorless, coffin-sized cubicle deep in the innards of a cost–obsessed colossus.

Specialization has its advantages. If you work for an artiste, you don't have to spend half your day defending the very *idea* of innovation to a boss who believes that penguins could fly if only they tried harder.

Most companies don't have the luxury of focusing exclusively on innovation. They have to innovate while stamping out millions of widgets or processing millions of customer transactions. Still there is much that can be learned from the artistes. While your company may never be an innovators' paradise, you should still be able to weave a few of IDEO's innovation principles[7] into the design of your next staff meeting:

1. Encourage wild ideas
2. Build on the ideas of others
3. Stay focused on the topic
4. One conversation at a time
5. Be visual
6. Go for quantity
7. Defer judgment

CYBORGS

Fourth are the *cyborgs*, companies like Google, Amazon, and Apple that seem to have been purpose-built to achieve superhuman feats of innovation. You won't find much industrial-age DNA in these organizations. Their management practices have been built around principles like freedom, meritocracy, transparency, and experimentation. They are so endlessly inventive and strategically flexible that they seem to have come from another solar system—one where CFOs are servants rather than gods.

The cyborgs don't just have innovative business models, they are filled with alien management practices—like Google's 60:1 span of control or Apple's top-to-bottom obsession with "joy-of-use." Like the tyros, many of the cyborgs are run by charismatic founders, but unlike other entrepreneurs, these visionaries haven't been taken hostage by one particular business model. They have worked hard to embed within their organizations a capacity for continuous renewal—and have mostly succeeded. Over the past few years Amazon has morphed from a web-based bookseller to an Internet shopping giant to a leader in cloud computing. Google has spawned dozens of new online services that complement its core search business. And Apple has conquered a series of businesses (including digital music and smartphones) that lie far afield from its home computer roots.

Unlike the laureates, the cyborgs are innovative on multiple dimensions, and unlike the rockets, they're probably going to show up on *next* year's "most innovative" list and the one after that.

Problem is, with their bionic capabilities, the cyborgs can make the rest of us feel like dolts. If you work in a company that's merely human—one that's riddled with stale, conformance-inducing management practices—another chirpy anecdote about Google's free-wheeling culture may make you puke. Your organization wasn't built from the ground up to be innovative, and you figure you'd have an easier time getting a date with a supermodel or George Clooney than turning your company into an innovation hottie. That's where you'd be wrong.

BORN-AGAIN INNOVATORS

Truth is, there are a few geriatrics out there who've cracked the innovation code. These *born-again* innovators—companies like Procter & Gamble, IBM, and Ford—are, perhaps, the most notable of all. For decades these behemoths were top-down and buttoned-down, hierarchical and stultifying. Time and again they found themselves outmaneuvered by less orthodox upstarts. And then one day they faced up to their failings and got religion—not the twice-a-year-only-on-holy-days facsimile of faith, but the whole down-on-your-knees-reborn-from-the-inside-out conversion experience. And so they set about reordering their priorities and reassessing lifelong habits.

At Ford, Alan Mulally has been working tirelessly to dismantle the company's silos and rekindle a passion for making great cars. Before stepping down as chairman of Procter & Gamble in 2010, A. G. Lafley launched a major initiative aimed at opening up the company's innovation pipeline to ideas from around the world. IBM has been even bolder in rethinking its innovation processes. Over the past decade, its process for incubating "Emerging Business Opportunities" and its global "Innovation Jams" have helped the once-insular company generate billions of dollars in new growth. (IBM's EBO process is detailed in my previous book, *The Future of Management*.)

If you dive into these cases you'll discover that each underscores the same fundamental point: going from bumbler to benchmark requires a complete retooling of a company's *management* processes—the way it plans, budgets, organizes, allocates resources, measures performance, hires, and compensates. Most of our management rituals were invented (a very long time ago) to promote discipline, control, alignment, and predictability—all laudable goals. To out-innovate the upstarts, a company must reengineer all of these processes so they facilitate bold thinking and radical doing.

What limits innovation in established companies isn't a lack of resources or a shortage of human creativity, but a dearth of pro-innovation processes. For example, in most organizations one finds that:

- Few, if any, employees have been trained as business innovators.
- Few employees have access to the sort of customer and technology insights that can help to spur innovation.
- Would-be innovators face a bureaucratic gauntlet that makes it difficult for them to get the time and resources they need to develop their ideas.
- Line managers aren't held accountable for mentoring new business initiatives and lack explicit innovation goals.
- Executive compensation schemes don't put a high priority on innovation.
- The metrics for tracking innovation (inputs, throughputs, and outputs) are patchy and poorly constructed.
- There's no common definition of innovation and, therefore, no way of comparing innovation performance across teams and divisions.

Weirdly, neither *BusinessWeek* nor *Fast Company* ranks Whirlpool among the world's top 50 "most innovative" companies. This is surprising, as I know of no other company whose innovation conversion has been more complete. Over the past ten years, the Benton Harbor, Michigan, appliance maker has recrafted all of its management processes to serve the cause of innovation. The payoff: an innovation pipeline whose value has increased from close to zero to more than $4 billion over the past 7 years, this according to a conversation with Nancy Tennant Snyder, Whirlpool's vice president for innovation.[8] If you want a detailed guide on how your company can go from innovation chump to champ, have a look at Nancy's recent book, *Unleashing Innovation*. It is by far the best "how to" I've come across. If a hundred-year-old manufacturing company can make innovation everyone's job, every day, there's no reason your company can't.

INSPIRING GREAT DESIGN 2.3

In a landmark 1964 case, the U.S. Supreme Court reversed the obscenity conviction of an Ohio theater owner who had screened the French film *Les Amants*. In his concurring opinion, Justice Potter Stevens concluded that although he was unable to provide a precise definition of pornography, he knew it when he saw it. So it is with great design—we know it when we see it. Trouble is, we see way too little of it.

Here's a case in point. A few weeks ago I traveled 3,000 kilometers in the world's most spectacularly uncomfortable airline seat, aboard a United Airlines flight from Chicago to San Francisco. Though I was sitting in the front of the plane, the seat's ergonomics resembled nothing so much as a canvas campstool. A U-shaped metal frame supported what had once been a cushion, but was now little more than a sagging piece of fabric. The seat bottom sloped from back to front and offered nothing in the way of thigh support. For four hours I squirmed and wriggled, but try as I might I couldn't escape the seat's vise-like grip on my butt, nor thwart its dogged attempts to give me the mother of all wedgies. How in the name of all that flies, I wondered, could anyone knowingly design such an excruciatingly discommodious bum cradle? Surely, design this bad had to be intentional. Maybe Bill Stumpf, the inspired creator of the Aeron chair, had a sadistic twin who took delight in designing hideously uncomfortable airline seats.

Earlier in the same month I had attended a conference in Milan. There I came across Technogym, an Italian manufacturer of exercise equipment. I've been in lots of gyms, and most exercise equipment looks as if it had been designed by a half-blind, medieval dungeon master—not so Technogym's Kinesis, a multipurpose workout machine that attaches to a wall, and is about the size of an upended pool table. The Kinesis has four shiny arms that swing out from each corner of the device. Cables run out across the upper arms, down to the lower arms, and then back into the base. Six sliding acrylic handles are positioned at various points along the cables and allow the user to perform more than 200 toning movements. A small, iPod-like touch wheel is mounted chest-high and allows users to adjust resistance levels with one finger. In its sleekest guise, the Kinesis is covered in glass and virtually disappears in a room. Designed by Antonio Citterio, the Kinesis proves that Italians can make even exercise equipment sexy.

These two radically contrasting experiences got me thinking about the power and importance of design. Great design evokes an almost visceral reaction because it is . . .

Utterly unexpected. A brilliantly designed product is clever and amazing. You look at it and go, "Jeez, how cool!" Exhibit A: Soon after its U.S. introduction, I carted a shiny new iPhone to the United Kingdom, where it had yet to be released. During an interview with a journalist from the *Economist*, I dug out my sleek new baby and pushed it across the table. The scribe picked it up and within a minute was giggling like a 10-year-old girl. Now *that's* great design.

Amazingly competent. A well-conceived product excels at what it does. It's functionally flawless—like a Ziploc bag, a tabletop radio from Tivoli Audio, a Philips Sonicare toothbrush, a Nespresso coffee maker, or Google's home page. A great design is ingenious and intuitive, perfectly suited to its purpose, and devoid of anything superfluous.

Aesthetically exquisite. At the pinnacle of great design are products so gorgeous and lust-worthy that you want to hug them or lick them: a shiny Porsche 911, a Leica M9 camera, an Eames lounge chair, or anything by Loro Piana. A truly great design is to the eyes what a *cioccolato* gelato is to the tongue.

Conspicuously conscientious. To qualify as world-class, a design must also be conspicuously conscientious. Whether it's the Toyota Prius or Nike's Trash Talk sneaker (which is made from fabric scraps and a recycled sole), consumers are demanding socially responsible products that reflect a sense of stewardship for the environment and a passion for making a difference.

Sadly, design is still an afterthought in most companies. For every iPhone or Aeron chair, there are hundreds of examples of design idiocy—like the impenetrable packaging that surrounds just about every small, electronic device; the tiny, illegible script that adorns the shower amenities found in most hotels; the tortuously convoluted language that purports to explain the terms of a life insurance policy; the six-level tech-support phone menu that refuses to route your call to a carbon-based life form; or the entirely nonintuitive process for resetting your car's digital clock. I don't know whether the cosmos contains evidence of intelligent design, but I can assure you that thousands of everyday products do not.

Tim Brown would like to change this. As CEO of IDEO, the world's preeminent design firm, Tim believes that the power of great design is still underappreciated and underleveraged in most organizations—and he's right. Historically, most managers viewed design as a little pot of fairy dust that could be sprinkled on homely products to tart them up. Tim's argument: design should be seen instead as a fundamental business discipline that can produce insanely loyal customers and fat, chunky margins.

Tim argues that "design thinking" needs to permeate every organization and shape all of its interactions with its constituents. Given his job, it's hardly surprising that Tim is an apostle for design, but there's plenty of evidence to support his thesis.

Consider Apple. How is it that over the past few years the company managed to handily outperform the dreadful economy, given that there are cheaper alternatives to just about everything Apple makes? The answer, of course, is exceptional design. Apple infuses everything it does—hardware, software, packaging, retailing, and technical support—with design thinking. Whenever you rub up against Apple you rub up against hip and helpful design.

So what *is* design thinking? In a conversation,[1] Tim outlined its three core elements—observation, experimentation and prototyping:

You have to start with observation because it's the only way to illuminate the subtle nuances about how people actually get things done, or don't get things done, and it's these deep insights that lead to powerful new ideas. Intellectual experimentation is equally critical because there's no way to generate real breakthroughs unless people are willing to explore a lot of options in a divergent way. Finally, rapid and inexpensive prototyping is the most efficient way to move an idea from concept to reality. By "building to think" instead of "thinking about what to build," an organization can dramatically accelerate its pace of innovation.

Tim believes that good design is rare not because it demands esoteric skills, but because so few people have been trained in the basic principles of human-centered design.

I don't fly much on United Airlines anymore, even though my local airport is one of the carrier's "fortress hubs." (Gosh, doesn't that say it all?) Instead I trust my posterior to Virgin America. Since its launch in 2007, Virgin has run up four consecutive wins as "America's Best

Domestic Airline," this according to an annual survey run by *Travel and Leisure* magazine. As a passenger, one finds evidence of thoughtful design everywhere: seats that actually coddle, a touch screen that allows you to order food from your seat, healthy snacks, pastel mood lighting, a tray table that swivels and tilts to become an easel for your iPad, hip tunes playing softly in the bathrooms, power outlets at every seat, wi-fi on every flight, and flight attendants who are energetic and fun. On a recent flight, one cheeky member of the flight team promised to do "everything I can to restore the dignity you lost during security screening." All this, and prices that undercut its design-deprived competitors.

As this example illustrates, great design is less about genius than empathy—and it's often the tiniest things that make the biggest difference to consumers. For example, I recently came across a hotel shower with a strange accouterment: A small triangle of marble that had been wedged into one corner of the shower, about 20 inches up from the floor. Hmm, I thought, too low to be a soap shelf, what could it be? And then the "aha": a place where a woman can perch her toes while shaving her legs. Multiply a small touch like that a dozenfold, or a hundredfold, and you have a business that will decisively outperform the competition. So here's a suggestion: if you're a manager, post these simple questions on your company's idea wiki: First, what are the thoughtless little ways we irritate customers and what can we do to change that? And second, what are the small, unexpected delights we could deliver to our customers at virtually no additional cost? Get a few hundred or thousand folks thinking about these questions and you'll be well on your way to embedding design thinking in *your* organization.

TURNING INNOVATION DUFFERS INTO PROS

2.4

There isn't a sport on the planet that delivers less adrenaline per unit of time than golf. For years, that simple fact kept me off the links. When compared to hurling oneself down a black diamond ski run or diving on a wreck, the idea of spending the better part of a day struggling to propel a small round object toward a pint-sized hole with a device ill-suited to the task, seemed to me both pointless and effete.

Yet there I was a few months back, hacking my way around two of the most extravagantly beautiful golf courses on the planet. Kauri Cliffs and Cape Kidnappers, on New Zealand's North Island, offer staggering views across the Pacific. And soon I'm off to join a few of my English friends for week-long golf orgy on Canada's Prince Edward Island, where the violent slash of my golf swing will once again be the subject of amusement and ridicule: "Next time, see if you can slow it down to a blur."

My journey from sneering skeptic to helpless addict began a dozen years ago when I set out to write a cover story for *Fortune* on the Internet. In the process, I visited eBay's nascent website and more or less randomly entered a bid for a set of golf clubs. I was confident my lowball offer would get bested, so I didn't bother to check back in on the auction. A few days later, I walked into my office and discovered an elongated box propped up in one corner. "Oh crap," I said, as a shiny set of Callaway irons tumbled out of the packaging. Nevertheless, within a few days I was down at the Stanford University driving range with a 7-iron in my hand and a bucket of balls at my feet. My first swing slammed into the ground a foot behind the ball. Another hideous spasm sent the golf ball whizzing sideways, provoking startled stares from my fellow range rats. "Jeepers," I thought, "this is hard." And then, ten or twenty lunges later, I connected—and with a whizzing sound sweeter than the air intake on a Ferrari Italia, the little white orb started to soar. Up it went, suspended in the sparkling autumn sky. And then, 150 yards downrange, it returned to earth, bouncing softly on the grass.

Gee whiz. I had just hit a ball farther than an A-Rod home run! In that first euphoric moment, I had no idea I had just inhaled a drug more powerful than crack. Like all addicts, my craving has cost me dearly. Green fees, new clubs every 18 months or so, coaches, training aids, and trips to exotic golfing locales.

The golf swing has been called "the most difficult move in sports"— a label that does little to lessen one's sense of inadequacy. To send your ball rocketing precisely toward its intended destination, you must think of nothing but the target, while resisting the temptation to actually *look* at the target; you must keep your arms and hands relaxed, while torquing your torso like a rubber band; and you must accelerate the club head from a standstill to more than ninety miles an hour in less than a second, while resisting the temptation to "swing hard." And yet, with a bit of application, a middle-aged boomer with virtually no athletic ability can become a respectable golfer. And once or twice a round, that diligent amateur will hit a golf shot that is the equal of anything you're likely to see on the PGA Tour. This fact brings me neatly to my point: Despite the old adage that says otherwise, gray-haired dogs really *can* learn tricky new tricks.

That's why I'm optimistic that your company can dramatically improve its innovation performance. Over the years, my colleagues and I have demonstrated again and again that with the right tools and training, you can turn "ordinary" employees into extraordinary innovators.

Progressive CEOs increasingly understand that innovation is a company's lifeblood, but not many CEOs have put every employee through an intensive training program aimed at boosting their innovation skills. Sure, companies have electronic suggestion boxes, slush funds for new ideas, pipeline management tools, and innovation awards—but in the absence of a cadre of well-trained and highly skilled innovators, much of the investment in these innovation enablers will be wasted.

Imagine that you've coaxed a keen but woefully inexperienced golfer onto the first tee at Pebble Beach. After arming the novice with the latest titanium driver, you challenge him or her to split the fairway with a monster drive. You offer a $100 bonus for every drive that stays out of the rough, and another $100 for every hole where the ball goes down in par. But what you don't do is this: you don't give your apprentice any instruction—no books, no tips from Dave Pelz or David Ledbetter, and no video feedback. Neither do you set aside any time for practice. Given this scenario, how many 200-yard drives will your neophyte land in the fairway? How long will he or she persevere with the sport? And what kind of return will you get on the $2,000 you shelled out for a bag full of high-tech clubs and Pebble's eye-watering green fee? The answers: not many, not long, and not much. And no one who knows anything about golf would ever do anything so stupid.

That's why I'm dumbfounded by the fact that so few companies have invested in the innovation skills of their frontline employees. The least charitable explanation for this oversight is that senior managers subscribe to a sort of *innovation apartheid*. They believe that a few fortunate souls are genetically equipped to be creative, while most everyone else is a lunkhead, unable to come up with anything more exciting than suggestions for incremental improvement.

Having said this, I understand how a CEO might come to such a conclusion. Every day senior executives get bombarded with new ideas, and most of them are either woefully underdeveloped or downright batty. After a while, it's easy to believe that all those dopey ideas must be coming from dopes, rather than from individuals who've never had the chance to hone their innovation skills.

This disappointment is typically multiplied when a company sets up its first "idea market." Executives quickly discover that most of the proffered ideas fall into one of two buckets: incremental no-brainers or flaky no-hopers.

When I try to convince a CEO to invest in systematic innovation training, I often get the following reaction: "I don't know why we'd do that, we have too many ideas already. We can't begin to fund them all." "But," I ask, "how many of those ideas are radical *and* practical, potential gamechangers that are actually feasible?" "Oh," most executives reply, "we don't have many of those." And that's the problem. Although innovation is a numbers game, where quantity matters, so, too, does quality, and to improve the quality of an organization's innovation pipeline, you have to improve the quality of its innovation thinking.

THE PERCEPTUAL HABITS OF SUCCESSFUL INNOVATORS

Obviously, you can't teach someone to be an innovator unless you know where game-changing ideas come from. You need a *theory of innovation*—like Ben Hogan's theory of the golf swing.[1] This is why, a few years back, I led a project that analyzed more than a hundred cases of business innovation. Our goal: to understand why some individuals see opportunities that others miss. Here, in a pistachio-sized shell, is what we learned. Successful innovators have ways of looking at the world that throw new opportunities into sharp relief. They have developed, often by accident, a set of perceptual habits that allow them to pierce the fog of "what is" and catch a glimpse of "what could be." How do they do this? By paying attention to four things that usually go unexamined.

Unchallenged Orthodoxies

To be an innovator you have to challenge the beliefs that everyone else takes for granted—the long-held assumptions that blind industry incumbents to new ways of doing business.

Within any industry, mental models tend to converge over time. Executives read the same trade magazines, go to the same conferences and talk to the same consultants. As the years pass, the intellectual gene pool becomes a stagnant pond.

Success accelerates this process. Effective strategies get translated into operating policies, which spawn best practices, which harden into habits. Inevitably, fossilized strategies create opportunities for less orthodox competitors to upend industry rules. One such insurgent is Salesforce.com, a leading vendor of customer management software and an early advocate of the "software-as-a-service" business model. Traditionally, enterprise customers licensed software programs and installed them on their own servers, and then paid an annual fee for upgrades and maintenance. The Salesforce.com model changed that. Its software runs in the cloud and customers pay a monthly usage fee, a delivery model that reduces costs and increases flexibility.

Innovators are natural contrarians ("What box?"), and with a little practice, anyone can learn how to uncover and challenge long-static beliefs. Here are a couple of questions you can use to arouse the contrarian instincts of your team: First, in what respects is our business model indistinguishable from that of our competitors? To what extent is our value proposition, service bundle, pricing, customer support, distribution, or supply chain undifferentiated? And second, what aspects of our business model have remained unchanged over the past 3–5 years? Whenever you identify a convergent belief, ask, does this rest on some inviolable law of physics, or is it simply an artifact of our devotion to precedent? By working systematically to surface these invisible dogmas, you can turn reactionaries into rebels.

Underappreciated Trends

Innovators pay close attention to emerging trends, to the nascent discontinuities that have the potential to reinvigorate old businesses or create new ones.

In my experience, innovators don't waste a lot of time speculating about what *might* change; they're not big on scenario planning.

On the other hand, they pay a lot of attention to the little things that are *already* changing, but have gone unnoticed or discounted by industry stalwarts. Innovators are constantly on the lookout for emerging discontinuities—in technology, regulation, lifestyle, values, and geopolitics—that could be harnessed to overturn old industry structures. What this requires is not so much a crystal ball as a wide-angle lens. You have to learn in places your competitors aren't even looking. Building a strategy that leverages an emerging but powerful trend which your competitors barely perceive can give a company a big jump on the future.

An example: For more than a decade it's been obvious that a big shift is coming in how individuals consume video media. Today, in most countries, people get their video programming from cable or satellite television providers. These companies bundle up hundreds of channels and then charge viewers a hefty monthly fee for the total package. Problem is, most of us watch only a fraction of the available channels, yet pay for all of them. What's been obvious to some—like the folks at YouTube, Roku, Vudu, Hulu, Netflix, and AppleTV—is that this model is grossly inefficient and ripe for change. One omen: in the recent recession, fifty percent of American consumers got in touch with their TV company in a bid to lower their monthly subscription costs.[2]

Behind this potential sea change are two enabling discontinuities: Ever-fatter broadband "pipes" and ever-better technology for delivering full-motion video over the Web. It's notable that the traditional distributors of television content are not, for the most part, the ones most vigorously exploiting these trends. Their lassitude has opened the door for a gaggle of new, web-centric, competitors. In a world of head-snapping change, a company that fails to exploit a discontinuity, or dithers because it might imperil a beloved business model, will end up as the disruptee rather than the disrupter.

So how do you help people uncover the harbingers of change? By getting them out on the fringe where they can have a first-person encounter with the future. This might mean taking a Korean marketing team to Silicon Valley, getting a bunch of Finnish engineers to marinate in Tokyo's club scene, or asking some savvy teenagers to run a social media training session for a group of senior brand managers.

In my experience, there are five questions that can help a team to zero in on potentially important discontinuities. First, as you think about culture, politics, technology, and so on, what are the things you've read, seen, or experienced in recent months that have been surprising, perplexing, or disconcerting? Second, which of these anomalies seem to have some momentum behind them? When you look across the world, or back over the last few months, do you see these trends expanding in scope or accelerating? Are they blooming if not yet booming? Third, if you "run the movie forward," how might these discontinuities play out? What are the chain reactions that might be set in motion? Fourth, which of these discontinuities aren't yet topics of conversation within your industry? Which ones were missing from the agenda of the last industry confab you attended? And then fifth, how might we exploit these discontinuities in ways that would wrong-foot our competitors? By coaching individuals through these questions in disciplined way, and creating opportunities for them to dig deep, you can strengthen their ability to spot the next wave and ride it.

Underleveraged Competencies and Assets

Every company is a bundle of skills and assets. Typically these things are embedded in legacy business models, but if repurposed, they can often serve as platforms for innovation and growth.

Innovation gets stymied when a company defines itself by what it does rather than by what it knows or owns—when its self-conception is built around products and technologies rather than around core competencies and strategic assets. To innovate, you need to see your organization and the world around it as a portfolio of skills and assets that can be endlessly recombined into new products and businesses.

Disney has frequently demonstrated a talent for redeploying its competencies in new ways. Examples include the company's highly successful theatrical division (which produces live shows like *The Lion King*), and its cruise ship line. One of the company's recent ventures is Disney English, a business that employs a specially trained staff to deliver English-language training to Chinese youngsters, aided, of course, by a menagerie of Disney characters. Launched in 2008, the business now has learning centers in seven Chinese cities. Andrew Sugarman, the general manager of Disney English, believes the Chinese market for English education will grow at nearly 30 percent over the next several years.[3] When viewed from the perspective of theme parks or animated films, Disney English may seem an odd fit. But if you start with Disney's core competencies (which includes recruiting peppy staff and developing kid-centric content), and fold in some of its strategic assets (like a roster of beloved cartoon characters), the business suddenly makes sense. Add to that a powerful discontinuity—the rapid growth of the Chinese middle class, who share a belief that English is a "get ahead" skill—and you've got the foundations for a compelling new business.

Here again, there are questions that can help your team to uncover the hidden wealth within your organization: As a starter, you might ask, what are the skills and assets we have that are (a) relatively unique and (b) important in creating customer value? Second, where else might these skills and assets add value? How could they be used as gamechangers in other industries? It's this sort of thinking that recently led Procter & Gamble to stamp its Tide brand on a small chain of dry-cleaning outlets. While still an experiment, this venture represents a logical extension of a venerable P&G brand to a highly fragmented industry. The question about how to leverage one's strategic resource can also be asked in reverse: if Google, Facebook, Amazon, Virgin, or some other highly admired company was intent on reinventing your industry, how would they use their competencies and assets to do so, and what could you gain by partnering with them? As individuals learn to see their company and others from this perspective, the opportunities for innovation will multiply.

Unarticulated Needs

Serial innovators are good at spotting the inconveniences, encumbrances, and vexations that customers have come to take for granted, and that industry veterans mostly ignore.

The goal with innovation is to amaze customers with something they never could have imagined, but having once experienced it, can't imagine living without. What falls into that category for you? My list would include digital video recorders (thanks, TiVo), online restaurant reservations (way to go, OpenTable), free international video conferencing (gracias, Skype), and customized Internet radio (bravo, Pandora).

To amaze customers with the unexpected, you must first uncover their unspoken needs. Customers have their own orthodoxies; like the rest of us, they are prisoners of the familiar. So asking them what they want seldom yields fundamentally new insights. Instead, you have to observe them, up close and over time, and then reflect on what you've learned: Where are we wasting our customers' time? Where are we making things overly complex? Where are we treating customers like numbers instead of people? Where are we forcing them to solve problems we should solve for them?

In my experience, two skills are essential to excavating unarticulated needs, and with a bit of practice, just about anyone can strengthen these aptitudes. The first skill is the ability to read the emotional state of customers as they interact with your company and its services or products. The good news is that most of us are pretty good at deciphering emotional clues. What people need, though, is an opportunity to get out in the field and witness those emotions firsthand, before they're filtered and aggregated by market research specialists. Depending on your industry, you might have employees watch customers fill out online insurance forms, navigate the maze of a shopping center, struggle to program their car's GPS, or file a report for a missing piece of airline baggage.

There's a simple framework I often use as the foundation for this sort of "empathetic" thinking. On one axis I list the various stages of the "customer experience chain":

Discovering: How does a customer become acquainted with our products or services? What prompts awareness and outreach?

Learning: How does a customer get smart about our products and those of our competitors? Where do they go to learn and compare?

Buying: How does a customer transact with our company? What are the dynamics of the purchasing process?

Acquiring: How does a customer take delivery of our product or service? What are the logistics of getting it from here to there?

Using: How does a customer use our product or service in his or her daily life? What do they have to do to take advantage of its benefits? What are the various components of the user experience?

Connecting: How does a customer interact with our company post-purchase? What are the interactions that promote loyalty and affection, or frustration and disenchantment?

And on the other axis I enumerate the various emotional states a customer may experience at each stage of the experience chain. I usually put them in a column down the left, with the positive states up top and negative ones below.

Positive Emotional States

I feel:

Valued	Trusted
Informed	Respected
Involved	Confident
Amused	Engaged
Empowered	At ease

Negative Emotional States

I feel:

Neglected	Mistrusted
Misinformed	Belittled
Ignored	Confused
Bored	Alone
Helpless	Anxious

You can number each cell, and then ask employees to "code" the particular emotional states they observe as they watch a customer work through each stage of the experience chain. Giving employees a simple tool where they can record both the emotions they witness and the circumstances that triggered those emotions can be a powerful way of bringing unarticulated needs to the surface. In this context, it can be useful to ask a customer what prompted a particular feeling—"Gee, you seem perplexed. What just happened?" Capturing real-time reactions can add a lot of nuance to one's understanding of unmet needs.

Teaching people to be inquiring anthropologists is just the first step. What's also needed are concrete ideas for reengineering the customer experience in ways that astonish and enthrall. To generate those ideas, people must be trained to find and exploit analogies from other industries. You can ask, what does Disneyland, Singapore Airlines, Fandango, or Lexus do, for example, to engender great customer experiences, and how might those practices be applied in our industry? Innovation isn't always about invention; often it's about borrowing great ideas from other industries.

Again, there's a simple exercise that can help a team to sharpen this skill. Get a group of colleagues or customers together and ask each person to identify a product or service that dramatically reshaped their expectations—something that made them go "Wow! How amazing!" The goal here, using the matrix described above, is to identify an experience that provoked a gusher of good feelings. Next, ask folks, what were the unique attributes of that experience that made it so memorable? How, exactly, did it defy their expectations? Answers might include: "It was unbelievably easy to use. They walked me through every step." "It was amazingly fun. They made it a game." Or, "It seemed so personal. Everyone remembered my name." Having extracted the distinctive elements of each experience, you can ask, "How might we leverage this idea to redefine customer expectations in our own industry?"

For example, why shouldn't a textbook manufacturer be able to develop an online algebra course that's as engaging as the *World of Warcraft*? Why shouldn't a supermarket treat its most profitable customers as well as an international airline does—maybe a dedicated checkout line and someone to load your groceries in your car? Why shouldn't insurance agents make their commission fees public like real estate agents and stockbrokers do?

In building a theory of innovation, I talked to dozens of trailblazers. They weren't all super-smart, or artistically inclined, or the product of an unconventional upbringing. But all of them had developed perceptual routines that helped them see beyond the ordinary—by turning industry dogma on its head, by amplifying weak signals, by exploiting competencies and assets, and by tuning in to customer emotions.

Through training and practice you can help your colleagues internalize these routines. It takes time, but it's eminently doable. Whirlpool's strong innovation performance in recent years owes much to the fact that the company trained more than 30,000 of its employees to be business innovators, and certified more than 1,000 of them as innovation "black belts."

I can't state the point strongly enough: the first and most important step for any organization intent on building a capacity for continuous, gamechanging innovation is to teach its people how to view the world around them with fresh eyes. Until *your* company steps up to this challenge, it will be filled with innovation duffers whose ideas rarely find the fairway.

DECONSTRUCTING APPLE

2.5

In 1997 I bought an e-tablet from A.T. Cross, the pen company. Codeveloped with IBM, the CrossPad was hailed as a breakthrough product that would open up a whole new category—portable digital notepads. I'm a copious notetaker, so the idea of turning my scribblings into digital files was too good to pass up.

Truth is, I'm not so much an early adopter as an easy mark. Who was I to argue with "Ozzie" Osborne, head of IBM's Pen and Speech Business Systems business unit, when he declared that the CrossPad would "redefine how users perceive pen and paper?"[1] So I ran out and bought the CrossPad, but a month later, it was sharing shelf space with all the other "revolutionary" products that had promised to change my life but somehow hadn't.

Over the years I've become a tad less susceptible to the utopian visions of technology's self-proclaimed prophets. Recently, for example,

73

I walked out of a Sony store *without* a 3-D television. I've learned to my sorrow that a lot of geeky gadgeteers are hucksters, not oracles.

Given that, you might have expected me to be at least a teensy bit skeptical of the hype that accompanied the announcement of Apple's first generation iPad in January 2010—but I wasn't. Not that there weren't doubters. Some questioned the need for an iPhone on steroids, others bemoaned the lack of a stylus, while still others panned the device as a wildly overpriced e-reader. By contrast, I have always found it difficult to bet against the pride of Cupertino. Not because I'm a hopeless fanboy, which I am, but because Apple has innovation embedded more deeply in its DNA than any other company I know.

With hindsight, the skepticism over the iPad appears downright silly. In its first nine months, the shiny tablet generated nearly $10 billion in revenue—that's 10 with a "b." If the iPad were a company, it would have gone from incubator to the middle of the Fortune 500 in less than a year! A feat that is, I think, unprecedented in the annals of business history.

Over the past decade, Apple has produced a mind-boggling parade of accomplishments.

- Having once been dismissed as a footnote in the personal computer industry, it is now the market leader in computers costing $1,000 or more. Apple's share of the industry's most profitable segment is estimated to be a whopping 90%.[2]
- Apple is today the world's largest music retailer, a milestone reached just six years after the launch of its online music store in 2003. The 10 billionth song sold on iTunes was downloaded on February 24, 2010.[3]
- Though it was a late entrant into the mobile phone business, Apple currently makes more money from its roughly 5% of the global handset market than Nokia makes with its 30-plus share.[4] To appreciate the magnitude of this accomplishment, consider the following. According to the website Asymco.com, at the time of the iPhone's launch in June 2007, Nokia accounted for 63% of industry profits. Thirty-six months later, Nokia's global profit share had tumbled to 22% while the iPhone's had rocketed to 48%.[5]

- Apple opened its first retail store in 2001. At the time, many analysts panned the strategy. Today, though, Apple's sparse, elegant shops generate four times the revenue per square foot of its big box competitors,[6] and its Fifth Avenue store in New York is rumored to be the most profitable retail outlet in the world.[7]
- Since the launch of the company's App Store in 2008, Apple has become the world's largest software distributor. Thus far, developers have created more than 425,000 applications for the company's iOS operating system, and consumers have downloaded more than 10 billion apps.[8]
- As I'm writing this, Apple's market value is $361 billion, making it the most valuable company in the world. For comparison, Hewlett-Packard, a company with twice the revenues of Apple, is valued at only $54 billion.

All this is more than extraordinary—it is nearly unimaginable. It's the business equivalent of an athlete setting world records in half a dozen different sports. Apple may one day fall victim to its own success (most companies do), but if that happens, Apple will still stand as one of history's most remarkable companies. Indeed, if I were compiling a list of the most important companies of all time, Apple would be in the top three—alongside Ford, which invented large-scale manufacturing, and General Electric, a company that has been a management bellwether for more than a century.

How in the world could one company accomplish all this? How in the heck do you build an organization that is capable of reinventing not just one industry, but five or six—including computing, music, retailing, mobile phones, software, and (just maybe) media and publishing as well? Most companies never reinvent one industry; no other company in history has reinvented a handful.

Some would argue you have to start with Steve Jobs, the inspired and uncompromising visionary who led Apple from 1976 to 1985, and then again from 1997 to 2011. In that latter fourteen-year period, Apple's share price increased 110-fold. When Jobs stepped down from his CEO post in August 2011, only two months before he lost his battle with cancer, he left behind a legacy that is nearly unparalleled in business history. As a business icon, he's in the same pantheon as Henry Ford, Thomas Edison, and, well, I can't think of another. Apple would never have existed without Steve Jobs—that's obvious. Equally obvious is the fact that the company's unparalleled accomplishments are the product of more than one fertile mind. Even if Jobs had never slept, he couldn't have spawned all the ingenious ideas that have made Apple the world's most innovative company.

Other observers might credit Apple's unique business model. Ask an industry analyst or MBA student to deconstruct the company's gravity-defying performance and they would probably point out some of the distinctive elements of Apple's strategy. These might include:

Redefine the basis for competition. Apple differentiates itself through design and ease-of-use. Its competitors, by contrast, seem determined to create products that are as homely and nonintuitive as possible.

Fuse hardware and software. While most of Apple's competitors specialize in either hardware *or* software, Apple pursued excellence in both. By tightly integrating hardware and software design, the company optimizes system performance to the benefit, and relief, of its customers.

Master a broad array of complementary technologies. With the possible exception of Samsung, Apple encompasses a broader array of technological competencies than any of its competitors. Though it does little of its own manufacturing, Apple's mastery of semiconductor design, advanced materials, batteries, power management, component packaging, application development, and industrial design gives the company a distinct advantage in launching groundbreaking products—and in controlling its own destiny.

Lock up customers with velvet hand-cuffs. Apple is highly adept at locking customers in and competitors out—all with the goal of delivering a delicious end-to-end experience (and making boatloads of money). That's why the only place you can buy music for your iPod or apps for your iPad is in Apple's online store.

Build a giant network of third-party developers. Apple understands that competition isn't device versus device, it's ecosystem
versus ecosystem. That's why the company has put so much energy
into nurturing a global community of passionate developers for the
iPhone and iPad—a network that none of its competitors can match.

Extend the company's core competencies into new markets.
Apple's self-definition isn't centered on a particular product or market, but on a portfolio of deep competences. Before his death, Jobs
described Apple as the world's largest "mobile devices company"
(ahead of Nokia, Samsung, and Sony), rather than a computer
company.[9] A decade ago, no one would have lumped Apple in
with these companies—the comparisons would have been with
Microsoft and Dell.

As logical as this analysis seems, it is unsatisfying. It reveals something
of the "how," but nothing of the "why." Why has Apple been able
to rewrite industry rules again and again? Why does it seem to take
such pride in defying conventional wisdom? Why is it able to routinely
deliver the exceptional?

I don't think it's a particular strategy or person that makes Apple
Apple; rather, it's the company's unstinting devotion to a particular set
of ideals. Within the universe of inventors, designers, and artists, these
ideals aren't all that remarkable, but within the universe of Fortune 500
companies, they're as rare as water in the Gobi.

Before going further, I should make it clear that my take on Apple's
signature values isn't the product of in-company research. Steve Jobs
lived nearby, but he never had me over for a chinwag. Nevertheless,
when you ask yourself, "What sort of values would a company have to
venerate if it wanted to duplicate Apple's success?" the answers seem
almost intuitive.

BE PASSIONATE

Great success is the product of a great passion; it arises from the tireless
and inventive pursuit of a noble ideal. And for Apple, that virtue is
beauty. At several points during his unveiling speech for the iPad, Jobs

paused, looked at the new device, and said, "It's just so amazing to hold." Can you imagine one of HP's recent chairmen enthusing over a product in that sort of way—taking joyous pride in a technological coup d'art. To deliver years of exceptional performance, a company must first dedicate itself to the pursuit of an exceptional ideal.

LEAD, DON'T FOLLOW

I'm guessing that most of the folks at Apple hate being derivative. Sure, they'll occasionally borrow an idea from Microsoft or Amazon, but what gets them up in the morning is the chance to break new ground. I'd be amazed if anyone at Apple has ever defended the proposition that it's best to be a fast follower. While Apple doesn't always pioneer a new product category—there were MP3 players before the iPod and smartphones before the iPhone—it always sets itself the challenge of radically redefining the status quo.

AIM TO SURPRISE

As a company, Apple seems committed to exceeding expectations—to wringing little gasps of delight from even its most jaded customers. That's why I think the company's penchant for prelaunch secrecy is more than competitive paranoia; it's the way you produce the sort of gee-whiz delight that a parent aims for on Christmas morning. Apple wants to bewitch us. On this point, listen to Jonathan Ives, the company's head of design: "When something exceeds your ability to understand how it works, it sort of becomes magical." That's the bar Apple has set for itself. By the way, when was the last time your bank did something magical for you, rather than something diabolical?

BE UNREASONABLE

Greatness doesn't come from compromise, from resigning oneself to the trade-offs others blithely accept. It comes by transcending trade-offs, by turning either/or into both/and. Apple gets this, and frequently challenges itself to do the impossible—like producing products that are both gorgeous and functional. Apple proves that a company doesn't have to choose between high value and low cost. Not only is it one of the world's most innovative companies, it's also one of the most efficient—when it comes to lean, Apple gives nothing away to Toyota, Wal-Mart, or Dell. There's an important lesson here: You can't outperform your competitors if you live by their trade-offs. Reasonable people don't produce breakthroughs.

INNOVATE INCESSANTLY AND PERVASIVELY

At Apple, innovation isn't a strategy or a department; instead it's the basic material that goes into everything the company does. From the wafer-thin MacBook Air to the App Store to the Genius Bar, innovation is ubiquitous. Apparently there are a lot of people at Apple who realize that innovation—in products, services, and business models—is the *only* strategy for creating long-term value. If so, they must be relieved that innovation is still a sideshow for so many of their competitors.

SWEAT THE DETAILS

Apple is justifiably celebrated for its sense of aesthetics—but great design isn't just about bold strokes, it's about getting all of the tiny things right that conspire together to make a product truly exceptional. In Apple's case, it's the magnetically-attached power cord on every laptop, it's the gorgeous packaging that surrounds every iPod, it's the single billet of aluminum that gives structural integrity to every MacBook—plus a lot more stuff you can't see. "It just works"—that's another thing you often hear from Apple's top executives. The company aims to produce products that work intuitively, seamlessly, and reliably—and this can only happen when hundreds of people take the trouble to sweat the details.

THINK LIKE AN ENGINEER, FEEL LIKE AN ARTIST

A company can't produce beautiful products if bean counters win every argument. That thought occurred to me a few years back when I first visited Apple's Fifth Avenue Store in New York. This is now one of the most photographed landmarks in the city—a giant glass cube with the Apple logo floating in the middle. If you haven't seen it, Google it. Now ask yourself, is this the cheapest way to build a store entrance? Obviously not. Can you imagine something so extravagant getting past your CFO? No way. So why does it happen at Apple? Because there are lots of people there whose cranial cavity contains both left and right hemispheres—and they understand their customers are similarly equipped. Apple's executives know that something lovely and sleek and unexpected can provoke a visceral reaction in customers—a reaction that may not be easily quantified but can nevertheless be monetized.

To be clear, I don't think Apple has it all figured out. There are plenty of people who will tell you that Apple has all the monopolistic tendencies of its competitors, or that its success owes more to hype than to truly outstanding products. And no one would accuse anyone on the top team of being humble. The thing that can't be argued, though, is this: Apple is one of the most successful companies *ever*.

So let's do a bit of compare and contrast. If the values in the left-hand column distinguish Apple (or my airbrushed rendering of it), what are the values that characterize your company? I'm guessing it's something closer to what appears on the right.

Be passionate	Be rational
Lead, don't follow	Be cautious
Aim to surprise	Aim to satisfy
Be unreasonable	Be practical
Innovate incessantly	Innovate when necessary
Sweat the details	Get it mostly right
Think like an engineer and feel like an artist	Think like an engineer and feel like an accountant

Unlike Apple, most companies are long on accountants and short on artists. They are run by executives who know everything about cost and next to nothing about value. Does that sound like an overstatement? If so, here's a recent case in point: a few weeks ago I once again found myself forced to fly on a United Airlines flight. (Sorry, another airline rant.) I had paid well over $1,000 for my one-way, first-class ticket, so when I was served a cup of the world's worst decaffeinated coffee, I couldn't help but enquire politely as to its provenance. "It comes from a 'tea bag,'" the flight attendant explained apologetically. "We stopped serving fresh-brewed decaf a few months back." I don't know how much money United will save by this move, but the airline's penny-wise, pound-foolish approach to customer service has already cost it tens of thousands of dollars in lost revenue from at least one business traveler—*me!*

Like many other cost-obsessed managers, United's bean counters seem to have forgotten that productivity is determined by two factors: the efficiency with which the organization uses its inputs, and the value customers place on its outputs. Executives often wrongly equate "good value" with "low price." Instead, "good value" should mean outstanding value *for* the price. Historically, many of Apple's products carried a premium price tag, but customers anted up because they also delivered superior fun and functionality. Put simply, hyper-rational executives produce hyper-boring products.

The bottom line: Apple's unique success is a product of its unique values, which are uniquely innovation-friendly and customer-centric. That's why I don't think any other company will soon duplicate the kind of run Apple has had over the past decade. I hope I'm wrong, and maybe I will be. Imagine if Apple's passions were the norm rather than the exception. What if the world's leading insurance company or publisher or bank or airline or hotel chain was driven by these ideals? What if you encountered them every time you talked to someone at the Internal Revenue Service or had to apply for a building permit? OK, now I'm hallucinating. But still, I can't help but dream of a world in which Apple has become a lot less exceptional because its core values have become a lot less exceptional. Apple may have patented a lot of things, but it hasn't patented the values that have made it, for a time at least, the world's most successful company. Apple is proof positive that innovation matters now!

SECTION 3

Adaptability Matters Now

CHANGING HOW WE CHANGE

3.1

What will people make of our age a thousand years hence? What will they find remarkable about the waning years of the second millennium and the coming of the third? The invention of the Web? The fact that human beings decoded their own genome or sent a vehicle to Mars? The emergence of digitally empowered democracy movements around the world? The ways in which we responded, or didn't, to the specter of climate change? All of this will be notable, but most of all, they'll be struck by the fact that in our generation, the pace of change went hypercritical.

Truly, change has changed. We are surrounded by all sorts of things that are changing at an exponential pace: the number of mobile phones in the world, CO_2 emissions, data storage, the power of semiconductor chips, the number of devices connected to the Internet, the number of genes that have been sequenced, world energy consumption, and knowledge itself. As human beings, we don't have much experience with exponential change. It's little wonder, for example, that regulators and risk officers struggled to control the contagion-like growth of mortgage-backed securities. In 1998, the value of outstanding credit default contracts was a relatively measly $300 billion, but over the next ten years that number would grow to $62 trillion—that's a compound annual growth rate of more than 70%.

Obviously nothing grows exponentially forever, yet as some trends slow (like the growth rate in mobile phone penetration), others catapult forward (for example, the explosive growth of social media); and when these trends interact, they spawn radically new phenomena—like flash mobs, global terror networks, or location-specific web apps. Other centuries were convulsed by famine, disease, and war, but never before have so many things been changing so rapidly.

We live in a world that seems to be all punctuation and no equilibrium, where the future is less and less an extrapolation of the past. Change is multifaceted, relentless, seditious, and occasionally shocking. In this maelstrom, long-lived political dynasties, venerable institutions, and hundred-year-old business models are all at risk.

Today, the most important question for any organization is this: are we changing as fast as the world around us? Most CEOs would have to answer "no." In industry after industry, it's the insurgents, not the incumbents, who've been surfing the waves of change—it's Google, not Microsoft; Zynga, not Electronic Arts; Hyundai, not Chrysler; Amazon, not Barnes and Noble; Apple, not Nokia; Air Asia, not JAL; Vizio, not Sony; and so on. The vanguard, though, are just as vulnerable to change as their victims. Success has never been more fleeting.

Reflect for a moment on the recent history of the mobile phone business. Motorola hatched the industry in 1983 with its brick-shaped DynaTac phone and for a time seemed invincible as the world's leading cell phone maker. A decade later, Nokia surprised the industry with its easy-to-manufacture "candy-bar" phone. By the end of the century, Nokia's fetching designs and torrid expansion had given the Finnish company a 40% share of what was now an enormous consumer market. In 2002, the Canadian company, Research in Motion, introduced its iconic "Blackberry," transforming the simple phone into an indispensible business tool. And then, in 2007, Apple rocked the industry with the iPhone, a powerful, handheld computing platform. Four leaders in four decades—that's the reality of competition in a world where change is shaken rather than stirred.

In web-based businesses, the whiplash can be even more sudden. Consider social networking. In less than a decade, leadership passed from Friendster to MySpace to Facebook. Like a bucking bronco, change frequently tosses its riders into the dirt.

Given all this, the only thing that can be safely predicted is that some-time soon your organization will be challenged to change in ways for which it has no precedent. Your company will either adapt or falter, rethink its core assumptions or fumble the future—and to be honest, a fumble is the most likely outcome.

Of course, change brings both promise and peril, but the proportion facing any particular organization depends on its capacity to adapt. And therein lies the problem: our organizations were never built to be adaptable. Those early management pioneers, a hundred years ago, set out to build companies that were disciplined, not resilient. They understood that efficiency comes from routinizing the nonroutine. Adaptability, on the other hand, requires a willingness to occasionally abandon those routines—and in most organizations there are precious few incentives to do so. That's why change tends to come in only two varieties: the trivial and the traumatic. Review the history of the average corporation and you'll discover long periods of incremental fiddling punctuated by occasional bouts of frantic, crisis-driven change.

In Global 1000 companies, as in poorly governed dictatorships, deep change occurs belatedly and convulsively. Doesn't this strike you as odd? Why should it take a "regime change" to change strategy? Why should an organization have to lose its way and surrender billions of dollars in market value before getting serious about change? A turnaround is a poor substitute for timely transformation. That's why we need to change the way we change.

The body's autonomic systems give us some useful metaphors. When you jump on a treadmill or pick up some weights, your heart starts to pump more blood, automatically. When you stand in front of a large audience to speak, your adrenal glands ramp up the production of adrenaline, spontaneously. When you catch a glimpse of someone who's physically attractive, your pupils dilate reflexively. (Truly, dear, it can't be helped.) *Automatically, spontaneously, reflexively*—these aren't the words we use to describe how our organizations change, but they should be. That's the holy grail—change without trauma.

In a world of mind-flipping change, what matters is not merely a company's competitive advantage at a *point in time*, but its evolutionary advantage *over time*. A few years back, the CEO of a vibrant, young company boasted to me that his business was "growing like a rocket." "Have you noticed," I asked, "that rockets follow a parabolic path, and that the satellites they launch into space ultimately come back to earth in little pieces?"

So how do you keep a company in orbit? That's the question we're going to explore in the next few chapters. As we'll see, building a truly adaptable company is a lot of work. It requires a shift in aspirations, behaviors, and management systems. Yet I have no doubt that tomorrow's most successful organizations will be the ones that master the challenge of high change/low pain.

The payoffs to investing in adaptability are many. First, a resilient organization should be able to avoid the sort of big earnings shocks that can slice a company's market value in half. Executives often complain that investors overreact to small earnings misses, but I'm not so sure. In recent years, investors have seen a lot of companies self-destruct when they missed a paradigm shift, underestimated a new competitor, or simply stopped innovating. When a company's earnings disappoint, investors have to ask themselves: was this a blip, the result of an easily corrected operating glitch, or is this an early warning sign of a structural decline in the long-term profitability of this company's business model? Executives will always claim it's a blip, but investors have learned to be wary of glib assurances. The safest thing to do is dump the shares, and then buy them back later once the problems have been remedied.

Investors like predictability and will pay more for a less volatile earnings stream. Though short-term earnings can be manipulated with accounting tricks, adaptability is the only thing that can deliver a smooth, upward slope over the long run. An adaptable company rethinks its strategy without having to walk through the valley of the shadow of death; it reinvents itself before getting mugged by the future. As a result, it experiences fewer financial reversals and its share price commands a premium. This is reason enough to care about adaptability, but there's more.

An adaptable company is one that captures more than its fair share of new opportunities. It's always redefining its core business in ways that open up new avenues for growth. If it had been more adaptable, Best Buy might have seen the opportunity for delivering movies online and beat Netflix to the punch; Coca-Cola might have preempted Gatorade in the sports drinks business; and General Motors, rather than Toyota, might have developed the world's best-selling hybrid. An adaptable company is always reinventing itself, always pioneering new markets.

An enterprise that is constantly exploring new horizons is likely to have a competitive advantage in attracting and retaining talent. When a once-successful company runs aground and starts to list, its most talented employees usually don't stick around to bail water, they jump ship. A dynamic company will have employees who are more engaged, more excited to show up to work every day, and thus more productive.

And finally, an adaptable company will be more proactive in responding to emerging customer needs. It will take the lead in redefining customer expectations in positive ways. The result: higher levels of customer loyalty and better margins.

Building organizations that are as resilient as they are efficient may be the most fundamental business challenge of our time. Adaptability *really* matters now.

BECOMING AN ENEMY OF ENTROPY

3.2

There aren't many institutions that have been around since the time of Julius Caesar, but the Christian church is one of them. Despite its longevity, Christianity has recently been on the defensive, particularly in Europe and North America.

Mainstream denominations have been losing mindshare among the planet's richest and best-educated inhabitants. Like their CEO counterparts, church leaders are being forced to confront a simple but profound truth: in a world of accelerating change, relevance can never be taken for granted.

That was the gist of my message when I stood in front of 7,000 clergy at a conference organized by the Willow Creek Community Church in Barrington, Illinois. Willow Creek is one of America's pioneering mega-churches, and since 1999 it's been running an annual "Leadership Summit" that draws together evangelical church leaders from around the world. Most of the speakers are not pastors but public personalities such as Carly Fiorina, Bono, and Tony Blair.

I found the experience a bit intimidating. I'm used to flashing my PowerPoints in front of people who are richer and more powerful than me, but this was the first time I had to face thousands of individuals who were undoubtedly more virtuous.

I agreed to speak for two reasons. First, I'm professionally interested in the challenges of organizational renewal—and I was eager to think about what this means for institutions that have been around for hundreds of years. And second, I believe the church (in the broadest, ecumenical sense of that word) plays an essential role in constructing the moral foundations of a democratic society—a view advanced 147 years ago by that famous French tourist, Alexis de Tocqueville:

Champions of freedom...should hasten to invoke the aid of religion, for they must know that without morality freedom cannot reign.[1]

Let me expand for a moment on this point.

Obviously, you don't have to be religious to be moral; and beastly people are sometimes religious. Yet despite the claims of neo-atheists like Richard Dawkins, Christopher Hitchens, and Sam Harris, religion has, on balance, curbed rather than exacerbated the human potential for evil.[2] Yes, terrible things have been done in God's name, but for every tyrant and terrorist who has claimed a divine warrant, there are thousands of faithful souls whose selfless acts have made the world a more just and tranquil place.

At the heart of every faith system is a bargain: on one side, there's the comfort that comes from a belief in the cosmic significance of human life, and on the other, there's a commitment to live up to certain moral standards that can, at times, be jolly inconvenient. I believe we should be grateful when an individual, however deluded, willingly assents to this bargain. For although there may be some who share a two-year-old's belief that we'd all be better off in a society free of moral constraints, most of us realize we wouldn't much like a world in which our neighbors, bosses, and bankers were unprincipled knaves.

Of course, in an ideal world, others would treat us charitably even when we stuck it to them; we could take advantage of their goodness while not being very good ourselves. But this doesn't scale. When that sort of one-sided selfishness becomes the norm, life gets brutish for everyone—a spiritual tragedy of the commons.

The fact is, society is made more hospitable when every individual acts as if "do unto others" really *is* a rule. And Dawkins notwithstanding, the evidence suggests that "religious people" actually *are* nicer, in practical feed-the-hungry, clothe-the-naked sorts of ways.[3] (And if *you're* one of those big-hearted believers, you're undoubtedly embarrassed by the minority of adherents who seem more eager to condemn than to love.)

Human morality is one generation deep, so if we want our children to live in a world where there is more benevolence than animosity, we must work to replenish the stock of spiritual capital we inherited from our forebears. In theory, at least, churches should be allies in this effort.

So that's why I went to Willow—and the experience was like a daylong group hug. Good golly, what a bunch of nice folks. Which made it even tougher for me to deliver my pointed message.

The fact is, the church is in trouble, particularly among young adults. Having lived in Britain for a decade, I am well aware of religion's marginal status in Europe, but I hadn't given much thought to the state of the church in America. Here's what I learned when I started prepping for my Willow talk:

- Since 1990, the number of Americans with no religious affiliation has nearly doubled, and the number of people who describe themselves as atheist or agnostic has quadrupled—this according to the 2008 *American Religious Identification Survey*.[4]
- The same survey revealed that two-thirds of Americans believe religion's influence is waning in our society, and just 19% say it's growing. The proportion of Americans who think religion "can answer all or most of today's problems" is at a historic low of 48%.[5]

- On an average weekend, just 17.5% of the population attends a Christian church service, down from 20.4% in 1990. This downward trend has been accelerating and if it continues, only 1 of 7 individuals will be attending church regularly in 2020.[6]
- In 2006 there were 91 million more Americans than in 1990, and 70 million of them were under the age of 17. Yet over this time frame, church attendance stayed flat.[7]
- The Christian "brand" has also taken a beating, particularly among young people. When polled, around half say they have a neutral view of Christianity, but among those who feel more strongly, the ratio of negative to positive views of "Christianity" and of those who are "Born Again" is 2:1. When asked about "Evangelicals," the ratio of negative to positive jumps to 16:1.[8]
- Between 1990 and 2008, the percentage of Americans identifying themselves with a large, traditional denomination (Catholic, Baptist, Methodist, etc.) dropped from 64.2% to 53.8%.[9]
- All of this means that churches are struggling to add new members. Church consultants Tom and Sam Rainer define a "healthy" church as one with a "conversion ratio" of 20:1 or better; that is, it takes twenty or fewer congregants to bring in one new member over the course of a year. By that modest standard, only 3.5% of America's 400,000 churches are evangelistically fit.[10]

Not surprisingly, pastors often place the blame for these trends on secular forces. The problem isn't "the church" but "the world," or more specifically:

- A consumer-driven society where the size of your paycheck counts for more than the quality of your character.
- The near-infinite number of diversions offered up by our media-saturated culture—distractions that crowd out time for spiritual reflection.
- The deeply cynical view young people have of large institutions—a view that lumps big religion together with big business and big government.
- The growing and reflexive skepticism of anyone who claims to have "the truth."

While these realities have undoubtedly played a role in the recent "de-churching" of America (and in the more advanced secularization of Europe), I don't believe this is the whole story, not by a long shot, and during my Leadership Summit talk I took pains to explain why.

Yes, church attendance is lagging, but 70% of Americans still believe there is "definitely a personal God."[11] Although they are becoming less religiously observant, Americans are still spiritually inclined. "So," I asked my audience, "Is it the gospel that is becoming less relevant, or your churches?" For pastors, this is a rhetorical question. The gospel is timeless. In other words, I argued, the problem confronting churches is not a decline in spiritual belief, but a decline in their spiritual effectiveness.

Organizations lose their relevance when the rate of internal change lags the pace of external change. That's the problem facing many churches today; and a whole lot of secular organizations, including yours, most likely, are in the same boat.

Think about General Motors, Sony, Motorola, Microsoft, AOL, Yahoo, Sears, Starbucks—how have these companies been doing in recent years? Not so great. Sure, the recession didn't help, but the real problem was something else. These companies were taken hostage by heritage; they locked themselves up in prisons of precedent.

So, I continued, as church leaders, you shouldn't feel too sorry for yourselves. Your problem isn't materialism, atheism, skepticism, or relativism—it's institutional inertia. And if it makes you feel better, it's not entirely your fault. Like leaders everywhere, you've been run over by change.

In our topsy-turvy world, you're either going forward or going backwards—but you're never standing still—and, at the moment, a lot of organizations, churches included, are going backwards.

Historically, business leaders and church leaders didn't have to worry about fundamental paradigm shifts. They could safely assume that their basic business models would last forever. In the case of church, that meant loyal pew-warmers who showed up each week, sat passively through the same unvarying service, dropped five bucks into the plate as it passed, and politely shook the pastor's hand as they headed off for lunch.

But business models *aren't* eternal, and in recent years their mortality rate has been rising. In industry after industry we've witnessed profound paradigm shifts. Some of the most notable:

- In the airline industry we've seen the majors lose ground to more focused competitors such as jetBlue and Virgin America.
- In pharmaceuticals, we've seen a transition from scattershot drug discovery to disease-focused, gene-based drug design.
- In the car industry, we've watched plug-in hybrids and all-electric vehicles challenge the long reign of the combustion engine.
- In software, we've seen a shift from software-as-a-product to software-as-a-service.
- In publishing, we've observed the explosive growth of e-books and a diminishing role for traditional bookstores.
- In health care, we've watched as "fee for service" business models have lost ground to "integrated care" models.

Most businesses, churches included, end up shackled to one business model—and when it atrophies, so does the institution.

In other words, the Second Law of Thermodynamics applies to organizations just as it does to physical systems. Over time, entropy increases. Visionary founders pass the baton to steadfast administrators who milk the legacy business but fail to reinvent it. The bureaucrats extrapolate but they don't rejuvenate. As the years pass, the mainspring of foresight and passion slowly unwinds. The organization gets better but it doesn't get different, and little by little it surrenders its relevance.

Over the centuries, Christianity has become institutionalized; it has become encrusted with elaborate hierarchies, top-heavy bureaucracies, highly specialized roles, and reflexive routines. (Kinda like your company, but more so.) Religion won't regain its relevance until church leaders chip off those calcified layers and rediscover their sense of mission.

What are some of the inertial forces that have prevented churches from reinventing themselves in ways that might make them more relevant to a post-modern world? A partial list would include:

- Long-serving denominational leaders who have little experience with nontraditional models of worship and outreach.
- A matrix of top-down policies that limits the scope for local experimentation.
- Seminaries that perpetuate a traditional view of religious observance and clerical roles.
- Promotion criteria that reward conformance to traditional church practices.
- And a straitjacket of legacy beliefs around how to "do church."

On this last point, it is worth noting that most denominations adhere to the same "delivery model" for "spiritual services," and that the standard template is less the product of Biblical injunction than of habit. Some of the unchallenged assumptions:

- Church happens in church.
- Preaching is the most effective way of imparting religious wisdom.
- Clergy lead while lay people follow.
- More programs equal more impact.
- The church service follows a typical order: greet, sing, read, pray, preach, bless, dismiss (repeat weekly).
- Believers, rather than curious skeptics, are the church's primary constituency.
- Going to church is the primary manifestation of a spiritual life.
- Church is a lecture, not a discussion.
- The primary mission of the church is to serve its members, rather than those outside of the church who are searching for a spiritual connection.
- The best way to grow the Christian community is to plant little churches that are replicas of big churches.
- To bring people to faith, churchgoers need to market their beliefs more professionally rather than live them out more convincingly.

(You may want to take a break here and make a list of what are the things that mindlessly perpetuate the past in your organization.)

If organized religion has become less relevant, it's not because churches have held fast to their creedal beliefs; it's because they've held fast to their conventional rituals, roles, and routines. In other words, the problem with organized religion isn't the "religion" bit, but the "organized" bit.

In the first and second centuries, the Christian church was communal, organic, and unstructured—a lot like the Web today. It wasn't politically powerful (it couldn't raise an army or depose a monarch), but it had enormous influence. Within the Roman Empire, the Christian church grew from a handful of believers in AD 40 to 31 million adherents by AD 350, making it the world's first viral organization. By contrast, today's mainline churches are institutionally powerful, but spiritually weak, at least in the developed world.

What's true for churches is true for other institutions: the more "organized" and tightly "managed" they are, the less adaptable they are. Not surprisingly, the most resilient thing on the planet, the Web, is loosely organized and lightly managed, and so was the first century Christian church. The lesson here? To thrive in turbulent times, organizations must become a bit more disorganized and unmanaged—less structured, less hierarchical, and less routinized.

In the next chapter, I'll dig deeper into the causes of organizational entropy, but for now, let's think about what you can do to become an enemy of entropy.

First, you have to protect yourself against denial. The longer one lingers in a state of denial, the longer the work of renewal gets postponed. The good news is that denial follows a familiar pattern, and when you recognize it, you can guard against it. To illustrate the cycle of denial, let's look at how a guy reacts when he finds himself in a slowly deteriorating relationship—with his spouse, let's say.

A man's first instinct in this situation is to simply dismiss the problem. He'll tell himself, "Every couple fights," or "All relationships go through rocky patches." In other words, if I just hang loose, the problem will go away. Now, where's the remote control? Sadly, though, the relationship continues to fray. Molten anger bubbles just below the surface, and the strained silences are frequently punctuated by heated emotional outbursts.

At this point, our male protagonist moves from dismissal to rationalization. It's obvious that his partner's barely contained fury is, well, a tad unusual, so he starts to speculate about its source. Maybe she hates her job. Maybe she's harboring childhood resentments, or maybe she's working out some misplaced anger over her feckless father. Note that all of these explanations are exculpatory. Whatever the problem, it's his wife's, not his. Things get worse. Shouting matches send the children running for cover, and hubby often finds himself spending nights on the couch. Rationalization will no longer suffice. It's time to do something. Our bewildered husband finds a quiet moment and gingerly approaches his spouse. "Have you thought about Prozac?" he asks. Her response rocks him back: "You idiot, I'm not depressed, I'm pissed off." With any luck, the penny finally drops and our consort moves on to confrontation. What must be confronted, though, is not his spouse, but his own shortcoming—the impatience, nitpicking, and ingratitude that have fueled his wife's frustrations.

This pattern of dismiss, rationalize, mitigate, and confront is as common in boardrooms as it is in bedrooms. Take, for example, the music industry's laggardly response to file-sharing. The first reaction of industry experts was ridicule. Who would want to listen to music on a computer? Searching the Web, downloading MP3 files, burning CDs—average listeners would never put up with something so complicated. Soon, though, Napster and its ilk were booming. Well yes, executives admitted, a lot of people were downloading music—but only because it was free. Eliminate that, and consumers would go scurrying back to their compact discs. As downloads soared, rationalization gave way to mitigation: Let's sue those teenage bandits. We can get the genie back in the bottle if we put the cheats in jail. In the end, though, the future couldn't be denied. By the time industry CEOs finally awoke to the inevitable demise of their hundred-year-old business model, CD sales were in freefall and Apple was dictating prices for online music.

There are three things you can do to inoculate yourself against denial. First, be humble. Regard all your industry beliefs as mere hypotheses, forever open to disconfirmation. Executives often say to me, "Gary, this is how our industry works." My stock reply: "Yeah, until it doesn't." If you want to deify God, go right ahead—but don't deify tradition or your own long-held assumptions. In a world of discontinuous change, arrogance is a mortal sin.

Second, be honest. Seek out the most discomforting facts you can find and share them with everyone in your organization. A leader has to confront the future, not discredit it. So find the dissident voices inside your organization and give them a platform. Search out anomalous business models (if you're a church leader, that might be www.xxxchurch.com) and ask yourself, what industry orthodoxies are they overturning? The canaries in the coal mine are there. You have to find them.

Another way to head off entropy is keep the mission paramount. It is easy, over time, to elevate form over function and confuse programs with purpose. The point of a newspaper is to connect people with the events that are shaping their world, not to distribute newsprint. A lot of publishers missed this point and left the door open for interlopers like Google News, the Huffington Post, and the Drudge Report.

Many of the world's top-rated universities suffer from a similar confusion between means and ends. Despite all their lofty rhetoric about advancing human knowledge, most deans and chancellors seem to believe that the purpose of an elite university is to provide a grand setting in which a small number of carefully screened and highly privileged students can acquire the exclusive credentials they will need to penetrate the ranks of other similarly elite institutions. This narrow, tradition-bound perspective has opened a gaping hole in the market for education—one that's being filled by organizations like the University of Phoenix, and by even more radical initiatives such as P2PU (Peer-to-Peer University).

Back to church. No pastor would ever tell you that the goal of his or her church is to create a place where members can gather each week to be expertly entertained while congratulating themselves on their moral superiority. And yet this seems often to be the case. I put another question to the Willow Creek crowd: "Is there a difference between 'doing church' and 'doing Jesus'?" "Of course," they responded. "So," I queried, "where do your loyalties lie? Is it with the mission of redemption and reconciliation, or with the traditional programs and policies of your church? And if it's the former, how would people know? What would be the evidence? Wouldn't it be your willingness to sacrifice some of those familiar practices on the altar of a bigger purpose?"

I've never met a leader who swears allegiance to the status quo, and yet few organizations seem capable of proactive change. How do we explain this? I think the answer lies, in part, with the difficulty we have in identifying our deeply engrained habits. While conceptually, one may understand the idea of industry "orthodoxies," how does one distinguish between an innovation-cramping habit and a time-tested policy that works?

There are only two things, I think, that can throw our habits into sharp relief: a crisis that brutally exposes our collective myopia, or a mission so compelling and preposterous that it forces us to rethink our time-worn practices. That's the point I made a few years back at a conference for MBA program directors and business school deans.

$250.00. That's the number I threw up on the screen. Then I asked, "Why can't we offer students an MBA degree for $250.00? Today, the all-in cost of an MBA degree at a top-flight university can run to $100,000 or more. If, as business educators, we really want to improve the quality of management around the world, we have to find a way to radically reduce the cost of a management degree."

To push their thinking, I shared a case study. The Aravind Eye Care System was founded in Madurai, India in 1976 by Dr. Govindappa Venkataswamy. Dr. V's vision: eliminate needless blindness by dramatically rethinking ophthalmic care. Modeled on McDonald's low cost, fast food model, the chain of eye clinics has developed highly efficient protocols for cataract surgery. Those who can afford the surgery pay for the procedure, but approximately 70% of Aravind's patients receive their care for free. Surgeons are paid competitive salaries, but perform as many as 100 surgeries during each 12-hour shift. More than 300,000 surgeries are performed each year in Aravind's five purpose-built hospitals, where operating rooms are in use 24 hours a day. The cost per surgery is around $18, about 1% of the cost for a similar procedure in the United States.[12] Even so, Aravind's complication rates are as good or better than the average in Western hospitals. The system is also financially self-supporting—thanks to the extraordinary efficiencies that have been engineered into its facilities and practices.

So, I asked my B-school friends, if it's possible to perform eye surgery for less than $20, why can't we offer a basic MBA degree for $250? Yeah, teaching is more complicated than surgery, but still . . . . Like health care, higher education is an extraordinarily inefficient business. Think about it: One professor in front of 80 kids. Hundreds of millions of dollars devoted to bricks and mortar. Huge research budgets devoted to the production of impenetrable articles for obscure journals. These taken-for-granted features of a typical business school seem sensible, and indispensible, until you redefine success. Instead of training a few hundred young managers each year, what if a business school aimed to train a few hundred thousand?

The Christian church in its various forms, and the great universities it spawned, have proven to be some of humanity's most durable institutions. From the beginning, they have been missional at their core—but as change accelerates, they will have to become even more so, and so, too, will your organization. It won't be easy.

As institutions mature, the positive thrust of mission diminishes and the pull of habit strengthens—until, one day, the organization can no longer escape the gravitational field of its own legacy. We will dissect these dynamics in the next chapter. For now, though, we need to remind ourselves that it's impossible to build adaptable organizations without adaptable people—individuals who are humble, honest, and inspired. These are the human roots of renewal. They aren't the only things that are needed to build an evolutionary advantage, but they're undoubtedly the most important.

DIAGNOSING DECLINE

I grew up in Michigan, so the bankruptcy of General Motors in 2009 struck close to home. There was a time when GM made more than half the cars sold in America. And then it was a ward of the state. GM's demise wasn't the result of one spectacularly ill-conceived decision; the company didn't jump off a cliff. Instead, it stumbled into mediocrity, one small, short-sighted step at a time. Thanks to the U.S. taxpayer, it got a shot at redemption, but no one's betting it will regain its former glory.

A company can coast for a long time when it starts with a dominant share of an enormous, hard-to-penetrate business in the world's largest economy—but given enough time, and enough myopia, it will eventually run out of momentum.

GM is not the only company that's sputtering right now. EMI, *The New York Times*, Johnson and Johnson, Nokia, Kodak—these are just a few of the companies that have lost their mojo in recent years. Truth is, every organization is successful until it's not—and today, there are a lot that aren't.

How does this happen? How do icons become also-rans? How does excellence expire? Typically, there are three forces at work.

FIRST, GRAVITY WINS

There are three physical laws that over time flatten the arc of success. The first is the law of large numbers. We all know it's harder to grow a big company than a small one. To add 25% onto the top line of a $40 billion company, one must create ten new billion-dollar businesses. To grow a $40 million company by the same percentage requires only $10 million in new revenue. In business as in biology, big things grow more slowly.

Then there's the law of averages. No company can outperform the mean indefinitely. During the last five years of Jack Welch's tenure at GE, the company's market value grew from less than $90 billion to more than $500 billion. To maintain that torrid pace, Jeff Immelt, who took over from Welch in 2000, would have had to grow GE's value to nearly $3 trillion dollars during the first five years of his tenure. That was never going to happen. As you lengthen the relevant time frame from one year to five, and then ten, the probability of outperforming the average rapidly approaches zero. In the long run, there are no growth companies.

Finally, there's the law of diminishing returns. The payoff to revenue- and margin-enhancing initiatives tends to shrink over time. Growth slows as a market matures, and productivity gains get harder to come by as the knife scrapes closer to the bone. Whatever the performance program, the ratio of outcome-to-effort will dwindle over time.

While these laws aren't as unyielding as gravity, they're tough to overcome—and few companies manage it. The best bet: break large, monolithic businesses into smaller ones, give them challenging growth targets, move aggressively to reallocate resources to faster-growing areas, spin off units where growth is decelerating, and search everywhere for new sources of differentiation.

Managers too often see themselves as farmers. They've been given a plot of ground to cultivate, a business or a market segment, and their goal is to grow the biggest possible crop of profits. Over time, though, yields fall as the soil becomes more saline (markets saturate), or as vital nutrients are depleted (differentiation wanes). By now, though, that VP is in love with his forty acres, so he responds by spending even more on fertilizer (marketing), and digs deeper and more expensive wells (raising capital investment even as ROI declines). It would be better if managers saw themselves as ranchers whose grass-fed herds were always on the move. A rancher's loyalty isn't to a piece of ground, or even a particular animal. When a pasture gets grazed out, you move the herd on. When an animal falls behind, it gets culled. And over time, the entire herd gets replaced, as older animals go off to slaughter and new calves get born.

In this regard, I think of the U.K. conglomerate, Virgin. Sir Richard Branson, Virgin's founder, has probably started more businesses than any other CEO on the planet, and he's killed almost as many. Though he's passionate about every new venture, like Virgin Galactic, he's never allowed Virgin's identity to become rooted in one particular business. There's a simple, but oft-neglected lesson here: to sustain success, you have to be willing to abandon things that are no longer successful.

SECOND, STRATEGIES DIE

No strategy lives forever, and in recent years, strategy life cycles have been shrinking. For human beings, the leading causes of death are heart disease, cancer, and stroke. By contrast, strategies die when they are:

Replicated. Over time, innovative strategies become less so. JetBlue took a chapter out of Southwest Airline's playbook. Cialis and Levitra aped Viagra. And Google's Android platform in many ways mimics Apple's iOS. While some strategies are harder to imitate than others (particularly those that exploit network effects), most can be decoded by dedicated rivals.

Superseded. Good strategies get supplanted by better strategies when newcomers invent more efficient ways of meeting customer needs.

Digital cameras made film obsolete. Skype allowed its users to sidestep expensive international phone tariffs. Wikipedia created a free alternative to traditional encyclopedias. Sometimes a high-flying strategy gets imitated, but other times it gets shot out of the sky.

Eviscerated. Powerful customers or new competitors can kill a strategy by slicing away at the profits of what once was a high-margin business. The Internet, in particular, has produced a dramatic shift in bargaining power from producers to consumers. Armed with near-perfect information, customers have battered down the prices of just about everything—cars, insurance, hotels, and luxury watches. For many companies, well-informed customers are now a bigger threat to margins than well-financed competitors. Increased competition can also eviscerate profits. Historically, most industries have been oligopolies. The incumbents were protected from newcomers by regulatory hurdles, patent walls, distribution monopolies, and economies of scale. Today, these barriers are crumbling. Deregulation, the commoditization of technology, the Web's global reach, and the abundance of venture capital have knocked down barriers, and a horde of newcomers have overrun what once seemed to be impregnable fortifications. A few of the most notable gate-crashers: Huawei in networking equipment, Embraer in commercial aircraft, HTC in mobile phones, and Ryanair in the airline business.

For human beings, death is sometimes sudden and unexpected. Strategy decay is more like cancer—it happens little by little, and the longer you wait to deal with it, the more deadly it becomes. By paying attention to the right metrics, strategy decay can usually be anticipated. Telltale signs include shrinking margins, slowing growth, declining asset productivity, eroding market share, higher customer churn rates, a declining share of revenues from new products, the proliferation of new and unorthodox business models, a downward kink in the pricing trend line, a falling price-to-earnings ratio, or an increasing ratio of marketing costs to revenue. If executives get surprised when a strategy finally collapses, it's because they weren't paying attention to the right metrics.

THIRD, SUCCESS CORRUPTS

Gravity and senescence are, to an extent, inevitable, but these aren't the primary reasons organizations stumble. There are human and organizational factors that conspire to make success a self-correcting phenomenon. Among the most dangerous are . . .

Defensive Thinking

Once a company crests the peak of industry leadership, its employees, from top to bottom, start to think defensively. The organizational ethos shifts from entrepreneurial to custodial. Executives who once challenged the status quo now defend it. When presented with a bold idea, their first question is, "How does it affect the base?" In consequence, risk taking shrivels and internal rebels emigrate elsewhere. Even worse, executives who are unwilling to cannibalize their own success use their political power to erect regulatory barriers that are designed to slow the advance of industry newcomers.

Inflexible Business Systems

As a company grows, its attention shifts from innovation to improvement, from exploration to exploitation. Discipline, focus, and alignment take center stage. Years of kaizen-style improvement yield an ultra-efficient and highly optimized business system. As this happens, assets, skills, and processes become more specialized, and change becomes more incremental. All of this is great for efficiency but deadly for adaptability. After a while, all of the components of the business system are so tightly interlaced that almost any sort of change is apt to be seen as dangerously disruptive.

Fossilized Mental Models

By reinforcing policy decisions that were made years or even decades earlier, success hardens strategic choices into creedal beliefs. Over time, what was once the "best" way becomes the "only" way. Success also turns luck into genius. A CEO who, by a collision of circumstances, chanced upon a game-changing business idea, gets enthroned as an all-wise seer. Unfortunately, most entrepreneurs never get a second epiphany. Nevertheless, they will often use their positional and reputational power to discount ideas that would challenge their own doctrinal beliefs. It's tough to make the case for revamping a vintage strategy when that strategy is the brainchild of the founder and chairman. It's hard to argue with success, and even harder to argue with a successful CEO.

Abundant Resources

With success comes plentitude—more employees, more cash, and more market power. Trouble is, abundance makes executives intellectually lazy; they start to believe that success comes from outspending your rivals rather than from outthinking them. Abundance also breeds sloth. Executives in market-leading companies often assume they have the luxury of time; they can let newcomers take the risks, and then overpower them later. This is always a dicey bet. It's not often that superior resources beat a superior strategy. Finally, affluence dulls the appetite for innovation. Groundbreaking ideas are born in the gap between aspirations and resources; they are the product of stretch, not slack. When resources start to substitute for creativity, it's time to short the shares.

Contentment and Entitlement

Decades of steady growth can lead executives to believe that continued success is preordained. Senior administrators who've never been entrepreneurs and have never created something out of nothing are prone to view success as the default setting, as something that *usually* happens, rather than as something that is inherently rare and fragile. It takes a whole lot more imagination and courage to *build* something than it does to *run* something, and perhaps even more effort to *change* something—a point that career bureaucrats seldom grasp. Like the loyal and well-mannered children of wealthy parents, caretaker executives often feel they *deserve* a grand inheritance, but have neither the incentives nor the skills to multiply that fortune. Contentment and entitlement are the inevitable by-products of *past* success, and the implacable enemies of *future* success.

How, then, do you counter the corrosive effects of success? By being alert to the small signs that it's metastasizing into arrogance and complacency; by drawing attention to the little precancerous cells which, if not lopped off, will one day pose a mortal risk. Like a dermatologist who's developed a well-trained eye for incipient tumors, you must develop a well-trained ear for the seemingly innocuous statements that suggest success is turning in on itself.

Here are the markers I listen for, and some responses you may want to employ if you hear them in *your* organization.

When an executive says:	You say:
"Whatever we do, we can't screw it up."	"Whatever we do, we can't play it safe."
"They wish they had our resources."	"They're glad they don't have our fixed costs."
"This is how we make money in this industry."	"So far as we know."
"We're the leading player in our segment."	"How are we different from all the companies that used to be the leaders in *their* segments?"
"Strategy is the easy part, execution is the hard part."	"Strategy seems easy only because we haven't created one that's truly differentiated."
"We're outspending our nearest competitor two-to-one."	"Do customers think we're out-innovating our competitors two-to-one?"
"We're running on all cylinders."	"Yeah, but are we adding new cylinders, and what about that new plug-in hybrid thingy?"
"This is our core competence."	"So what are our *in*competencies?"
"That's not part of our strategy."	"Is that because it's a dumb idea or because it threatens the status quo?"

When an executive says:	You say:
"We're the biggest."	"So was the Titanic."
"Our most valuable asset is our distribution (or R&D or manufacturing or brand)."	"So how would a competitor turn that into our biggest liability?"
"We're really focused on (*fill in the blank*)."	"And by being focused, what are we ignoring?"
"We don't really consider them a threat."	"I'm sure they're counting on that."
"That's how we built this company."	"True enough, but what got us here won't get us there."

Success doesn't have to produce sclerosis, but it will unless you and others in your organization have the guts to challenge defensiveness, dogma, rigidity, and complacency at every turn. Do that, and today's success will be a launching pad for something even grander.

MOURNING CORPORATE FAILURE

3.4

In the next chapter I'm going to talk about how you can design a company to be truly resilient; how you bake in an evolutionary advantage. But first, we need to tackle a fundamental question—one that may have already occurred to you. In a dynamic economy, is there any reason to *care* whether a particular company lives or dies? Or to put it another way, does organizational longevity have any intrinsic value—for shareholders, employees, customers, or society at large? If you're a venture capitalist or a free market ideologue, you'll likely answer "no." I get that. In an open economy, there are a variety of mechanisms that make it difficult for a company to consistently misuse society's resources. Robust competition, a market for corporate control, and a vibrant entrepreneurial sector protect customers and shareholders from protracted bouts of managerial incompetence. When these insurance policies are in place, a corporation that fails to adapt to changing circumstances loses its customers, its best employees, and, eventually, its independence. That's what happened to Sun Microsystems, the once-brilliant company that in 2009 ceded its sovereignty to Oracle. And if all these mechanisms fail, there's always bankruptcy. Sooner or later the resources of a perennial laggard get reallocated to more productive uses. In this view, no company dies before its time. In my view, however, the issue of corporate life and death is rather more complicated.

First, many important institutions aren't publicly traded companies: the U.S. Department of Homeland Security, Britain's National Health Service, the European Central Bank, and NATO, for example. For the most part, these organizations have no direct competitors, nor can they be taken over. Within the public sector, there is little that safeguards society from management teams that are less creative and energetic than they should be. Think about the last time you paid a visit to the Department of Motor Vehicles. How would you rank that experience as compared to, let's say, getting a Kindle book from Amazon or downloading a movie from Netflix? Without the threat of defecting customers, hostile takeovers, and bankruptcy, the only thing that keeps public sector bureaucrats on their toes is the surveillance of more senior bureaucrats, who are even further removed from the point of service. The impetus this provides for proactive change is more wet noodle than cat-o'-nine-tails.

Second, the machinery that strips resources from poorly managed companies operates slowly and unreliably. Overly compliant boards often show a remarkable amount of patience with CEOs who fiddle while a business burns, or use a penknife instead of a machete to trim bloated overheads. Consider, for example, how long Jerry Yang was able to hold on to his CEO job at Yahoo, despite his company's failure to reinvent itself around a Web 2.0 business model. Yang even convinced his board to spurn two takeover offers from Microsoft—deals that priced Yahoo at more than twice its current market value.

Read the board minutes of a faltering company and you'll soon discover there are many ways for nostalgic and pain-averse executives to postpone the day of reckoning. They can erect barriers against hostile takeovers; use rebates and price cuts to camouflage uncompetitive products; dress up retrenchment programs in the rhetoric of bold transformation; or sell off assets to keep moribund businesses afloat. To put it simply, big companies die slowly. The death throes can last for years, and all the while resources are being squandered.

And then there are the unavoidable adjustment costs, a third reason to be less than sanguine about corporate failure. Reallocating the highly specialized skills and assets of a floundering company is a grossly inefficient process. It can take months or years for displaced employees to find new jobs, and when they do, those jobs will probably pay less than the old ones. It can take even longer to find new uses for idled facilities and mothballed equipment. A laid-off autoworker isn't likely to find a job in Silicon Valley, and an empty car plant can't easily be transformed into gentrified housing.

Added to this are the negative externalities—the costs failing companies impose on society in the form of unemployment benefits, reduced tax revenues, and a general loss of social well-being. To see these costs close up, visit the vast industrial wasteland that surrounds Detroit, a rusted, shuttered, and socially benighted testament to the inability of America's car companies to reinvent themselves in a timely manner. Consumers and competitors win when a corporate dinosaur succumbs to the inevitable. Taxpayers and citizens, on the other hand, must often bear the costs of the funeral.

Fourth, large established companies are critical to any economy. Young companies are generally less efficient than older companies— they're innovative, but their business processes aren't yet optimized. Moreover, start-ups typically depend on established companies for funding, managerial talent, and market access. Classically, Microsoft's early success was dependent on its ability to harness IBM's brand and distribution power. There's a critical symbiosis between large and small companies. Given all that, start-ups are not an alternative to established companies; they are, however, an insurance policy against the costs imposed on society when large corporations fail to adapt. As is true for insurance generally, it's better to avoid disaster than to make a claim. Silicon Valley and other entrepreneurial hot spots are a boon, but they are no more than a partial solution to the problem of nonadaptive incumbents.

Those who regard institutional death with equanimity often view businesses as organisms. In the natural world, animals compete for food and mates, and the strong devour the weak. When a lion brings down a gazelle, there are few who mourn the loss of life (other than young viewers of the Discovery channel). I believe it is wrong, though, to view a substantial company, such as Citigroup, Hewlett-Packard, or Sony, as a single organism. The size and scope of these organizations, and the economic consequences of their success or failure, dwarf that of a sole proprietorship. Thus the biological equivalent of large-scale corporate failure is not the death of a lone polar bear or cheetah, but the collapse of an entire ecosystem or the extinction of a species, events that most biologists would lament.

The ecologists are right about one thing, though: resilience requires variety—a menagerie of competing ideas where the winners are cho-sen not by a few sagacious judges, but by the collective wisdom of the marketplace. Silicon Valley, a loosely constructed marketplace for ideas, talent, and capital, spawns hundreds of new start-ups every year. Strangely, many organizational theorists seem to believe that tightly coupled social networks—large companies—are incapable of playing the same numbers game; that is, they are incapable of launching a host of new-rules experiments internally. Out of this prejudice grows the belief that economic resilience is critically dependent on competition between a large number of highly focused start-ups. It should be possible, I think, to recognize the importance of entrepreneurship to economic vitality without denying the value that would be gained if incumbent institutions were dramatically more experimental themselves.

Let's return to our question: Can an organization die an untimely death? Most economists, like venture capitalists, would answer "no." Institutions die when they deserve to die, that is, when they have shown themselves habitually unable to meet the demands of their stakeholders. Yet this crude tautology conceals a more subtle point. Organizations don't die from "natural causes." They may die from predictable causes (as I argued in the last chapter), but "predictable" is not the same thing as "inevitable." There aren't any two-hundred-year-old human beings, but there are lots of two-hundred-year-old institutions. When organizations die, it is usually from suicide, from the decisions made, and not made, that rendered the institution unfit for the future. Most of us would regard any act of human suicide as untimely (save that, perhaps, of a terminally ill patient). So why should we be indifferent to corporate suicide? We shouldn't, and for the same reasons: it breaks hearts and narrows the future.

Time—years, decades, and centuries—enables complexity. It took millions of years for evolution to produce the mammalian eye and, eventually, the human brain. If some climactic event had destroyed life on Earth in the millennia preceding the Cambrian explosion, the possibility of human reason would have been aborted. Whether anything would have been "lost" by such a catastrophe is a metaphysical question, but the point becomes quite practical when we veer back to the world of organizations. Organizations grow and prosper by turning simple ideas into complex systems—from the idea of mobility for the masses came the Ford Motor Company, and from the notion of Internet search, Google. Yet the process of turning inspiration into value takes time, proceeding as it does through iterative cycles of experiment, learn, select, and codify. If a poor executive decision prematurely interrupts this process, a society may lose the benefit of an inspired idea, if only for the period of time it takes another organization to pluck that idea from the ashes of the failed pioneer.

Imagine, for a moment, that Larry Page and Sergey Brin, Google's founders, had failed in their quest to wrap a revenue-producing business model around their original page-link algorithm. Sooner or later, another upstart would have come along to help us navigate the Web, but in the meantime, an important avenue of human progress would have been closed off. In general, complex things are more valuable to human beings than simple things—a MacBook Air versus a chunk of aluminum, for example. Complexity, though, takes time. That's a fifth reason to be less than relaxed when a company fails to adapt.

There's a final reason to bemoan the death or incapacitation of a once-successful business. Leaving aside the promise of a hereafter, human beings have only two ways of transcending death: by passing on their genes and by building institutions that last. Cambridge University, Microsoft, Toyota, and Amazon: these are vessels into which tens of thousands of individuals have poured their energies and ideas; they are living monuments assembled out of human ingenuity. As such, we owe them the same care and respect we would accord the Pyramids, the Elgin Marbles, or Salisbury Cathedral. Like curators everywhere, we have a duty to protect what we've inherited, not by propping up failing companies and roping them off from reality, but by helping them to change and adapt in ways that will make them evergreen.

Truth is, we *care* about our institutions, or at least those in which we have invested our skills and passions. The tenured economist who takes a coldly dispassionate view of corporate failure will nevertheless rally to the support of his own university when its future is threatened by administrative incompetence or a funding crisis. We can't expect others to care about *our* institutions if we don't care about theirs, or at least about the health of institutions in general.

Now before anyone starts fibrillating, let me be clear: I'm not arguing that policymakers should insulate companies from the consequences of executive stupidity. While I don't believe that institutional death is inevitable (in theory, every company could be immortal), I do believe there are many organizations that *deserve* to die, and that policymakers should leave them to their fate. Subsidies (of whatever sort) are expensive and usually ill-conceived. Subsidies and bailouts distort economic decision making, reward bad management practices, lock in archaic industry structures, and inhibit growth. So I mostly agree with the free market advocates. On the other hand, institutional failure can be hideously expensive—in lost competencies, inefficient adjustment mechanisms, and related social expenses. (That's why I thought the Obama administration did the right thing when it threw General Motors a lifeline.) Nevertheless, as a taxpayer, consumer, citizen, investor, and employee, I want to avoid *all* of these costs, and the only way to do that is to help organizations of every type and size to become more adaptable.

Yes, I believe that institutional longevity has value, but I also believe that every organization must continually earn its right to exist—whether it's the local high school, the U.S. Army, or General Motors. Longevity should be the reward for resilience, rather than the product of protection. Although, as a practical matter, some institutions may be too big or too important to fail in the short run, policymakers must never grant any institution immunity from economic Darwinism.

FUTURE-PROOFING YOUR COMPANY

This chapter should have been a book, but then I would have had to write two books instead of one, and you might have felt compelled to read both of them. That's too much work for you and me. So I'm going to give you the CliffsNotes version instead. Not that this abbreviated treatment will rob you of any fundamental insights. The average business book is a *Harvard Business Review* article with extra examples, and the average *HBR* article is three PowerPoint slides with a lot more words. So I'm going to spare you all that superfluous prose and give you the pared-down, no-added-fat version of my manual for future-proofing your company.

I've explained why adaptability matters, and outlined the reasons why companies so often fail to change. Now I'll try to outline the essential "design rules" that must be followed if you want to build a company that can change as fast as change itself. This is a tall order. I don't think any company today is as adaptable as it's going to need to be in the years ahead. Benchmarks are few. Google, Amazon, and Apple have all shown an ability to morph their core business while inventing new ones, and have done so in the absence of a performance slump. But as I argued in an earlier chapter, these companies are relatively young, have been revolutionaries since birth, and have been blessed with leaders who are serial visionaries.

Your company, by contrast, has probably been around for decades, is inherently conservative, and is led by sober-suited administrators rather than T-shirt-wearing rebels. Most critically, its management processes—the tools and systems it uses to set goals, create plans, allocate resources, manage operations, and measure performance—were built years ago with one goal in mind: efficiency. That's why we have organizations that are focused, methodical, and rigorous (Yea, Six Sigma!), but not very inspired, proactive, or experimental.

Around the world, companies have been working hard in recent decades to reengineer their *business* processes for efficiency and speed. The focus has been on things like logistics, inventory, and customer support. In the decade now unfolding, companies will need to devote a similar degree of effort, if not investment, to reinventing their *management* process around the challenge of zero-trauma change.

But what is it, exactly, that makes a company adaptable, or not? In this chapter I'll outline six critical factors. Three of these focus on various forms of flexibility: intellectual, strategic, and structural. The other three focus on anticipation, variety, and resilience-friendly values. As appropriate, I'll recapitulate a few points from earlier chapters. The goal: a comprehensive framework that can help you identify the adaptability challenges and leverage points for *your* organization.

ANTICIPATION

You can't outrun the future if you don't see it coming.

A. Face the Inevitable

More often than not, companies miss the future not because it was unknowable, but because it was disconcerting. Think about how long it took for GM to admit the need to trim its bloated U.S. brand portfolio, which, before the company's bankruptcy, included Saab, Hummer, Saturn, and Pontiac (all sold or closed), as well as Cadillac, Buick, Chevrolet, and GMC. All these competing lines might have made sense when the company had more than half of the U.S. market, but amounted to an enormous liability when GM's share shrank to less than 20%. Nokia was another ostrich. Even though it was a smartphone pioneer (with the Nokia Communicator in 1996), the company failed to get out in front of the mobile data revolution. Nokia's halfhearted attempts to transform itself from a hardware-centric device company into a software-centric platform company opened the door for Apple and Google. There were undoubtedly employees at GM and Nokia who saw the handwriting on the wall, but senior management had its emotional equity invested in the past. To guard against this sort of nostalgia, you have to ensure that the top team doesn't dominate the strategy discussion. One way to do this: create an online forum where those who are alert to emerging challenges can raise the alarm and suggest potential responses. To put it bluntly, the conversation about "where we go next" should be dominated by individuals who have their emotional equity invested in the future rather than in the past. It needs to be led by individuals who don't feel the need to defend decisions that were taken ten or twenty years ago.

B. Learn from the Fringe

What's true for music, fashion, and the arts is true for business as well: the future starts on the fringe, not in the mainstream. As William Gibson once noted, "The future has already happened, it's just unequally distributed." To see it coming, managers have to pay attention to nascent technologies, unconventional competitors, and unserved customer groups. A good rule of thumb: spend an hour a day, or a couple of days a month, exploring emerging trends in technology, lifestyles, regulation, and venture capital funding. Get out into the field. Talk to inventors, academics, journalists, social campaigners. It's hard to see the future when you're sitting behind a desk. Given the disproportionate amount of power they wield, it's particularly important that senior executives spend time "future hunting." If they don't have their own first-person experience with the future, they'll be inclined to discount the discomforting views of junior colleagues who've been out on the fringe. Remember, the future will sneak up on you unless you go out looking for it.

C. Rehearse Alternate Futures

It's not enough to spot trends; you have to think through their implications and how they'll interact—and then develop contingency plans appropriate to each potential storyline. The more time a company devotes to rehearsing alternate futures, the quicker it will be able to react when one particular future begins to unfold: "Hey, we've already seen this movie and we know what comes next, so let's get moving."

INTELLECTUAL FLEXIBILITY

An adaptable company requires adaptable minds.

A. Challenge Assumptions

In most organizations, deep-rooted assumptions are the biggest barrier to adaptation. Twenty years ago, just about everyone in the U.S. airline business believed you needed a diversified fleet of aircraft and a fortress hub or two to run an airline profitably. And that was true, until Southwest Airlines proved it wasn't. A decade ago, we all assumed you sat on your butt when playing video games—and that was true, until the Nintendo Wii got gamers up off their backsides with a motion-detecting game controller. In a world of unprecedented change, there's only one way to protect yourself from creative destruction—do the destructing yourself. As a first step, though, you have to deconstruct your own industry beliefs. Some helpful questions in this regard: How could we take 30 or 50 or 90% out of the industry cost structure (as LegalZoom.com did with basic legal services)? How could we access an entirely different category of customers (as the University of Phoenix did when it pioneered university degree programs for mid-career adults)?

How could we offer customers a 10X-plus performance improvement (as Amazon's Kindle did by reducing the time it takes to acquire a book to a minute or less)? How could we "enchant" customers, to use Guy Kawasaki's evocative term, rather than merely satisfy or please them? To uncover conventional beliefs, you have to challenge yourself to image how you might achieve unconventional outcomes.

B. Invest in Genetic Diversity

What's true in nature is true in business—a lack of diversity limits the ability of a species to adapt and change. Fact is, despite all those diversity programs, most companies are still diversity-challenged. All too often the executive committee is comprised of long-serving veterans whose experiences and attitudes are more alike than different. Homogeneity has its virtues—it facilitates communication and speeds decision making—but it also limits a company's ability to respond to unconventional threats and opportunities. Teams at every level in the company need to reflect diversity in age, gender, culture, skills, and industry experience. Change usually takes a catalyst, and the best catalyst in my experience is someone whose views and life experiences differ considerably from your own. One simple way of increasing diversity is to overweight every team and decision-making body with individuals who are younger than the company average, have worked in other industries, and aren't based at the head office.

C. Encourage Debate and Dialectic Thinking

Diversity is of little value if senior executives value conformance and alignment above all else. One of the reasons that McKinsey & Company has remained atop the consulting game for so many decades is that it encourages internal dissent. It believes that vigorous debate improves the quality of decisions. Within any organization, it's usually the malcontents and rebels who are the first to sense the impending demise of a long-cherished business model, and the first to see the value in wacky, new ideas. Yet these folks are often muzzled rather than encouraged to speak up. On every important issue managers need to ask their subordinates and colleagues, "Where do I have this wrong? What would you do differently? Is there an option I haven't considered?" The best leaders are the ones who get the most options on the table before making a decision, and the most adaptable companies will be those that encourage folks to voice heretical viewpoints.

STRATEGIC VARIETY

To give up the bird in the hand, you have to see a flock in the bush.

A. Build a Portfolio of New Strategic Options

Without a lot of exciting new options, managers will inevitably opt for more of the same. That's why renewal depends on a company's ability to generate and test hundreds of new strategic options. There's a power law here: Out of 1,000 crazy ideas, only 100 will merit a small-scale experiment. Of those, only 10 will be worth serious investment, and out of that bundle, only 1 or 2 will have the power to transform a business or spawn a new one. Google gets this. Within its core search business, the company tests more than 5,000 software changes a year and implements around 500—this according to *BusinessWeek*.[1] The fact that Google has thus far managed to maintain its overwhelming lead in online search is in large part the result of this blistering pace of experimentation. In the end, the pace at which Google or any other company is able to evolve is a function of the number of new strategic options it is able to generate and test.

B. Build a Magnet for Great Ideas

In the quest to expand the option set, it's important to cast the innovation net as widely as possible. IBM did this in both 2006 and 2008 when it hosted worldwide "Innovation Jams." The online conversations were designed to help IBM identify new ways of using its resources to address some of the world's most vexing challenges. In the first Jam, more than

150,000 experts, vendors, employees, and clients participated in two 72-hour brainstorming sessions that generated 46,000 postings IBM. distilled this torrent of ideas into ten major new growth initiatives, and set aside $100 million to fund them. Dell has done something similar with Ideastorm, a website where customers post suggestions for new features, products, and services. The battle for renewal is, at least in part, a battle to capture more than your fair share of the world's great ideas. You can't be adaptable if you're not open to learning from unexpected places.

C. Minimize the Cost of Experimentation

A company can't explore a lot of new options if it costs millions of dollars (or even thousands) to test each one. Problem is, big companies aren't very good at quick-and-dirty. To outpace change, an organization must master the art of rapid prototyping. Here the goal is to maximize the ratio of learning over investment in order to find the sweet spot of demand for a new product, or perfect a nascent business more rapidly and inexpensively than your competitors. Again, Google gets this. In one conversation, Google's Executive Chairman Eric Schmidt told me: "Our goal is to have more at bats per unit of time and money than anyone else." To experiment more, organizations will have to learn to experiment more cheaply, by developing storyboards, simulations, role-playing scenarios, and cheap mock-ups that allow customers to interact with early-stage ideas. Learn early, learn cheap, learn fast—three essential rules for any company that wants to outrun change.

STRATEGIC FLEXIBILITY

Nine times out of ten, nimble beats big.

A. Disaggregate the Organization

Big things aren't nimble. That's why there aren't any 200-pound gymnasts or jumbo jet–sized fighter aircraft. It's why the biggest creatures that ever walked this planet disappeared 60 million years ago, and why the smallest, bacteria, are still here—all 5 million billion trillion of them. It's also why Gore & Associates, the manufacturer of Gore-Tex and 1,000 other high-tech products, limits its business units to around 200 individuals. It's why Morning Star, the world's largest and most efficient tomato processor, has more than twenty business units in a company with only 500 full-time employees. And it's why Google's average team size is 4–7 individuals. In a company comprised of a few, very large organizational units, there is often a lack of intellectual diversity, since people within the same unit tend to think alike. Big units also tend to have more management layers, which means new ideas have a longer gauntlet to run. In addition, elephantine organizations tend to undermine personal accountability. An employee who's one of thousands, rather than one of a few, is unlikely to feel a personal sense of responsibility for helping the organization adapt and change. (Surely, that's someone else's job.) For all these reasons, small, differentiated units are a boon to adaptability. Most executives overweight the advantages of scale and underweight the advantages of flexibility—hence the enduring and often perverse managerial preference for combining small units into big ones—a preference that all too often turns lithe acrobats into muscle-bound giants. It's fine for a company to look big on the outside, but it should always feel small on the inside.

B. Create Real Competition for Resources

Businesses fail when they over-invest in "what is" at the expense of "what could be." This happens with depressing regularity. Why? Because in most organizations, well-established programs and product lines have a distinct advantage in attracting resources. Conversely, the champions of the new are usually at a profound disadvantage when it comes to competing for talent and capital. This is true for two primary reasons. First, in a bureaucracy, personal power is a function of the resources one controls; that's why managers are invariably reluctant to give up headcount and budget, even when those resources could be more profitably used elsewhere in the organization. And second, the funding criteria for new projects tend to be highly conservative.

This makes sense for large investments in the core business, where experience provides a robust fact base, but it's just plain dumb for small, exploratory investments in new areas. No one should have to build an unimpeachable business case to invest a few thousand dollars in a small-scale experiment. In most companies, existing businesses enjoy a kind of "squatter's rights"—only a small percentage of their budget and headcount is "up for grabs" in the annual budgeting cycle.

There are several solutions to this problem. First, executives should set aside a share of the company's capital budget for projects that are truly innovative. That way, when a legacy business fails to come forward with enough breakthrough projects, a big chunk of its resources gets automatically reallocated to more innovative units. Second, it's important to relax the investment criteria for small, experimental projects. Venture capitalists think about risk at the level of the portfolio, rather than project-by-project. They know that most start-ups fail, but invest anyway. Their hope is that in a portfolio of 15 or 20 companies, one of them will turn out to be the next eBay or Facebook. As the noted venture capitalist Steve Jurvetson once put it to me, "On average we're wrong, but when we're right, we're *really* right." So while the modal (or most likely) return on any particular investment may be close to zero, the average return for the portfolio can be strongly positive. Companies need to learn to take fewer big risks and a lot more small risks. Third, executives must create incentives for talent mobility. For example, a talented manager who changes jobs to take on the challenge of building a new business should be more highly rewarded than one who opts for a safe caretaker role in a long-established business.

C. Multiply the Sources of Funding for New Initiatives

In most companies there is a monopsony for new ideas. (You'll remember that a monopsony is one buyer, while a monopoly is one seller.) All too often there's only one place an employee can go to get funding for a cool new idea—up the chain of command. If the project doesn't dovetail with the boss's priorities or prejudices, it doesn't get funded. This paucity of funding sources puts a huge damper on innovation.

Imagine, for example, what would happen to Silicon Valley if there were only one venture capital firm and it was run, let's say, by a veteran from Microsoft. Google and Salesforce.com might have never been funded. In the world of venture capital, it's not unusual for a would-be entrepreneur to get turned down half a dozen times before finding a willing investor, yet in most companies, it takes only one *nyet* to kill a project dead.

The solution here isn't an internal venture fund or incubator. That doubles the number of funding sources, but doesn't go far enough. In a large company, there will be hundreds of people who have some sort of discretionary budget. Imagine giving each of those individuals the permission to invest 2 or 5% of their budget in any project they see as promising. Suddenly, internal entrepreneurs would have dozens of "angel" investors that could be tapped for funding. No longer could a single, reactionary executive deep-six a new idea. While it's important to create an open forum in which ideas compete, it's even more critical to ensure that innovators have multiple sources of funding. No single executive, or "venture board," should be given control over funding decisions for new projects. When it comes to resource allocation, most companies are still more like the Soviet Union than Silicon Valley. That has to change.

STRUCTURAL FLEXIBILITY

Surrender your freedoms reluctantly; guard your flexibility diligently.

A. Avoid Irreversible Commitments

Major capital investments. Multiyear labor contracts. Specialized facilities. High fixed costs. All these things are dangerous in a world where the future is unlikely to mirror the past. Historically, managers have often traded away long-term adaptability for short-term economic advantage (like temporary labor peace, better long-term lease rates, or a larger scale factory). Going forward, they will need to explicitly evaluate the "adaptability costs" of every decision. Critical questions to include: "How might this decision lock us in?" "Where does it reduce our degrees of freedom?" "What would it cost us to get out?" Though the recession battered luxury travel, the Toronto-based Four Seasons hotel chain resisted the temptation to slash published room rates. Instead, it offered travelers a fourth or fifth night free. While cutting tariffs might have helped to fill hotel rooms in the short run, it would have undermined the company's pricing flexibility in the long run. To build an adaptable company, you have to make "reversibility" a critical parameter in every business decision.

B. Invest in Flexibility

It's not enough to avoid inadvertent lock-in; every company must also act positively to increase its room to maneuver. In a world of fractured markets, fickle customers, and whipsaw demand shifts, any company that figures out how to reduce its breakeven point, or accommodate greater variety in its product mix, will gain a decisive advantage. Consider Toyota. Long renowned for its flexibility, Toyota became more limber still when it rolled out its Global Body Line manufacturing system earlier this decade. When compared to its aptly named predecessor, the Flexible Body Line, the GBL reduced the cost of building multiple vehicles on the same assembly line by an additional 70%. It also reduced the assembly line's footprint by 50% and halved the associated capital costs.[2] Paradoxically, building a flexibility advantage often requires standardizing a few critical variables. The ability of the GBL to handle a wide variety of Toyota models is based in part on the fact that every vehicle is designed around common dimensional standards that allow assembly line robots to move seamlessly from one car model to another. Toyota's ultimate goal: to be able to manufacture any of its products on any of its production lines, anywhere in the world. *That's* flexibility.

C. Think Competencies and Platforms

To be adaptable, a company must decouple its fortunes from the fate of any particular market or product category. This requires a corporate "self-definition" that is elastic and extensible, one that is built around deep competencies and broad platforms rather than around specific products and services. If Apple had defined itself as a computer maker, rather than as a company that brings world-class design skills and user engineering to digital devices, it would have never reinvented the music industry or transformed the mobile phone business. Another example: Gore & Associates has made money every year since its founding half a century ago, a testament to the company's adaptability. Gore's secret? It has no "core business." It sees itself instead as a portfolio of chemistry-based competencies that can be exploited in dozens of markets.

RESILIENCE-FRIENDLY VALUES

You have to build adaptability into your company's DNA.

A. Embrace a Grand Challenge

You can't build an adaptable organization without adaptable people, and individuals change only when they have to, or when they want to. As noted earlier, deep change is usually crisis-driven. People are usually pushed to change by circumstances outside of their control. But every day human beings all over the world rush out to *embrace* change, because they are seduced by an opportunity to do something big, exciting, or virtuous. If you want people to change ahead of the curve, you have to give them something worth changing *for*. You have to set in front of them some enticing challenge that draws them forward, or let them define their own. Sounds simple, and it is, but in most companies, there's no glistening, Everest-like peak of purpose that draws people out of their comfy down sleeping bags and up the icy slopes of change and challenge, and that's a problem, because in the absence of purpose, the only thing that will disrupt the status quo is pain.

B. Embed New Management Principles

As I argued in the introduction to this section, modern organizations weren't designed to be adaptable; they were designed to be disciplined and efficient. That's why getting a big company to change is like getting a dog to walk on its hind legs. If you dangle a treat in front of Bowser's nose, you may coax him into taking a few, halting steps on his hind feet, but the moment you turn your back, he'll be down on all four paws again. That's because he's a quadruped, not a biped. Walking upright isn't in his DNA. Similarly, most companies don't have adaptability DNA in their corporate genome. Their core management processes weren't built with adaptability in mind. Changing this will require the equivalent of gene therapy: organizations must complement their efficiency DNA with adaptability DNA. What does that mean practically? It means working hard to learn from the things in our world that have demonstrated their adaptability over decades, centuries, and eons—things like biological systems, democracies, cities, and stock markets. By digging into these highly adaptable systems, we can uncover the principles for building an adaptable company. A few of the most critical: variety (you have to try a lot of new things), decentralization (you need to create mechanisms for bottom-up change), serendipity (you have to create more opportunities for unexpected encounters and unscripted conversations), and allocational flexibility (you have to make it easy for resources and ideas to find one other). The real challenge, of course, is figuring out how operationalize these principles in the every day practices of your organization. For deeper insights on how to do just that, see chapters 4.3, 4.4, 5.2, 5.3, and 5.4.

C. Honor Web-Inspired Values

The Internet is the most adaptable thing human beings have ever created. From Google to Craigslist to Twitter, and from YouTube to Flickr to Facebook, the Web has morphed in ways that few of us would have imagined a decade ago. It has also spawned a host of amazing new social technologies, including crowdsourcing, folksonomies, opinion markets, wikis, mash-ups, and microblogging. Unlike our management systems, which are based on a top-down model of control, the Web is all periphery and very little center—its architecture is end-to-end, not center-to-end. The distinction between the technology of management and the technology of the Internet is more than merely architectural, though. At the heart of the Web lies a bundle of social values that stand in stark contrast to the values that predominate in the average company. Community, transparency, freedom, meritocracy, openness, and collaboration—these comprise the fundamental ethos of the Web. Within the precincts of corporate-dom, the values of control, discipline, accountability, reliability, and predictability reign supreme. Twenty-first-century organizations must integrate these counterposed values—and in Section Five, we'll look at how that can be done.

So that's the recipe for building an adaptable company. It's daunting, I know—more like trying to make seafood vol-au-vent than ready-mix pancakes. But think back to those early management pioneers, individuals like Henry Ford and Frederick Winslow Taylor, who were born into an agrarian and craft-based economy. What inspired and sustained them in their quest to master the intricacies of large-scale, hyper-efficient manufacturing, a mission that from their vantage point must have looked equally intimidating? A dream, I think; the possibility of enhancing millions of lives by making labor-saving, life-enhancing machines more affordable. So what's our dream?

Today our world is dominated by large-scale organizations. We rely on them as consumers, work for them as employees, and depend on them as investors. And yet, these organizations often seem to fail us. As consumers, we are often the victims of their indifference, of rules and policies that are efficiency-focused rather than service-focused. As employees, our voices are often ignored and our creative energies wasted. And then, when the inevitable crisis occurs, we are asked to bear a disproportionate share of the costs. As investors, we watch our portfolios shrink when once-great companies miss a turn in the road. All of us have a huge stake in our organizations, and we need them to be far more resilient than they are today.

Like those long ago management innovators, we can dream, too. We can dream of organizations that are forever looking forward and jump at every opportunity to better the human condition. We can dream of organizations where the enthusiasm for change is palpable and pervasive, where individuals, ennobled by a sense of mission and unencumbered by bureaucracy, rush out eagerly to meet the future. We can dream of organizations where the fearless renegades always trump the fearful reactionaries, where the constituency for the future always outguns the constituency for the past. We can dream of organizations where the drama of renewal occurs without the trauma of a turnaround. And, if we're daring and inventive and determined, we can build these organizations. That's what matters now.

SECTION 4

Passion Matters Now

EXPOSING MANAGEMENT'S DIRTY LITTLE SECRET

4.1

How would you feel about a physician who killed more patients than she helped? What about a police detective who committed more murders than he solved? Or a teacher whose students got dumber rather than smarter as the school year progressed? And what if you discovered that these perverse outcomes were more the rule than the exception, that they were characteristic of *most* doctors, *most* policemen, and *most* teachers? You'd be more than perplexed. You'd be outraged. You'd demand that something be done!

Given this, why are we complacent when confronted with data that suggests most managers are more likely to douse the flames of employee enthusiasm than to fan them? Why aren't we a little bit angry that our management systems are more likely to frustrate extraordinary accomplishment than to foster it?

Consider the 2007–2008 *Global Workforce Survey*[1] conducted by Towers Perrin (now Towers Watson). In an attempt to measure the extent of employee engagement around the world, the company polled more than 90,000 workers in 18 countries. The survey covered many of the key factors that determine workplace engagement, including the ability to participate in decision making, the encouragement given for innovative thinking, the availability of skill-enhancing job assignments, and the interest shown by senior executives in employee well-being.

Here's what the researchers discovered. Barely one-fifth (21%) of the employees surveyed were truly engaged in their work, in the sense that they would "go the extra mile" for their employer. Nearly four out of ten (38%) were mostly or entirely disengaged, while the rest were in the tepid middle. There's no way to sugarcoat it: this data represents a stinging indictment of management-as-usual.

So why aren't we scandalized by this data? I talk to thousands of managers each year and for most of them, employee engagement isn't Topic A, or B, or even C. How do we account for this apparent disregard? There are several possible hypotheses.

1. **Ignorance**. It may be that managers don't actually realize that most of their employees are emotionally tuned out at work. Maybe corporate leaders haven't seen the many other studies that mirror the results of the Towers Watson survey. Or maybe they just don't have enough emotional intelligence to recognize the low-grade disaffection that afflicts most of their workforce.
2. **Indifference**. Another explanation: managers know that a lot of employees are flatlining at work but simply don't care, either because a callous corporate culture has drained them of empathy, or because they view engagement as financially unimportant. It's nice to have, but not an imperative.
3. **Impotence**. It could be that managers care a lot, but can't imagine how they could change things for the better. After all, a lot of jobs are just plain boring. Retail clerks, factory workers, call center staff, administrative assistants—of *course* these folks are disengaged, how could it be otherwise? Like prison wardens, managers would be shocked if their charges suddenly started bubbling with *joie de vivre*.

Let's evaluate these hypotheses. The first seems to me unlikely. Anybody who has ever read a *Dilbert* strip knows that cynicism and passivity are endemic in large organizations. Only an ostrich could have missed that.

The second hypothesis has more to recommend it. I believe there are many managers who have yet to grasp the essential connection between engagement and financial success. Companies that score highly on engagement have better earnings growth and fatter margins than those that don't—a fact borne out by the Towers Watson study,[2] as well as by the work of Professor Raj Sisodia of Bentley College.[3] This correlation between enjoyment and profitability is likely to strengthen in the years ahead. Let me use the example of the Apple iPhone to explain why.

Ask yourself: What allowed Apple to jump into the mobile phone business so quickly, despite a complete lack of industry experience? The answer? It was able to leverage a lot of commodity knowledge and standardized components from third-party vendors. A lot of companies, mostly in Asia, know how to make a mobile phone. While this helps to explain how Apple got into the business so speedily, it doesn't explain why the iPhone succeeded so spectacularly. In the first quarter of 2011, Nokia sold nearly six times as many phones as Apple, but Apple made more money. Why? Because the average wholesale selling price for an iPhone was $638 versus $87 for a typical Nokia product, this according to a proprietary report by Strategy Analytics quoted in a *Computer World* blog.[4]

The lesson here: you don't have to be the biggest to be the most profitable, but you have to be the most highly differentiated. Apple made the iPhone a money machine by injecting it with a lot of *non*-commodity knowledge. When it debuted in June 2007, the iPhone offered users a unique portfolio of functions: a touchscreen display, a built-in music player, a highly capable Web browser, and a suite of useful applications that let users check the weather, track stocks, and watch YouTube videos.

The fact that Apple's margins are so much better than Nokia's reflects a simple reality: in making a mobile phone, Apple adds a lot more differentiation to the standard componentry than does Nokia, and

Apple adds it in a highly efficient manner. Or to state it another way, among all the various players in the iPhone value chain, Apple has, by far, the highest ratio of differentiation-to-cost, and thus the fattest margins.

In a world of commoditized knowledge, the returns go to the companies that can produce nonstandard knowledge. Success here is measured by profit per employee, adjusted for capital. As you would expect, Apple's profit per head is significantly higher than its major competitors, as is the company's ratio of profits to net fixed assets.

It doesn't matter much *where* your company sits in its industry ecosystem, nor how vertically or horizontally integrated it is. What matters is its relative "share of customer perceived value" and the costs it incurs to produce that value. The greater one's share of differentiation, the greater one's share of industry profits.

Of course, Apple isn't immune to the forces of commoditization. Within a few months of its launch, many of the iPhone's original features had been duplicated by its competitors. So Apple had to innovate again. It invited third-party developers to write applications for the iPhone and thereby laid the groundwork for a revolution in portable computing. But once again, competitors like Blackberry and Google are in hot pursuit.

So what does all this have to do with engagement? Just this: in a world where customers wake up every morning asking, "What's new, what's different, and what's amazing?" success depends on a company's ability to unleash the initiative, imagination, and passion of employees at all levels, and this can only happen if all those folks are connected heart and soul to their work, their company, and its mission.

In my last book, *The Future of Management*, I introduced a simple framework—my version of Maslow's hierarchy—except that in this case it's not a hierarchy of human needs, but of human capabilities at work (see Figure 4.1.1). At the bottom you have obedience—employees who show up each day and follow all the prescribed rules and procedures. Obedience is important and large-scale enterprise would be impossible without it. On the next step is diligence—employees who work hard, who stay till the job is done and take personal responsibility for delivering great results. Again, this is critical. You can't build a winning organization with slackers. Next is intellect, or personal competence. Every business

Figure 4.1.1 A Hierarchy of
Human Capabilities at Work

Level 6: **Passion**
Level 5: **Creativity**
Level 4: **Initiative**

Level 3: **Expertise**
Level 2: **Diligence**
Level 1: **Obedience**

wants employees who have world-class skills, who are well trained and eager to learn more. Trouble is, obedience, diligence, and competence are becoming global commodities. You can buy these human capabilities just about anywhere in the world, and in places like India and China, they can be bought for next to nothing. Recognizing this, companies have out-sourced millions of jobs to countries that have a surplus of well-trained, biddable workers. Nevertheless, wage arbitrage is not a strategy for long-term competitive advantage, as every competitor has more or less the same access to these low cost factors of production. In other words, if obedience, diligence, and knowledge are the *only* things you're getting from your employees, your company will ultimately lose.

So we have to move up the capability pyramid. Beyond expertise is initiative—employees who spring into action whenever they see a problem or an opportunity, who don't wait to be told, who aren't bound by their job description and are instinctively proactive. Up another notch is creativity. Here, employees are eager to challenge conventional wisdom and are always hunting for great ideas that can be imported from other industries. Finally, at the apex, is passion—employees who see their work as a calling, as a way to make a positive difference in the world. For these ardent souls, the dividing line between vocation and avocation is indistinct at best. They pour all of themselves into their work. While other employees are merely *present*, they are *engaged*.

In today's creative economy, it's the capabilities at the top of this list that create the most value. Audacity, imagination, and zeal are the ultimate wellsprings of competitive differentiation. And there's the rub. These higher order human capabilities are *gifts*; they cannot be commanded. You can't *tell* someone to be passionate or creative. Well, you can, of course, but it won't do much good. Individuals choose each day whether or not to bring these gifts to work, and as we've seen from the data, they mostly choose not to.

Throughout history, managers have seen their primary task as ensuring that employees serve the organization's goals—obediently, diligently, and expertly. Now we need to turn the assumption of "organization first, human beings second" on its head. Instead of asking, how do we get employees to better serve the organization, we need to ask, how do we build organizations that *deserve* the extraordinary gifts that employees could bring to work? To put it bluntly, the most important task for any manager today is to create a work environment that *inspires* exceptional contribution and that *merits* an outpouring of passion, imagination, and initiative.

Let's recap:

- In every industry there are huge swathes of critical knowledge that have been commoditized, and what hasn't yet been commoditized soon will be.
- Given that, we have to say good-bye to the "knowledge economy" and wave hello to the "creative economy."
- What matters today is how fast a company can generate *new* insights and build *new* knowledge, of the sort that enhances customer value.
- To escape the curse of commoditization, a company has to be a gamechanger, and that requires employees who are proactive, inventive, and passionate.
- Problem is, the human capabilities that matter most in the creative economy are precisely those that are most difficult to "manage."
- Given all this, we need to shift our focus from "managing" to "unleashing."

Today, no leader can afford to be indifferent to the challenge of engaging employees in the work of creating the future. Engagement may have been irrelevant in the industrial economy and optional in the knowledge economy, but it's pretty much the whole game now.

Fair enough, you might say. I'd love to create a highly engaging workplace, but the folks who work for me are not creating gorgeous products at the cutting edge of technology; they're answering phones in a call center, cleaning hotel rooms, or bagging groceries. How can you expect people to be engaged in their work if their work isn't engaging? A lot of jobs are kind of crappy. Isn't that what the data is telling us?

Actually, no. Eighty-six percent of the employees in the Towers Watson study said they loved or liked their job. So why not more engagement, then? Julie Gebauer, who led the Global Workforce Study, points to three things that are critical to engagement: first, the scope that employees have to learn and advance (are there opportunities to grow?); second, the company's reputation and its commitment to making a difference in the world (is there a mission that warrants extraordinary effort?); and third, the behaviors and values of the organization's leaders (are they trusted, do people want to follow them?).

All of these are *management* issues. It is managers who empower individuals and create the space for them to excel, or not. It is managers who help to articulate a compelling and socially relevant vision and then make it a rallying cry, or not. It is managers who demonstrate praise-worthy values, or not. Here, again, the survey data is disturbing.

Only 38% of employees believe that "senior management [is] sincerely interested in employee well-being." Fewer than 4 in 10 agree that "senior management communicates openly and honestly." A scant 40% believe that "senior management communicates [the] reasons for business decisions," and just 44% of employees believe that "senior management tries to be visible and accessible." Perhaps most damning of all, less than half of those polled believed that "senior management's decisions [were] consistent with our values."

My conclusion from all of this: if we're going to improve engagement we have to start by admitting that if employees aren't as enthusiastic, impassioned, and excited as they could be, it's not because work sucks; it's because management blows.

PUTTING INDIVIDUALS AHEAD OF INSTITUTIONS

4.2

I live half a mile from the San Andreas fault—a fact that bubbles up into my consciousness every time some other part of the world experiences an earthquake. I sometimes wonder whether this subterranean sense of impending disaster is at least partly responsible for Silicon Valley's feverish, get-it-done-yesterday work norms. Build your company quick 'cause tomorrow we may all get flattened.

Like many sorts of change, major tectonic events happen very slowly and then all of a sudden. The earth's wandering plates are held in check by friction for decades or centuries, and then one day the forces of change finally break loose and the planet erupts.

Social convulsions aren't usually as abrupt as earthquakes, but they can still be startling, particularly to those who weren't paying attention. Years of repressed resentments and bottled-up frustrations can suddenly

145

burst forth and fracture long-standing relationships. It happened in 1773 when angry colonists dumped 300 chests of British tea into Boston Harbor. It happened in 1966 when determined civil rights campaigners marched from Selma, Alabama, to the state capitol. It happened in 1989 when euphoric Germans tore down the Berlin Wall, and again in 2011 when a Twitter-enabled citizen's revolt forced Egypt's Hosni Mubarak from power.

And it's happening right now, along the fault line that runs between individuals and institutions.

Over the past few years, we have seen a fundamental breakdown in the trust that individuals are willing to place in large organizations and in the people who run them. When asked to rate the ethics of various professions in a recent Gallup poll,[1] Americans ranked those who represent big business and big government near the bottom. Only 15% of respondents rated the ethical standards of business executives as "high" or "very high." Members of Congress fared even worse at 9%.

	Percentage of respondents who ranked each profession "high" or "very high" in ethical standards
Nurses	81%
Doctors	66%
Police officers	62%
Clergy	53%
TV Reporters	23%
Bankers	23%
Lawyers	17%
Business executives	15%
Members of Congress	9%
Car salespeople	7%

In the 2010 Edelman Trust Barometer,[2] barely one-quarter of Americans said they would regard the information they receive from a company CEO as "highly credible" or "extremely credible."

While some might argue that this trust deficit is the by-product of a few high-profile scandals, like those involving Italy's Parmalat or Lehman Brothers, I believe something deeper is going on. The tectonic plates of individual interests and institutional interests are moving in different directions, and have been for some time, at least from the perspective of "ordinary" workers and voters.

When a politician bends the truth or a CEO breaks a promise (as Kraft's Irene Rosenfeld did when she reneged on her premerger pledge not to close Cadbury's chocolate factory in Somerdale, England),[3] trust takes a beating. Nevertheless, I think the disaffiliation of individuals and institutions is the product of something more fundamental than a few fibs or an occasional Enron-scale delinquency.

It's not just that individuals have lost faith in the integrity of their leaders, it's that they no longer believe society's most powerful institutions are acting in their interests. As I write this, only 6% of Americans believe their legislators in Washington are doing a "good" or "excellent" job.[4] And, as we saw in the previous chapter, fewer than 4 out of 10 employees believe their managers are seriously concerned with their well-being.[5]

Trust is not simply a matter of truthfulness; it is also a matter of amity and goodwill. We trust those who have our best interests at heart, and mistrust those who seem deaf to our concerns. Deceit and dereliction can undermine a relationship, but so too can a slow erosion of affinity and accord.

When legislative bodies are dominated by politicians who put the interests of their financial patrons before the interests of their constituents, or sacrifice their country's long-term economic security for short-term political advantage, then the institutions of government will be mistrusted, whether or not any ethical guidelines have been breached. Likewise, when business leaders treat employees like expendable resources while pocketing huge bonuses, or hack away at employee benefits while retaining their own lavish perks, corporations will be viewed suspiciously, whether or not any laws have been broken.

I don't have any empirical evidence that would prove leaders have become less honest in recent years, but it does seem they've become less responsive to the interests of citizens and employees, or at least that's the way most people feel. The causes of this disconnect are many. In the case of the U.S. federal government, they include: (1) a campaign finance system that turns legislators into special interest lapdogs; (2) gerrymandered voting districts that shield incumbents from challengers; and (3) a candidate selection system that gives undue influence to party extremists. In business, the misalignment is the result of: (1) competitive pressures that create incentives for wage arbitrage; (2) executive compensation systems that discourage long-term thinking; and (3) authoritarian management practices that undermine morale and frustrate contribution.

Another more insidious culprit is the centralizing impulse of both corporate and public sector leaders. Those who have power often want more of it, and are usually skilled at concocting arguments for why they should have it. Who can argue with the need for a "comprehensive solution," for "harmonization," "shared services," "best practices," or "economies of scale?" Yet as power moves away from the periphery and toward the center, individual influence wanes and policies become less attuned to local circumstances. The result: a population that feels aggrieved and impotent.

I believe the growth of the Internet has also been contributing to the rift between individuals and institutions. In recent years, millions of us have rushed to take advantage of the Internet's open and meritocratic architecture. We have used the Web to express our opinions, to expose the misdeeds of the powerful, to build online communities, and to launch new, grassroots initiatives. As we have done so, we have become less tolerant of the closed, top-down power structures that we encounter in the offline world.

Whatever the cause, the data is clear: more and more of us feel that our institutions are run for the benefit of the plutocrats. My Catholic friends feel dishonored by their church's laggardly response to the cancer of sexual abuse. Tea Party activists feel disenfranchised by politicians who take their orders from Beltway lobbyists. The Occupy Wall Street brigade feels aggrieved by a financial system that lavishly rewards imprudent bankers. And across the world, frontline employees feel marginalized by managers who see them as semi-programmable robots.

When viewed from the bottom of the pyramid, the problem at the top is less blatant dishonesty than imperial disregard. It's hardly surprising, then, that populism is an increasingly potent political force in the United States, or that job-hunting MBA students now rank "caring about employees" almost as highly as "starting salary" when evaluating a future employer.[6]

In the 2010 edition of the Global Workforce Study, Towers Watson found that employees are more willing than ever to trade employment perks (such as training, bonuses, and regular pay hikes) for job security.[7] Problem is, it's unlikely that any additional security will be forthcoming. Companies that didn't reward fidelity and devotion in a tight labor market are even less likely to do so in the midst of a recession when employees have fewer choices. Instead, it's more likely that executives will use their newfound bargaining power to squeeze even more out of employees while trimming benefits. The faltering economy may push turnover down, but resentment is likely to go up.

Whatever happens to the economy, the threads that weave individuals and institutions together will continue to fray until leaders of all sorts rethink their fundamental assumptions about the relationship between human beings and organizations.

Crack open the head of an average manager, and you'll find a way of thinking that puts the institution in front of, or on top of, the individual:

INSTITUTION → INDIVIDUAL → PROFIT

The company hires employees to produce goods and services that yield profits for shareholders. In this model, the individual is to the institution what human beings were to the *Matrix*—raw material, factors of production hired to serve the institution's goals. In real life, human beings aren't plugged into machines, but they're often plugged into roles that don't suit them and jobs that don't fulfill them. Usually, it is the individual who must conform to the institution rather than the other way around. If you doubt this, ask yourself what task would you take on if you were free to choose? What boss would you work for if it were up to you? What computer would you use on the job if you could pick any one you wanted?

We can, though, imagine a different model, one where the interests of the individual take precedence:

INDIVIDUAL → ORGANIZATION → IMPACT

Note here the substitution of the word "organization" for "institution." The latter word implies a lot of structure and a hierarchical distribution of authority. The word *organization* is a bit more ambiguous. It can encompass something cellular, like Alcoholics Anonymous, or something networked, like an open source software project. Here, the folks "in charge" are servant leaders who regard their constituents as volunteers, even if they're paid. There is an explicit understanding that the organization can only succeed if it meets the needs of those who support it. In this model, the organization, not the individual, is the instrument.

These two models form the endpoints of a continuum, and while few organizations (or institutions) inhabit the extremes, most large enterprises reside on the "institution first, employee second" side of the spectrum. I think we need to flip this for two reasons.

First, misaligned interests undermine competitiveness. A cynical and worried public will want to hogtie big companies in a snarl of rules and regulations, and as this happens, those institutions will become less flexible and responsive. In addition, low-trust, low-engagement institutions will fail to fully exploit the talents of their members, and consequently will be less innovative and resilient. This combination of heavy-handed regulation and underleveraged talent will result in institutions that are less competitive than they might be.

And second, we deserve better. No one should have to work in an organization that feels more like a centrally planned economy than a vibrant, open community. Nor should anyone in a democracy feel that they are more subject than citizen.

Building human-centered organizations doesn't imply a return to the paternalistic, corporate welfare practices of the nineteenth century. Most of us don't want to be nannied. We understand we live in an uncertain world, where no one can guarantee our job security. We also understand that individual interests vary, and that no single organization can reconcile all our competing demands. Nevertheless, we expect our institutions to be our servants and not the reverse. This implies organizations that are built around some simple but important principles:

- Decentralize wherever possible
- Emphasize community over hierarchy
- Ensure transparency in decision making
- Make leaders more accountable to the led
- Align rewards with contribution, rather than with power and position
- Substitute peer review for top-down review
- Steadily enlarge the scope of self-determination

But, you ask, can an institution-centric enterprise turn itself inside out? Can leaders change their mental models? Can they be induced to surrender their prerogatives? Can command-and-control types reinvent themselves as mobilize-and-mentor types? And can all this happen without undermining operational effectiveness? I think the answer is a tentative "yes," and in the next chapter I'll share a heartening example from a 500-year-old institution.

BUILDING COMMUNITIES OF PASSION

I wouldn't blame you for thinking I'm a bit of a romantic, not the roses and wine sort, but the soppy idealist sort. Come on, Gary, you might say, you can't really create organizations where ordinary folks come first, not unless you're starting from scratch. Maybe Whole Foods is into this *love* thing, but that's because its founder, John Mackey, was a hippie, and is still running the place. How would your theories work in a tradition-encrusted organization with an entrenched hierarchy? And what can you do if you're a mere team leader, rather than an EVP? Sure, I want to pump up the passion in my organization, but it's hard to do when you're buried in layers of bureaucracy.

I get that. Your skepticism is warranted. Old organizations are tough to change, but it can happen, and it can start anywhere, even with *your* team. Don't believe it? Stay with me and I'll share an amazing story about bottom-up change in an organization that was born during the reign of England's Henry VIII: the Church of England.

Today, less than 3% of the British population attends a Church of England service in a typical month.[1] Since 1969, attendance numbers have fallen by half.[2] A survey by Tearfund, a Christian charity, estimates that a third of Britain's population is now "de-churched"; these are former parishioners who no longer attend weekly services.[3] The fact that more than 50% of U.K. residents still describe themselves as Christians makes the decline of Britain's "established" church all the more perplexing. As one Christian website put it, "If the Church of England was the national football team, we would have sacked the manager long ago."[4]

The fact is, the Church of England has become irrelevant to millions of British citizens. At this point I should declare a personal interest. During the ten years I resided in the United Kingdom, I frequently attended an Anglican church that was distinguished by its energetic singing, impassioned preaching, and a vibrant children's program. And yet, I still found it easy to be a pew warmer, a consumer, and a back row critic. After all, the only thing the vicar seemed to want from me was a kind heart and a generous hand. I, like other congregants, was occasionally asked to donate time to one of the church's well-intentioned initiatives and help fund its various programs, but that was it. None of the clergy seemed eager for me or anyone else to actually take the initiative and *start* something. I was never challenged to lead, only to "serve." And if it sounds like I'm justifying my lethargy, you're right—but it's hard to get excited when there's little scope for initiative, and the categories of contribution have already been defined by others. To be blunt, I struggled to find my niche in a top-down, pulpit-led model of "church," and still do. In this regard I'm not alone; well, not if the experience of Drew Williams is anything to go by.

I met Drew a couple of years ago, nearly fifteen years after I had left Britain to move back to the United States. Drew, I learned, had recently made his own transatlantic move, to become the senior pastor of a church in Greenwich, Connecticut. Ten years earlier, he had also changed careers. Having trained as a corporate litigator, Drew practiced law for ten years before deciding to pursue a "higher calling." After completing his theological training in Bristol, he was appointed assistant vicar of an Anglican congregation 25 miles northwest of London, in Chorleywood, Hertfordshire.

Drew e-mailed me after hearing me speak at a conference where I had argued that organizations should be built around "communities of passion." In his note, Drew said, "I wanted to stand up and clap when you made this point, but since I'm English I didn't." When we finally connected by phone, I learned that Drew had helped to pioneer a radical new "management model" during his tenure at St. Andrews, one that started from the pews rather than the pulpit and radiated outwards rather than downwards. Wow, I thought, if this is possible in an institution that's been around for half a millennium, maybe we really *can* bridge the chasm between organizations and individuals.

When Drew took up his post in 2003 at St. Andrews, he joined a church that had 500 members, offered a full roster of programs, and ran several highly polished worship events every week; a church that was, by U.K. standards, large and successful.

Problem was, as Drew put it, St. Andrews had a back door that was bigger than its front door. Each year it was losing about 10% of its membership. Drew was bothered by what he saw as a "come to us" model of church, where the weekly services and the physical building were the focal points—both physically and spiritually—of the church's mission.

"There was a lot of excellence in worship," said Drew, "but we were pretty weak at getting folks involved. Church members would look at us, and say, What could I possibly offer here, everything is done so professionally? We had a congregation who saw themselves as an audience."

St. Andrews' vicar, Mark Stibbe, who was also troubled by this reality, asked Drew to take charge of developing a new strategy. Recalls Drew, "I was sitting next to Mark in church one week, when he told the congregation, 'I'd like to urge all of you to be here in two weeks for a very important meeting. Drew is going to present our new church plan.'" Drew was startled, to say the least, as this was the first he had heard of his new assignment. Says Drew, "I was on the hook—and had no idea where to begin."

Believing that the real mission of St. Andrews was to bring hope to those outside the building and beyond the congregation, Drew began to think about how he might build a "go-to-them" church, one that would encourage the spiritual growth of its members while multiplying their impact in the community.

As he struggled with this challenge, Drew was struck with another realization. While St. Andrews had small groups (typically 3–4 believers who'd meet during the week to chat and pray), and a really big group (the entire congregation), it had no midsized groups—nothing that was the equivalent of an extended family, more than three but less than fifty. This seemed odd, as the early Christian church had been built around communities of just that size.

With the clock ticking, Drew searched desperately (his word) for case studies that might point him in the right direction, and finally found one in Sheffield, England. There, Mike Breen, the vicar of St. Thomas Crookes, had been experimenting with programs built around midsized groups. Relieved to have stumbled across a potential exemplar, Drew drove up to Sheffield and spent several hours interviewing Mike about his novel approach. At the end of the meeting, Drew felt that while he might not have discovered the Holy Grail, he was at least on the right path.

Drew saw several advantages in organizing St. Andrews around medium-sized groups, or what he would later call Mission-Shaped Communities or MSCs.

First, they would be more open and inviting than the small groups. Over time small groups tended to become cliquish. When Drew would try to help a new member connect with a small group, he'd often be told that the group was full, or be asked whether the newcomer was overly needy. A midsized group was big enough that a newcomer wouldn't stand out, yet small enough that he or she wouldn't get lost.

Second, there'd be a lot more room for members to exercise their leadership gifts in intermediate-sized groups. A group of three or four wasn't big enough to tackle significant projects, nor did they offer gifted lay leaders much "leverage." On the other hand, few lay members were eager to volunteer for large-scale projects that involved the entire church, since they typically made poor use of specific congregational talents.

Finally, Drew hoped the MSCs would strengthen the social fabric of the church by creating a lot of new opportunities for members to connect with one another.

On a blustery November night, Drew stood in front of a nearly full sanctuary and sketched out his ideas. Those hoping for a grand strategy were disappointed. Instead, Drew pointed folks back to the early church. In the first few centuries after Christ, the church had been organized around small, local communities. Drew noted that those early believers had met in the biggest house they could find, and when they ran out of room would subdivide and form a new community.

Drew admitted that he didn't have a precise plan for putting his ideas into practice, but he asked everyone to think about the kind of difference they could make if they were part of a more intimate and impassioned community. He challenged his parishioners: What's your passion? Where's your heart? What service-oriented program would you like to start or help scale up? At the end of his talk, Drew announced that a follow-up meeting would be held in a month's time, and invited anyone who thought they might be willing to lead an MSC to come along.

In his heart, Drew was hoping 12 prospective leaders would respond to his plea. He thought 12 was about the number he'd need to start something new, and on December 6, exactly that many church members showed up.

After an opening prayer, congregants talked about their passion for children, for the disabled, for students, and the elderly. Drew encouraged them to start talking to others in the congregation, to start recruiting volunteers and laying out plans. Drew gave the would-be leaders very little direction. When they asked him, "How often should we meet?" Drew would say, "I don't know, why don't you pray about that." When they asked, "Where should we meet?" or "What should our strategy be?" he'd give them the same answer: "Just pray about it." Again and again, Drew pushed the responsibility for fleshing out the new model back onto the parishioners.

Drew was clear about one thing: every group had to have a purpose that went beyond merely meeting up. Each week Drew met with all of the nascent teams, praying for them and encouraging them to take risks and fail forward.

The first MSC got up and running in January. It brought together a group of members who lived in Watford, a large town near Chorleywood. The group met in a home to brainstorm around a possible mission. As they were deliberating, they noticed that a gaggle of children were playing football in a nearby park. Parents were standing around the frozen pitch, cheering on their kids. Milling on the sidelines were a few dozen younger siblings, cold and bored. Maybe, someone ventured, we could run a club for all of the kids who come out each week and don't get a chance to play. The club proved to be an immediate hit with kids and parents. Word spread and soon the newly hatched MSC had been asked to operate an after-school club at a nearby primary school. The MSC members were upfront about their intentions. They told parents, "We're going to talk about Jesus, is that OK?" and virtually all the parents said yes.

Another MSC found their mission in helping revelers get home safely after a night of partying. Congregants would take to the streets in the early hours of the morning when people were stumbling out of night clubs, often the worse for wear. Flip-flops were offered to bleary-eyed young women tottering down the street in high heels. A cup of coffee and a ride home were also available.

One MSC bought an old double-decker bus and turned it into a mobile coffee bar. Church members would park the bus in a disadvantaged neighborhood and offer teenagers, young moms, and others a cappuccino in a convivial setting.

Video was a key part of getting the MSC idea to go viral. Drew would film the MSCs at work, and then play the videos at church on Sunday, encouraging others to either get involved or start their own groups.

In addition to their community work, MSC members were encouraged to gather at least once a week outside of church to worship and plan. Typically the group would set up its worship space like a church, with rows of chairs and one member presiding from the front. Drew would remind them, "You don't have to replicate the church floor plan. You can do church any way you like."

Drew's mantra, borrowed from Mike Breen, was "low control and high accountability."

Every team was free to set its own mission, but members knew the whole church was expecting them to do something that would make a noticeable difference in the lives of others. Beyond that, there were few constraints. "As long as it wasn't immoral, illegal or heretical," says Drew, "we encouraged the teams to press forward."

At the outset, the MSCs were encouraged simply to shine the light of God's love into their communities. There was no heavy-handed evangelical push. But over time, many of those who were touched by the MSCs started to find their way to faith and into St. Andrews.

Initially, the MSC program had no budget. That lowered the political hurdles in getting the initiative started, because Drew didn't have to put his hand in someone else's cookie jar.

For the most part, the MSCs were self-funding, though eventually they were able to draw on church funds for minor operational expenses like renting a hall. At one point, Drew was supporting 30 MSCs on a budget of £30,000 per year.

Mark and Drew believed God could do even bigger things with St. Andrews. Even as the MSC program was taking off, Drew was praying that God would put some dynamite under his church and blow the last cobwebs of complacency out of the rafters.

The TNT came in the form of a major refurbishment, a remodel that closed the main church building for nine months. Rather than find an alternate facility, Mark and Drew told the congregation that if they wanted to continue to worship together, they'd have to hook up with an MSC. There were some who worried this might slim the church rolls by as many as 200 members. But over the next nine months, the church grew from 500 souls to nearly 1,000, as fence-sitting parishioners caught the MSC bug.

The MSC model gave individuals the chance to exercise their unique gifts. One person might emerge as a strong project manager, while another would design publicity materials. A particularly patient parent might supervise youngsters during meetings, while someone else organized a meal. Though the roles were flexible, one rule was fixed: whenever an MSC grew to 50 people, it had to divide.

Other doubters worried that giving would go down. When meeting outside the church, MSC leaders weren't keen to take up an offering.

So instead, the church set up a program where members could establish standing orders for weekly debits from their bank accounts or credit cards.

There was one fact, however, that no one could argue with. The new, community-based approach to church was getting folks off the sidelines and into the game. It was also unleashing a ton of latent leadership talent. Here's how one MSC leader, a profoundly deaf woman, described her role:

> **I can honestly say that leading an MSC for the last eight months has been the hardest and most challenging thing I have ever done, parenthood aside. In running the MSC I have discovered a lot of things about myself. Some I knew already and others were fresh revelations. I am not a brilliant administrator, neither am I a preacher. I don't think I am a worship leader or a kids ministry leader but I have had to do all these things and more at some stage or another and I discovered that I can passably lead prayers, make OK coffee, improvise a kids session, preach if necessary, and make difficult decisions.**

Once the church reopened, Mark and Drew realized that the congregation had become too big for the building, though this proved to be less problematic than might have been expected. Many of the MSC members had hoped the renovation work would continue indefinitely, since they were enjoying the adventure of actually "making a difference," rather than being "nailed to a pew." Most MSC teams had started meeting twice a month for worship and at other times to carry out their mission work. When team leaders asked Drew, "Do we have to come back to church?" he told them, "Pray about it and do whatever you feel led to do." Everyone, though, was encouraged to show up on the fourth Sunday of each month for a time of "celebration." To accommodate the entire congregation, the service was offered at four different times during the day.

While the disaggregation of St. Andrews multiplied opportunities for leadership and service, some feared it might also undermine the unity of the church as a whole. There was a risk that as members became more tightly knit together in their MSC teams, they would feel less of an identity with the larger community. Drew wanted subdivisions, not splinters.

To that end, he launched a weekly newsletter to help people stay connected. Periodically, he'd also bring the MSC leaders together to set priorities and identify new opportunities. Over time, many of the MSCs set up their own websites and this became another mechanism for keeping congregants informed.

Other common touchpoints included a teaching guide used by all the MSCs in their weekly worship discussions, and a compulsory training course for MSC leaders and members. In his linchpin role, Drew also spent a lot of time nurturing connections between MSC leaders and service-minded parishioners.

There were, of course, hiccups. Occasionally an MSC leader would fight tenaciously for a project that was only marginally effective. Another source of friction came from neighboring vicars. The Church of England is divided into geographically defined parishes and some nearby vicars raised objections when they learned that a St. Andrews team was operating outside its franchise. In hindsight, Mark and Drew admit they might have done more to anticipate these objections and smooth feathers along the way. Nevertheless, after witnessing seven years of growth and outreach, there were few at St. Andrews who wanted to undo the MSC experiment.

As Drew says, "This was a radically different model of doing church. It's not one where programs get established and blessed at the center. It's one where authority doesn't trickle down, and where the spokes of control don't run out from a hub." It is, though, a model that has been amazingly effective. In one representative month, MSC teams conducted more than 106 service projects.

By the time Drew left St. Andrews in 2009, the congregation had grown to more than 1,600 members, most of whom served on an MSC. In talking with me about his journey at St. Andrews, Drew recalled his first Christmas Eve service:

We did back-to-back carol services with a great orchestra and a gifted speaker. At both services we invited people forward for prayer, and everyone stayed seated; no one came forward. I thought, this is as good as church is ever going to be. It was an exemplary piece of "attractional" worship. We had drained

every church within 40 miles, but it was all transference, no new growth. I thought, we would have been better to break the congregation up and send them out caroling. It was just clear to me that this model wasn't working.

Drew went on:

Before we started the MSCs, we had a whole Sunday devoted to children's work, and the point was to get more volunteers. People wept at the end of the service, and yet we had zero response. It was so depressing. When we started doing the MSCs, people had to step forward. And suddenly, people realized they had gifts, unexploited talents. In the culture of excellence, people felt under-qualified. Once they were in an MSC, they had folks they could work with, other amateurs who said, "Come on, we can do this." You had friends rooting for you.

There are many lessons that could be drawn from this experiment in bottom-up change, but let me focus on two. First, if you're a formally appointed leader, and you want to turn sheep into shepherds, you have to take off your leadership mantle and say to people, "I don't have a plan, what's yours?" That's humbling, but it's the only way to release the latent talents within your organization.

Second, you have to let people find the work that best suits their interests. This is the key to building a community of passion. When you force people into slots, you get slot-shaped contributions; you don't get bold and astonishing contributions. If you want the unexpected, you have to give people the freedom to *do* the unexpected.

Now, can you run an airline this way, or a semiconductor fab line? I don't know, but I bet you can run parts of any organization like this. One thing I'm sure about: if you want to take full advantage of the extraordinary talents that exist in *your* organization, you'll need to ask yourself each day, "What can I do to make this place feel less like a hierarchy and more like a community?" And here's the good news: you don't have to be the Archbishop of Canterbury to get started.

REVERSING
THE RATCHET
OF CONTROL

In most organizations, the decision-making freedoms of frontline employees are highly circumscribed. Sales reps, call center staff, office managers, and assembly line workers are usually trussed up in a strait-jacket of rules and procedures. I believe that's a problem, for it's impossible to unleash human capabilities without first expanding the scope of employee autonomy. To create an organization that's adaptable and innovative, people need the freedom to challenge precedent, to "waste" time, to go outside of channels, to experiment, to take risks, and to follow their passions.

Interestingly, humanity's most adaptable social systems, democracies and markets, are the ones that extend the greatest freedom to their constituents. In a democracy, you don't need anyone's permission to start a political movement, organize a demonstration, or change your party affiliation; in open markets, individuals are free to buy and invest as they see fit.

Obviously, policies and rules are important—no organization can survive without them. Most organizations, though, are overcontrolled. That's because control works like a ratchet. Managers are incentivized to create rules, not abolish them. More rules mean more things to control, and that means more job security and more power. As the years pass, rules and regulations accumulate, layer by layer. That's why older organizations are usually more arthritic than younger ones. If you doubt whether this dynamic is at work in your organization, conduct a simple survey. Ask frontline employees whether they feel they have significantly *more* autonomy today than they had five years ago. Unless your company is truly exceptional, the answer will probably be "no."

Imagine, then, the controls you might find in an organization that will soon celebrate its 150th birthday, a venerable institution like, let's say, the Bank of New Zealand. BNZ is the 148-year-old subsidiary of National Australia Bank, but strangely enough it's also a case study in the power of empowerment.

AN IMPROMPTU EXPERIMENT

It started simply enough. In June 2007, Chris Bayliss, BNZ's general manager for retail banking, was visiting the bank's City Center store in Christchurch. (Within BNZ's retail-oriented culture, branch banks are known as "stores.") It was just after 9 A.M. and the bank wasn't open yet, but a long line of customers was already forming on the sidewalk. On most days, BNZ's stores opened at 9:00, but today was Tuesday, and on Tuesdays and Wednesdays, staff training sessions kept the doors locked until 9:30—hence the queue. At BNZ, corporate policy dictated opening hours, and all of the bank's 180 stores, from Invercargill in the south to Kaitaia in the north, adhered to the same schedule.

As the line of impatient customers continued to grow, Chris turned to Sue Eden, the store manager: "If you owned this store, would you open earlier and find another time for staff training?" "Of course," replied Sue, "just look outside!" Chris frowned. Here was a store manager eager to serve her customers, yet bank policy was tripping her up. "OK then," Chris said, "*you* choose when to open and close, but don't expect any extra money from me for more staff." The store manager quickly agreed, and Chris walked out of the store scarcely aware that he had just launched a mini-revolution in employee freedom.

Within days, news of the policy shift had spread across BNZ's retail network. Soon Chris was fielding requests from managers throughout New Zealand, all of whom, it seemed, were eager for the same freedom that had just been granted to the Christchurch store. With e-mails flooding in, Chris reached out to his colleague, Blair Vernon, general manager of marketing. Within the bank, opening hours were considered a "brand and customer experience issue," and that was Blair's bailiwick. As a teenager, Blair had flipped burgers at McDonald's, a company that lets its franchisees decide when to open and close. Reckoning that what worked for McDonald's might work for BNZ, Blair agreed that the petitioners should be able to set their own hours.

In Takapuna, a tiny Auckland suburb, BNZ became the first bank to open on Sunday mornings. This allowed the store to serve the thousands of customers who flocked to the local farmers' market. In South Island ski towns, store managers opted to stay open until late in the evening so skiers could do their banking after a day on the slopes. Within city centers, many store managers chose to synchronize their schedules with nearby retailers rather than keep bankers' hours. Within six months, nearly 95% of BNZ's 180 stores had altered their opening hours in some way.

NOT SO FAST

While store managers were moving quickly to exploit their newfound freedom, there were many at the head office who fretted about the loss of control. Chris and Blair soon found themselves fighting a rearguard action with head office staff who regarded the policy shift as rushed, if not reckless. Typically, a change of this magnitude went through a detailed risk assessment that gave every function the chance to weigh in.

Chris and Blair struggled to defend their hurried decision. They hadn't set out to bypass the usual decision-making process, but had simply been overwhelmed by the horde of frontline managers who were eager to operate more flexibly.

Within the bank's HR function, there was a concern that the bank employees union, Finsec, would raise a "ruckus" and object to any changes that extended the workday or compelled employees to come in on weekends. Others worried that store managers might choose to cut opening hours—a move that would jeopardize customer satisfaction. BNZ's risk management experts had their own issues. There were detailed policies that governed how a store was supposed to be opened, and cash transfers to and from armored vehicles had to be scheduled at precise times. Given this, how could managers be allowed to open up "any old time they felt like it?" Information technology was another sticking point. The bank's IT staff typically scheduled major maintenance during times when the stores were closed. What would happen if a store opened at an odd hour and the IT system was down?

Then there was corporate marketing. Charged with protecting the brand, senior staffers worried that a hodge-podge of opening times might damage the bank's carefully built reputation for consistency and reliability. And what about all those hand-lettered signs that were being used to announce new opening hours? They looked tacky.

Although many of the objections were more political than practical, some were well grounded and prompted policy adjustments. A software template was developed that allowed store managers to print out a simple sign displaying local opening hours. Team members were reminded they had to abide by the bank's security policies and could do nothing that would jeopardize employee safety. Furthermore, store managers were expected to consult with team members before making any changes to staff schedules; new opening hours required the agreement of every store employee. This caveat also helped to neutralize objections from BNZ's union. How could the union demur when the new work schedules had been set by employees rather than imposed from above?

"What everyone learned," says Blair, "is that when you treat people like adults, they act like adults." The operational Armageddon that some had feared never came to pass.

A DAY AT THE BEACH

Store managers understood that the new policy was the product of an ad-lib experiment, and not a corporate-level task force. That fact, as well as the oft-expressed enthusiasm of Chris and Blair for a bottom-up approach to innovation, encouraged store managers to take the lead in testing other offbeat ideas.

One of the zaniest was a "trailer" bank. Explains Blair: "It's a bank that's kind of like an ice cream cart. It's been shrunken so it can be pulled behind a vehicle." Although the concept had been in development for several months, a local store team caused a splash when they towed the trailer onto a beach on New Year's Day. Clad in BNZ T-shirts, local staffers started blowing up balloons. Soon children were circling with their parents in tow. As a crowd gathered, store employees fired up a barbecue and started passing out sausages, along with information about BNZ's latest products.

Although some on the HR staff worried that customers might think the bank was exploiting its employees by making them work on New Year's Day, or breaching health and safety regulations by cooking sausages, Chris and Blair were more sanguine. They viewed the bank-on-the-beach as a great example of what charged-up employees could do when they felt they had the freedom to experiment. Says Chris, "If we'd *told* them to do this, it never would have happened. But it was *their* idea, and no one bothered to ask permission."

WHY IT WORKS

So how has BNZ been able give employees more discretion and still run a disciplined and profitable business?

Incentives are part of the answer. A typical BNZ store has 4–7 team members: the store manager, a few tellers, and a couple of salespeople, or "advisors." Each store manager receives a salary plus a bonus for meeting the store's financial goals, usually 10% of base pay. In addition, the manager receives 10% of any profits earned in excess of the plan. Advisors receive bonuses based on the products they sell, such as credit cards and life insurance policies. Store employees also participate in a team-based incentive scheme that is linked to sales performance and customer satisfaction metrics.

In defending the move to flexible hours, Chris often argued that "there's nothing more frustrating for staff than being open when the town is dead, or closed when it's packed." There's an important lesson here. Companies often work hard to cultivate a passion for customers, and then turn that ardor into anger when rigid rules prevent employees from creatively addressing customer needs. When employees are incentivized to produce the right outcomes, senior executives can, and should, worry a lot less about prescribing the means.

The second component of BNZ's decentralized control system is data—lots of it. Says Blair, "If you empower people but don't give them information, they just fumble in the dark." To address this, an initiative was launched in 2004 that gave every store employee a clear window into the financial performance of the bank. Daily P&L statements provide detailed information on costs, revenues, and profits for each store, all of it broken down by product and service.

Nothing remarkable about this, except that in most banks, branch managers don't get a real P&L. Instead they get a set of synthetic accounts that give them only a rough indication of the store's real profitability, and they seldom get detailed information on the performance of other branches. These contrived performance measures allow head office executives to tweak incentive structures at will, and to exhort high-performing branches to do even better, but they also make it difficult for frontline employees to judge the real profit impact of their decisions.

BNZ, by contrast, provides its store managers with a high-definition picture of branch profitability; store managers even know the bank's wholesale cost of funds. Having been richly endowed with information, store managers are given a lot of decision-making latitude, and are held accountable for results. A store manager might, for example, discount a loan to win a new customer, but will think carefully before doing so because the loan stays on the store's books until it's paid off.

"It's amazing," says Blair. "If you get head office out of the way and give people accurate data about their performance, they quickly figure out what's a good decision and what's not!"

At BNZ, store managers have the incentives, the data, and the freedom that are typical of a small business owner. As a result, most regard themselves as more than clock-punchers; they're leaders who have a real stake in a real business, and they run it as if it was their own.

Blair summarizes the changes at BNZ with a telling anecdote. "I was walking by one of our stores on a Sunday morning with my kids, and my son said, 'Dad, the doors of the bank are open.' And I thought, crap, someone forgot to close the doors. But then I looked in, and saw that the entire store was open. No one is forced to roster on Sunday, but team members had come in from other branches in order to swap their hours. One mom was working on Sunday because she wanted to take Wednesday off. And it hit me: no one at head office even knows when the stores are open." Adds Chris, "The freedom to open when you want may not be the biggest thing we've done, but it's the most symbolic in terms of telling people, 'We trust you, and we're serious about empowering you.'"

None of this is rocket science, and by itself, a single policy change won't transform the fortunes of a company. But the story is telling nonetheless. Turns out, the ratchet of control can be reversed, when a small, seemingly insignificant breech in a culture of control opens the door to additional freedoms. Says Chris, "The empowerment horse is now out of the stable."

Take a moment and ask yourself: How many policies in your company exist only to preserve the fiction that the higher-ups really are in control? How many rules enforce standardization at the expense of initiative and passion, while delivering few if any performance benefits? Better yet, post those questions on an internal wiki and invite your colleagues to join forces in reversing the ratchet of control.

REINVENTING MANAGEMENT FOR THE FACEBOOK GENERATION

Like the inventors of the light bulb, the telephone, and the automobile, the inventors of modern management were born in the nineteenth century. Those long-dead pioneers—individuals like James Mooney, Alfred Sloan, and Donaldson Brown—would be surprised to learn that their inventions (which included workflow optimization, variance analysis, capital budgeting, functional specialization, divisionalization, and project management), are still the cornerstones of twenty-first-century management systems.

It is difficult for contemporary observers to appreciate the profound impact these revolutionary breakthroughs had on the organization of economic life in the early decades of America's industrial revolution. In 1890, nine out of ten white males worked for themselves, and the ones who didn't were referred to disparagingly as "wage slaves." At the time, the average manufacturing company had four employees, and few factories had more than 100 laborers. Yet within a generation, Ford Motor Company would be making half a million cars a year, Sears, Roebuck & Company would be running a continent-wide distribution system, and U.S. Steel would be boasting about a billion-dollar market value.

This transition from an agrarian and craft-based society to an industrial powerhouse required an epic resocialization of the workforce. Unruly and independent-minded farmers, artisans, and day laborers had to be transformed into rule-following, forelock-tugging employees. A hundred years on, this work continues, with organizations around the world still working hard to strap rancorous and free-thinking human beings into the straitjacket of institutionalized obedience, conformity, and discipline.

But now, for the first time since the early twentieth century, we're on the verge of another management revolution, and it may turn out to be just as unsettling as the one that spawned the Industrial Age. There are three forces at work that make such a metamorphosis likely; three discontinuities that will end management as we know it.

The first of these is a bundle of dramatic changes that have made the business environment substantially less forgiving. Companies around the world are struggling to cope with a wildly accelerating pace of change, an onslaught of new, ultra low-cost competitors, the commoditization of knowledge, rapidly increasing customer power, and an ever-lengthening menu of social demands. Traditional management models that emphasize optimization over innovation, and continuity over change, simply can't cope with these unprecedented challenges.

The second driver is the invention of new, web-based collaboration tools. For the first time since the pyramids were built, human beings have a new way of organizing themselves, via online, distributed networks. At long last, there's an alternative to formal hierarchy.

The third driver is the mash-up of new expectations that Generation Facebook will bring to work in the years ahead. If you're part of the first generation to grow up on the Web, you don't think of the Internet as something "out there"—as a tool you use to reserve a hotel room, buy a book, or rekindle an old flame. Rather, the Web is something you're perpetually *in*; it's as ubiquitous and transparent as water to fish. As a digital native, the Web is the operating system for your life, the indispensable and unremarkable means by which you learn, play, share, flirt, and connect.

The experience of growing up online will profoundly shape the workplace expectations of Generation F. At a minimum, they'll expect the social environment of their worklife to reflect the social context of the Web, rather than a mid-twentieth-century bureaucracy.

With that in mind, I compiled a list of twelve work-relevant characteristics of the social Web. These are the post-bureaucratic realities that tomorrow's employees will use as yardsticks in determining whether your company is "with it" or "past it." In assembling this short list, I haven't tried to catalog every salient feature of the Web's social milieu, only those that are most at odds with the legacy management practices that characterize most companies.

1. All ideas compete on an equal footing.

    On the Web, every idea has the chance to gain a following, or not. No one has the power to kill off a subversive idea or squelch an embarrassing debate. Ideas gain traction based on their perceived merits, rather than on the political power of their proponents. By disassociating "share of voice" and "share of power," the Web undermines the ability of the elites to control the conversation or set the agenda.

2. Contribution counts for more than credentials.

    When you post a video to YouTube, no one asks you if you went to film school. When you write a blog, no one cares whether or not you have a journalism degree. Position, title, and academic degrees—none of the usual status differentiators carry much weight online. On the Web, what counts is not your résumé, but what you can contribute.

3. Hierarchies are built bottom-up.

    In any Web forum there are some individuals who command more respect and attention than others, and have more influence as a consequence. Critically, though, these individuals haven't been appointed by some higher authority. Instead, their clout reflects the freely given approbation of their peers. On the Web, authority trickles up, not down.

4. Leaders serve rather than preside.

On the Web, *every* leader is a servant leader; no one has the power to command or sanction. Credible arguments, demonstrated expertise, and selfless behavior are the only levers for getting things done. Forget this online, and your followers will soon desert you.

5. Tasks are chosen, not assigned.

The Web is an opt-in economy. Whether contributing to a blog, working on an open source project, or sharing advice in a forum, people choose to work on the things that interest them. Everyone is an independent contractor and everyone scratches their own itch.

6. Groups are self-defining and self-organizing.

On the Web, you get to choose your compatriots. In any online community, you have the freedom to link up with some individuals and ignore the rest, to share deeply with some folks and not at all with others. Just as no one can assign you a boring task, no can force you to work with dimwitted associates.

7. Resources get attracted, not allocated.

In large organizations, resources get allocated top-down, in a politicized, budget wrangle. On the Web, human effort flows toward ideas and projects that are attractive (and fun) and away from those that aren't. In this sense, the Web is a market economy where millions of individuals get to decide, moment by moment, how to spend the precious currency of their time and attention.

8. Power comes from sharing, not hoarding.

The Web is also a gift economy. To gain influence and status, you have to give away your expertise and content. And you must do it quickly; if you don't, someone else will beat you to the punch and garner the credit that might have been yours. Online, there are lots of incentives to share and few to hoard.

9. Mediocrity gets exposed.

Online rating systems have become ubiquitous—for hotels, books, local businesses, and products of every sort. Though not every review is useful, in the aggregate they provide a good guide to what's remarkable and what's rubbish. In traditional organizations, employees don't get to rate much of anything. As a result, one often finds a "conspiracy of the mediocre"—"I won't question your decisions or your effectiveness, if you don't question mine." There are no such cabals on the Web. If you're inadequate you'll be found out. The Web gives disgruntled customers a global soap box. Few companies, though, seem eager to give employees an internal platform where they can challenge executive decisions and corporate policies.

10. Dissidents can join forces.

In a hierarchical organization (or political system), it takes a lot of courage to speak up. When communication channels run vertically rather than laterally, it can be difficult to know whether anyone around you is possessed of a similarly rebellious mind. Individuals who feel isolated and vulnerable are unlikely to protest. The Web, by contrast, makes it easy to find and connect with individuals who share one's own dissenting point of view. Agitators who might have been marginalized in a top-down organization can rapidly mobilize like-minded confederates in the Web's densely-connected "thoughtocracy."

11. Users can veto most policy decisions.

As many Internet moguls have learned to their sorrow, online users are opinionated and vociferous, and they'll quickly attack any decision or policy change that seems contrary to the community's interests. Only by giving users a substantial say in key decisions can you keep them loyal. It doesn't matter who built the online community; the users own it and, as a practical matter, policies have to be socially constructed.

12. Intrinsic rewards matter most.

The Web is a testament to the power of intrinsic rewards. Think of all the articles contributed to Wikipedia, all the open source software created, all the advice freely given, all the photos submitted to Flickr. Add up the hours of volunteer time and it's obvious that human beings will give generously of themselves when they're given the chance to contribute to something they actually care about. Money's great, but so are recognition and the joy of accomplishment.

All these features of web-based life are written into the social DNA of Generation F, and are mostly missing from the managerial DNA of the average Fortune 500 company.

If your organization hopes to attract the most creative and energetic members of Gen F, it will need to understand these Internet-derived expectations and reinvent its management practices accordingly. Sure, it's a buyer's market for talent right now, but that won't always be the case. In the future, any company that lacks a vital core of Gen F employees will find itself stuck in the mud.

Clay Shirkey writes persuasively about how the Web has harnessed humanity's "cognitive surplus"—the thinking time that went unused when our pastimes were mostly passive. The Web is also proving to be an outlet for a lot of pent-up passions (and no, I'm not talking about Internet porn). One not-so-small example is the Kahn Academy, an online treasure trove of more than 2,400 mini-lectures, all created by Salman Kahn, an MIT- and Harvard-educated polymath. The inspiration for this instructional supermarket came while Kahn was tutoring a cousin in mathematics via short coaching sessions he recorded on an electronic blackboard. Kahn wondered, why not make these video tutorials available to anyone around the world? Why not, indeed? Within three years of its founding, the Kahn Academy was dishing up more than 35,000 YouTube-hosted videos each day. Had he been born in an earlier decade, Kahn's passion for teaching would have been just as intense, but it wouldn't have found a global audience, and without that audience, Kahn probably wouldn't have been inspired to build a tutoring emporium.

Each of us wants to find and follow our passion. That may be especially true for Generation F, but it's probably true for you as well. Despite its drawbacks, we're enamored with the Web because it's a passion multiplier; we can mold it to our interests, search its vast realm for inspiration, and use it to recruit collaborators.

The Web compounds our passions because online . . .

No one can kill a good idea.
Everyone can pitch in.

Anyone can lead.

No one can dictate.

You get to choose your cause.

You can easily build on top of what others have done.

You don't have to put up with bullies and tyrants.

Agitators don't get marginalized.

Excellence usually wins (and mediocrity doesn't).

Passion-killing policies get reversed.

Great contributions get recognized and celebrated.

Now ask yourself, how many of these things can be said of your organization? Not enough, I warrant. But as we'll see in the next section, you can change this.

If you had been alive in 1890, it would have been difficult to imagine an organization as big and efficient as the Ford Motor Company. Today, it's equally hard to imagine a global-scale organization that exemplifies all the passion-boosting attributes of the Web. But that's the challenge we should set ourselves as twenty-first-century management innovators—because only by doing so will we create organizations that magnify rather than shrink human passions, and passion matters now like never before.

SECTION 5

Ideology Matters Now

CHALLENGING THE IDEOLOGY OF MANAGEMENT

5.1

Here's a word that probably doesn't get much airtime in your organization: *ideology*. Do a search of your company's internal website and I'm willing to bet you won't find a single reference. That's a problem. As managers, it's our creedal beliefs that prevent our institutions from being more adaptable, more innovative, more inspiring, and more noble-minded. We are limited by our management ideology.

Human history is a chronicle of ideological conflict: polytheism versus monotheism, materialism versus idealism, mercantilism versus free trade, totalitarianism versus democracy, and communitarianism versus individualism. Occasionally, an ideology trumps its rivals, usually because it produces better social outcomes. For example, most economists believe free trade is better for prosperity than autarky (self-sufficiency)—an assertion that's supported by a wealth of empirical data. In other disputes, the dust never settles, either because the debate is purely philosophical (so it's impossible to prove the efficacy of one proposition versus another), or because the opposing ideologies are complementary rather than antithetical. Within Christian theology, for example, the ideas of mercy and justice are counterposed *and* reciprocal. Neither ideological pole is viable on its own. Justice without mercy is vengeance; mercy without justice is license. All of us, I think, want to live in societies where these ideologies are robust competitors. Charles Simeon, a nineteenth-century cleric and fellow at King's College, Cambridge, put it well when he said of justice and mercy: "Truth is not in the middle and not in one extreme; it is in both extremes."[1]

It is difficult for us to imagine how two diametrically opposed ideologies could have equal sway. Instinctively, though, we know it's not enough to simply split the difference—to bring, for example, a meager morsel of mercy and a little dollop of justice to every situation. Sometimes justice needs to prevail in full, as when a child abuser is sentenced to an extended prison term. At other times, mercy needs to have the upper hand, as when a father-to-be is excused for speeding as he rushes his pregnant partner to the hospital. In the first case, we wouldn't wish the judge to be lenient, even if the abuser himself had been abused. The safety of our children is paramount. Likewise, if a cop pulls over a speeding car and discovered a woman in labor, we want him to provide an escort to the hospital rather than issue a ticket for a lesser infraction because of extenuating circumstances.

Finding an accommodation between competing ideologies isn't about compromise; it's about getting the weighting right in every circumstance and at every moment. Doing so requires four things: first, a sense of the ultimate goal (in the case of jurisprudence, this might be a society that is as fair as possible to as many as possible); second, situational awareness (a knowledge of the on-the-ground realities that must be considered in making critical trade-offs); third, a large dose of good sense (the intelligence, emotional and otherwise, that is needed to make Solomon-like decisions); and fourth, personal incentives for getting the balance right (a practical reason to care deeply about the consequences of one's choices).

If you're a parent, you already have lots of experience in managing paradox. Every day, for example, you're called upon to reconcile love and discipline. You give your four-year-old daughter lots of cuddles, but occasionally she gets a scolding and time-out as well. As a parent, you're constantly struggling to get this balance right. In every situation, you're thinking long-term *and* short-term. When you're exhausted at the end of a long day, you may decide to forego a battle of wills with your defiant toddler. But even in those moments, you remain aware of your ultimate responsibility: to positively shape her character. You know you won't get the weighting between love and discipline right *every* time, but you're deeply committed to getting it right *over* time.

Now imagine there was a vice president of parenting who didn't live in your home and didn't really know your children. Imagine further that this executive received monthly reports from a dozen parents and, in response, occasionally issued blanket edicts: "I see we're way over budget on tantrums. Next quarter we're going to focus on discipline. I want every parent to increase the number of time-outs by 30%." How helpful would *that* be?

To see how all this applies to management, we need to tackle three important questions. First, what is the ideology of management—what is its doctrinal core? Second, what is its conceptual rival—what's the yang to management's yin? And third, how can we create organizations where yin doesn't always win at the expense of yang—where there's genuine, productive tension, rather than a fudge or a perpetually one-sided battle?

With respect to the first question, we get a clue to the ideology of management when we consult a thesaurus. In most languages, the first synonym for the word "manage" is "control." This tight coupling between management and control is an artifact of the industrial revolution. The engineers and accountants who invented management were crusaders for efficiency. To them, waste was anathema, so they attacked it with division of labor, standardization, workflow optimization, performance monitoring, and efficiency-focused compensation schemes—all weapons in the arsenal of control. In the battle against inefficiency, managers were the enforcers. It was their job to ensure that rules were followed, variances were minimized, quotas were met, and slackers were punished. And so it is today. Employees manufacture products and services; managers manufacture control.

We can, of course, take a broader view of management. Grandly, management is the *technology of human accomplishment*. It encompasses the tools and methods we use to mobilize and organize resources to productive ends. As a species, our capacity to manage—to coordinate, allocate, evaluate, motivate, and all the rest—sets the boundaries on what we can achieve. This makes management one of humankind's most important "social technologies." In practice, though, management is something far more prosaic. At its core, it's a methodology for routinizing work.

If you have a car or two in the garage, a home packed with technological wonders, and a closet full of clothes made halfway around the world, you owe an enormous debt of gratitude to the intrepid souls who invented the means for hyper-efficient, high-volume production. All of humanity's scientific advances would have contributed little to our quality of life if they hadn't been accompanied by equally astounding breakthroughs in management science. Over the past century, much of this innovation was focused on getting people to be as reliable as machines, a challenge that required a new and systematic approach to the problem of control. The name for that approach: *bureaucracy*.

To get traction, a social ideology must ultimately be expressed in a tangible, organizational form. For Marxism, that was the communist party, and for management, bureaucracy. Writing in the early years of the twentieth century, the renowned German sociologist Max Weber extolled the virtues of this radically new organizational paradigm:

> **[Bureaucracy] is, from a purely technical point of view, capable of attaining the highest degree of efficiency and is in this sense formally the most rational known means of carrying out imperative control over human beings. It is superior to any other form in precision, in stability, in the stringency of its discipline, and in its reliability. It thus makes possible a particularly high degree of calculability of results for the heads of the organization and those acting in relation to it.[2]**

In this single, concise paragraph, Weber lays bare the ideology of management—control*ism*; and a hundred years later, it remains the philosophical cornerstone of virtually every large-scale human organization.

Note the bounties of bureaucracy which Weber celebrates: precision, stability, discipline, and reliability. These are undoubtedly blessings, but in most industries today, they are merely table stakes. They are prerequisites for competitive parity, but insufficient for real advantage. Today, our institutions are up against *new* challenges: a rapidly accelerating pace of change, hyper-competition, the commoditization of knowledge, and ever-escalating demands for social accountability. These imperatives demand something more than more control. As I've argued throughout this volume, we need organizations that are passion-filled, creative, and malleable. Problem is, these organizational attributes are inversely correlated with bureaucratic control.

Weirdly, human beings already have many of the qualities that our organizations lack. People are surprisingly adaptable. I have a physician brother who went back to school in his early fifties to get a master's degree in health administration, in order to become the CEO of a hospital group. I have friends who've moved across oceans to give their families a better life, who've sought out challenging new jobs in a quest for personal growth, and who've been strengthened, rather than crushed, by personal tragedy. People are resilient, and they're innovative. Every day I'm amazed by the cataract of human creativity one finds on the Web. We were *born* to create—we can't help ourselves. All we need are the right tools and a bit of encouragement from other creative souls. We are also intensely interested in one another—that's why reality television is universally popular, and why we love watching humanity tumble by while sipping a latte at an outdoor café. You, me, the person in the next cubicle, all of us have stories to tell, stories that can entertain, enlighten, and energize. How is it, then, that our organizations are less adaptable, less creative, and less inspiring than we are? Because they are hostages to an ideology that is, in a real sense, *inhuman*.

Weber may have composed an anthem for bureaucracy, but he was also mindful of its dehumanizing effects. In a speech he gave in 1909, he warned of its dark side:

[In a bureaucracy] the performance of each individual is mathematically measured, each man becomes a little cog in the machine and, aware of this, his one preoccupation is whether he can become a bigger cog....

[T]he great question is therefore not how we can promote and hasten [bureaucracy], but what can we oppose to this machinery in order to keep a portion of mankind free from this parceling out of the soul.[3]

Weber understood that in routinizing work, we risked routinizing human beings. Indeed, this was inevitable, since the goal of bureaucracy was (and is) to excise the human factor, to turn people into machines made of flesh and blood. It is easy to believe that, a century on, we are somehow more enlightened than those early management pioneers. After all, we no longer call subordinates "employees," but rather "associates" and "team members." As leaders, we tell ourselves we really *do* care about work-life balance, personal growth, diversity, mentoring, empowerment, transparency, and a dozen other human-friendly issues. Yet the fact remains: nearly 80% of employees around the world are less than highly engaged in their work. They show up on the job each day, but leave most of their humanity at home.

It's not as if we haven't tried to make our organizations more humane. Fifty-two years ago, Douglas McGregor, then an MIT professor, published his landmark book, *The Human Side of Enterprise*. If you're a student of management theory, you might recall the distinction he drew between "Theory X" and "Theory Y."

"Theory X" was McGregor's shorthand for a management mindset that regards employees as lazy and ill-disciplined. In this view, workers are shirkers. They will be industrious only to the extent they are monitored by supervisors and motivated by extrinsic rewards, such as money and the threat of punishment. Control, in a Theory X organization, comes from without, not within. "Theory Y," by contrast, holds that employees are inherently self-motivating. They are eager to do a good job and will happily do so if given the chance. Here, motivation comes from the pride of accomplishment rather than from a clever amalgam of sticks and carrots. Build a high-trust organization and employees will reciprocate by exhibiting a high degree of self-control.

Most of today's "progressive" people practices are rooted in Theory Y precepts. Sadly, though, all these well-intended policies haven't yet managed to de-bureaucratize our organizations. You may find it hard to believe that your organization is still Theory X at its core, because you hear so much Theory Y rhetoric–talk about empowerment, engagement, participation, trust, and openness. Nevertheless, as a practical matter, our organizations are still ideologically asymmetrical. The creed of control reigns supreme. If you doubt this, ask yourself: Is your organization any less rules-driven than it was ten or twenty years ago? Do people on the front lines feel any less controlled? Are their freedoms any less abridged? And are little cogs any less obsessed with becoming big cogs?

If you read the story of St. Andrews in Chapter 4.3, you know that autonomy and passion are positively correlated. Consider your own life: Have you ever been more enthused about something you were *told* to do, rather than something you *chose* to do? What stands in the way of genuine empowerment isn't the occasional control freak, but the deeply embedded control structures that strip employees of their discretion. What's worse, we take these authoritarian structures for granted. Step back for a moment, though, and they start to seem absurd. For example, doesn't it strike you as odd that a consumer can unilaterally decide to purchase a $25,000 car, while that same individual at work has to get permission to requisition a new office chair?

Passion and initiative are not the only victims of *controlitis*—so too are adaptability and innovation. In most companies, strategy making and resource allocation are centralized, a fact that seriously undermines resilience.

When the responsibility for setting strategy is concentrated at the top of a large organization, a handful of executives are able to stymie change, and will often do so rather than write off their own depreciating intellectual capital. Consider Microsoft. For years, Bill Gates held court as the company's "chief software architect." In this role, his endorsement was required for any major new software initiative. Unfortunately, Gates saw the world through a particular prism, one that was PC-centric, product focused, and oriented toward Microsoft's traditional, industrial customers. I believe it was this confluence of strategic orthodoxy and centralized power that doomed Microsoft to follower status when the industry paradigm shifted toward the Web, open source, and the cloud. The fact that Microsoft is, in so many respects, an extraordinary company, merely serves to underline the debilitating effects of centralization.

Control-oriented, top-down structures are similarly toxic for creativity. As I argued in Chapter 3.5, innovation, particularly of the disruptive sort, is unlikely to flourish when a few key executives have a choke hold on resource allocation. Experience shows they will frequently overinvest in existing businesses (the ones they understand and lead), while starving new initiatives of talent and capital. When it comes to getting the right resources behind the right opportunities at the right time, hierarchical organizations almost always get it wrong. Indeed, it's this fact that gives venture capitalists a leg up over resource-rich incumbents.

It is impossible, I think, to have an organization that is adaptable, innovative, and engaging when power trickles down from the top, when big leaders appoint little leaders, when a handful of executives make the critical calls, and when senior executives are less accountable to employees than the reverse. Put simply, you can't build an organization that's fit for the future around an ideology that *preemptively* and *structurally* empowers the few while disempowering the many.

Now let me be careful. I have no argument with control, *per se*. No organization can long survive without a strong spine of discipline. I do believe, though, that most organizations are *overcontrolled* and *wrongly controlled*. They are overcontrolled in the sense that managers try to control too many things, too tightly; and wrongly controlled in that control comes too much from supervisors and edicts rather than from peers and norms. The net effect is a low-trust workplace where individuals don't have the autonomy to make smart, real-time trade-offs between competing priorities.

Given all these limits to the ideology of control, why don't we yet have an *effective* philosophical competitor to classical bureaucracy? Why is Theory Y still mostly *theory?* Why, a half century after McGregor, are management professors *still* writing books about empowerment? Perhaps it's because the ideology of control got a big head start and is now deeply ensconced in management systems and processes. Perhaps it's because bureaucracy, however flawed, has been so darn effective. Better the devil you know than the one you don't. And then there's the fact that most managers have never seen anything that looks like a viable alternative to the bureaucratic model, one that yields the necessary degree of control *and* allows human beings to blossom. Most of us have grown up in and around organizations that adhere to a standard template. There are layers of managers with well-defined titles and clearly proscribed authority limits. Employees report to supervisors who set priorities and assess performance. Big decisions are taken by executives with big titles and salaries to match. Promotions are highly coveted and the competition for advancement is fierce. This is what organizations are *supposed* to look like.

Fact is, many things—like the first iPhone, J. K. Rowling's wizardly world, or Lady Gaga's sirloin gown—were hard to imagine until they were encountered. But all of these things now exist. (What? Hogwarts isn't *real?*) Someone imagined these things; so what prevents us from imagining organizations where the brambles of bureaucratic control have been entirely uprooted rather than merely pruned? Thus far, most of the attacks on bureaucracy have been tactical rather than existential; they've been friendly shoulder jabs (let's do 360-degree reviews) rather a left hook to the temple (let's tear down the pyramid).

Having unpacked the ideology of management, let's turn to the second question: does control have a viable philosophical rival? Sure, *freedom*. People who are free to follow their interests, choose their allegiances, and make their own commitments, *flourish*. And what we need now more than ever are organizations that allow human beings to do just that. An organization will never be fully capable unless it's fully human. The trick, of course, is getting beyond the rhetoric. We need an ideology that is radical *and* potent, one that emancipates employees, demolishes top-down hierarchy, and still produces solid business results.

Can we find smarter ways of managing the tension between control and freedom? Yes. Can we overcome the systemic incompetencies of our control-besotted management structures? Yes. In coming chapters I'll dig deeper into two extraordinary companies that have been built around the ideology of self-determination: W. L. Gore and Morning Star. These aren't poofy start-ups or flaky experiments. They are large, process-intensive businesses, and they're industry leaders. What you won't find in either of these companies is a formal hierarchy, a trickle-down power structure, or employees who feel like serfs. What you will find is a dynamic balance of yin *and* yang, of freedom *and* discipline, of accountability *and* autonomy.

Is it easy doing battle with bureaucracy? Nope. You can't empower the many without disempowering the few, and the few probably won't like that. Indeed, that's one of the reasons the bureaucratic model has been so sticky: it provides a powerful rationale for the organizational caste system. Like the rest of us, CEOs, VPs, and department heads are jealous of their prerogatives. They would like to believe that it's impossible to manage without a management hierarchy, but it's not.

The truth is this: As managers, we've been fiddling at the margins. We've flattened corporate hierarchies, but haven't eliminated them. We've eulogized empowerment, but haven't surrendered our decision-making privileges. We've encouraged employees to speak up, but haven't let them choose their own leaders. We've denounced bureaucracy, but haven't dethroned it. But now, at long last, we must do so, and we can learn much from the progressive organizations that have gone to war with bureaucracy. One of those organizations is HCL Technologies, an India-based IT services company, which you'll also meet in this section.

In the decades to come, our organizations will become less lopsided, because they must. Freedom and control will duke it out every day, moment-by-moment and issue-by-issue. When control wins, it won't be because a manager somewhere felt the need to be *in control* and pulled rank. Control will win, because at that particular moment, on that particular issue, it deserves to win. And in that moment, the decision about which way to jump won't be made by some far distant "parenting" executive who's long on data and short on context. It will be made down on the ground, by individuals who are richly endowed with information, who are intensely passionate about the organization's purpose, and who have the freedom to do the right thing.

To build this new organizational reality we'll need a bold and focused agenda for management innovation, and in the final chapter I'll lay that out.

MANAGING WITHOUT HIERARCHY

5.2

As a management researcher, I've had the opportunity to peer inside a lot of organizations. Most are boringly similar. Once in a while, though, one comes across an eye-popping exception like W.L. Gore & Associates. Known mostly for its Gore-Tex range of high-performance fabrics, the company makes more than 1,000 products and employs 9,000 associates in 50 locations around the world. Wherever it operates, Gore is ranked as one of the "best places to work."

I first visited Gore when doing research for *The Future of Management*. My friends at *Fast Company* magazine had labeled Gore "the world's most innovative company," so I was eager to learn more. That first visit was weird, even disconcerting. I found virtually nothing at Gore that matched up with the management practices I had observed in hundreds of other companies. There were no titles, no bosses, and no formal hierarchy.

I soon learned that Gore's progressive management model have been ahead of its time for more than half a century, ever since the company was founded in 1958 by Wilbert (Bill) L. Gore, a chemical engineer who left Du Pont with the goal of building a company where the entire organization felt like a skunk works. One measure of Gore's innovation-fueled resilience: in more than 50 years it has never made a loss.

Despite having no EVPs, SVPs, or plain ol' VPs, Gore does have a CEO. Terri Kelly got the job in 2005 in a peer-driven process. She joined Gore in 1983, after graduating summa cum laude from the University of Delaware with a bachelor's degree in mechanical engineering. During her career at Gore, she has exercised her considerable leadership gifts in a broad array of roles.

I met up with Terri near my California office and she took me on a deep dive into Gore's post-bureaucratic management model.

Gary: To an outsider, what are the strangest things about Gore's management practices?

Terri: First, we don't operate as a hierarchy, where decisions have to make their way up to the top and then back down. We're a lattice or a network, and associates can go directly to anyone in the organization to get what they need to be successful.

Second, we try to resist titles. We have a lot of people in responsible positions in the organization, but the whole notion of a title puts you in a box, and worse, it puts you in a position where you can assume you have authority to command others in the organization.

Third, our associates, who are all owners in the company, self-commit to what they want to work on. We believe that rather than having a boss tell people what to do, it's more powerful to let each person decide what they want to work on and where they can make the greatest contribution. But once you've made your commitment as an associate, there's an expectation you'll deliver. So there are two sides to the coin: freedom to decide and a commitment to deliver.

And fourth: Our leaders have positions of authority because they have followers. Rather than relying on a top-down appointment process, where you often get promoted because you have seniority, or are the best friend of a senior executive, we allow the voice of the organization to determine who's really qualified to be a leader, based on the willingness of others to follow.

Gary: Bill Gore founded your company more than 50 years ago. What was his vision? Where did these radical management ideas come from?

Terri: Bill was very passionate about new materials and saw a lot of promise for fluoropolymers. When he started Gore, his business plan was not all that developed, but he did have a set of deeply held beliefs about how you lead people and build an organization. What motivated Bill was an understanding that as a company we had to innovate. We wouldn't be successful unless we could bring innovative products to the market.

Bill spent a lot of time thinking about the human element in this. He was influenced by Douglas McGregor's book, *The Human Side of Enterprise.* He was influenced by Abraham Maslow and his views on how people react when they're not feeling safe and secure. These philosophies set the foundation for our company's values. He knew that if you can't engage your associates, if they don't feel they can make a difference, if they don't feel valued for what they bring to the business, and if they aren't encouraged to collaborate and share their knowledge, you won't get innovation. But there was a clear business purpose to all of this; the goal wasn't simply to create a happy work environment.

At Du Pont, Bill had had the opportunity to work on a small skunk works team, and he was struck by the fact that the people on the team behaved so differently from what he observed elsewhere. They'd drive to work together, they'd work around the clock to get something done, they'd get to know one another. So he wondered, why couldn't a whole company work this way?

Gary: Gore doesn't have a formal hierarchy, or titles, so how does someone become a leader at Gore?

Terri: One of my associates said, "If you call a meeting, and no one shows up, you're probably not a leader, because no one is willing to follow you." At Gore, the test of leadership is that simple:

are others willing to follow you? We use a peer review process to identify individuals who are growing into leadership roles. Who are our associates listening to? Who do they want on their team? At Gore, leaders emerge, and once they're in a leadership role, they understand their job is to bring out the strengths of their teams, to make their colleagues successful. Our model also flips the role of the leader; the way you use your power is quite different from what you'd find in most other organizations. At the end of the day, our leaders know their "followership" comes from their peers, and that they can easily lose this if they don't live up to their expectations and the company's values.

Gary: At Gore, it sounds like people earn their power by supporting others, and if they stop doing this, their power starts to erode. So how does this reality shape leadership behaviors and drive business results?

Terri: The challenge in this distributed leadership model is to make sure it's not just chaos. First of all, there are norms of behavior and guidelines we follow. These are our "rules of engagement." Every associate understands how critical these values are, so when leaders make decisions, people want to understand the "why." They know they have the right to challenge, they have the right to know why this decision is the right one for the company. This puts a tremendous burden on the leader to explain the rationale behind the decision, and to put it in the context of our culture: Why is this fair? Why is it consistent with our beliefs and principles? So again, the burden on leaders is different from what you'd find in many other companies, because our leaders have to do an incredible job of internal selling to get the organization to move.

Gary: I can understand how this painstaking consultation produces buy-in, but doesn't it slow things down?

Terri: The process is sometimes frustrating, but we believe that if you spend more time up front, you'll have associates who are not only fully bought-in, but committed to achieving the outcome. Along the way, they'll also help to refine the idea and make the decision even better. So yes, it takes more time, but we find that once the decision is made, you'd better get out of the way because now you have the whole organization eager to accelerate and execute. In many organizations, leaders make quick decisions but don't understand that the organization isn't behind the decision. Half the people don't know why the company is moving in this direction, and the other half is pulling in the opposite direction, either intentionally or unintentionally. So if you think about the entire process of decision-making and implementation, our approach is faster, because by the time you get to the decision, the whole organization is behind it, rather than just a few leaders.

Gary: Executives often try to get alignment by selling a decision once it's been made. For them, alignment is a communication exercise. Or they think they can get alignment through a consistent set of financial incentives, a shared scorecard. By contrast, it seems as if Gore sees the problem of alignment as one of involvement.

Terri: Absolutely. All of our associates are owners and they feel an incredible degree of responsibility for business outcomes. If they think we're going in the wrong direction, or believe a decision is wrong, they feel compelled to speak up, and they know our values give them the right to have a voice. For leaders, this can be troublesome at times, because you're not only evaluated by the outcomes you achieve, but by how you get the job done. One of the hardest jobs is to be a leader at Gore, because we expect so much of you.

Gary: I know that Gore puts as much emphasis on building great teams as it does on developing great leaders. Can you explain the thinking behind this?

Terri: I think it's wrong to believe that the most important decisions in an enterprise are made by senior leaders. Some of the most impactful decisions at Gore get made by small teams. Within any team you'll find people with very different perspectives; they don't all think alike, and we encourage this. We encourage teams to take a lot of time to come together, to build trust, to build relationships, because we know that if you throw them in a room and they don't have a foundation of trust, it will be chaotic, it will be political, and people will feel as if they're being attacked. We invest a lot in making our teams effective, so when they have those great debates; where a scientist doesn't agree with a sales associate, or manufacturing doesn't agree with a product specialist, the debate happens in an environment where everyone is looking for a better solution, versus "you win, I lose."

We want to avoid a situation where decisions have to bubble up to the center, because this undermines our goal of driving decisions through our most knowledgeable associates. We want to make sure that people know they have the authority to make decisions and are responsible for the outcomes.

Gary: I can understand why being a leader at Gore is a challenge. In most organizations, leaders have positional power, someone has made them head of a business or a function, and their subordinates must follow them. In addition, they have sanctions. They can fire or demote subordinates who don't get on board. But this isn't true at Gore. When you bring in leaders from outside, do they have difficulty adapting to this model? Do they struggle to figure out how to get things done?

Terri: We sometimes hire senior talent in, but we're very careful before putting them into a leadership role, because even though they may have great capabilities and experience, they don't know how to navigate our culture, so it's very dangerous to put them straight into a leadership role. Typically, we'll put them in a functional role to start with, or in some other role where they can demonstrate their capabilities and expertise. We help them learn how to lead in a way that is consistent with our culture. We've had some success here, but it's not easy. When we hire outside people and get them to talk about their values, they'll say, "I'm a people person. I believe in teamwork." But when we put them into our environment and strip away their positional power, it can bring them to their knees, because they hadn't realized how much of their success was a function of their position and power and their ability to command and control.

In other companies, the leader is often expected to be the most knowledgeable person on the team, the voice of the company, all-wise and all-knowing. We have a different view. If you want to tap into the whole organization, you have to distribute the responsibility for leadership to the associates who have the relevant knowledge. The Gore model changes the traditional role of the leader. The leader's job is to make sure the culture is healthy: Is it working as a system? Are teams coming together? Are we getting diverse points of view? Are the best ideas rising to the surface? Our leaders have to be comfortable with not being at the center of all the action, with not trying to drive every decision, with not being the most strategic person on the team or the one with the most thoughtful ideas. Their contribution is to help the organization scale and be effective.

Gary: What does it feel like when a new associate joins Gore? They aren't assigned to a boss, so how do you bring them on board? How do they learn about the culture?

Terri: On day one, they won't know what to work on, so we work with each associate to develop their starting commitments. They'll also get a sponsor, which is a very unique role within Gore and different than a leader. A sponsor makes a personal commitment to an associate's success and development. A leader can also be a spon-sor, but needs to be very clear about which hat he or she is wearing. If you're the leader of a business, you can be conflicted, since your success is around driving business results; but one of your valued team members might need to leave your business to develop and grow. That's a tension, but your responsibility as a sponsor is to help the associate reach their full potential.

A new associate will probably experience a lot of freedom they didn't have in their last job, but also a lot more responsibility, in terms of having to be self-driven and self-initiated. Even though the sponsor is there for you, you need to set your own career goals and determine for yourself where you can make the biggest contribution. For a lot of people, this is very different from what they would have experienced in a more structured environment.

Gary: Another unique thing about Gore is your approach to locating factories. For the most part, you've avoided building large, focused factories in low-cost labor locations. Your factories are clustered together. Gore also splits a business in two when it reaches a certain size. None of this sounds very efficient. What's the logic?

Terri: There are a couple of practices that have served us well. First is the three-legged stool. We like to have the functions co-located because innovation depends on having research, manufacturing, and sales all in the same place, where they can build off each other. This also helps us develop leaders.

Second, if a plant gets too big or a business gets too large—more than 250 or 300 people—you start to see a very different dynamic. The sense of ownership, the involvement in decision making, the feeling that I can make an impact starts to get diluted. So we look for opportunities to divide big business into smaller businesses. Bill Gore said that one of the most important responsibilities of the leader is to figure out how to divide so we can multiply. We look for opportunities where dividing a unit up and replicating some of its activities can accelerate growth.

Large businesses tend to stifle smaller businesses by hogging critical resources. When you split a business up, the smaller unit gets its own resources and can set its own priorities. Another bonus: new leaders emerge because you no longer have a single leadership team under one big roof, but now have two distinct leadership teams.

The last thing that's helped us in the current economic environment is that we co-locate different businesses together. If a particular industry has a downturn, you want to be able to move the associates to another opportunity. If our plants were all in isolated locations, this would be much more difficult. So we like the idea of campuses where a number of small factories are co-located within a 25-mile radius. This way, people don't fear moving on to something else, and are less hesitant to take on a new opportunity. This lessens the risk the associates will try to preserve a business or product area that may no longer be so profitable for the company.

Gary: To a typical hard-driving manager, the Gore model probably seems utopian, maybe even naive. You don't have a hierarchy. Leaders can't command. Employees choose their own commitments. It sounds like a slacker's paradise. No wonder the company is consistently ranked as a great place to work. But where does the discipline come from? Most managers view freedom and discipline as mutually exclusive trade-offs, but that's clearly not the case at Gore. You sell to demanding customers like Nike and Procter & Gamble, and have made money every year since the company was founded. What drives discipline at Gore?

Terri: Some days things are chaotic. I don't want to paint a picture of something that's perfect. You have teams coming together, storming and forming and building relationships. But there are some fundamental things that hold Gore together. Our values are paramount. They define how we're going to treat each other, and trust is at the center.

One of the most powerful things that creates discipline is that everyone in the organization knows they will be ranked by their peers, and that their compensation will depend on this ranking. Peer pressure is much more powerful than top-down pressure.

As I mentioned, our associates get to choose what commitments to make. If they didn't know they were going to be evaluated by their peers, they might be tempted to take on an assignment that is personally interesting to them, a hobby, but one that's not important for the company. But instead, every associate is constantly thinking, "I want to be viewed as making a big contribution to the enterprise," so they're looking for opportunities that will leverage their strengths. So there's a natural, built-in pressure: every associate wants to work on something impactful.

Typically, an associate will be evaluated by 20 or 30 peers and will, in turn, evaluate 20–30 colleagues. You rank your peers from top to bottom. It's a forced ranking. You're asked to rank only people you know. What we find is that there's typically a lot of consistency in who people view as the top contributors, and who they put at the bottom of the list. We don't tell our associates what criteria to use, we simply ask them to base their ranking on who's making the greatest contribution to the success of the enterprise. You don't evaluate people solely on the basis of what they're doing within their team, but in terms of the broader impact they may be having across the company. And then beyond their contributions, are they behaving in ways that are collaborative? Are they living the values? Sometimes someone will get great results but at great expense to the organization. These are the issues associates think about when they're putting together their rankings.

We have a cross-functional committee of individuals with leadership roles who look at all this input, debate it, and then put together an overall ranking, from first to last, of those particular associates. Then, in setting compensation, they ensure there's a nice slope to the pay curve so that the folks who are making the biggest contributions are also making the most money.

The process is a bit brutal, but it ensures that real talent gets recognized. This system avoids the problem of paying someone more because of seniority or title. New associates joining the organization—the scientists who don't want to be people leaders—we want these people to feel highly valued, because the next invention may come from them. No system is perfect, but ours levels the playing field and allows real talent to emerge and get compensated accordingly.

We don't need a bureaucratic system to hold people accountable. We don't need time cards, because we don't care when the person comes or leaves; we just care about their contribution. So you can deconstruct a lot of the typical bureaucratic processes that are typically used to measure and control performance. We've also found that by not having hard and fast performance metrics we can avoid a lot of unintended consequences. You get a lot of negative behavior when you have narrow metrics that really don't represent the complexity of the business. Instead, we ask our associates to view performance holistically, versus focusing on a few specific variables.

Gary: A lot of companies struggle to balance trade-offs between growth and earnings, short-term and long-term, and so on. Often these trade-offs are made at the top. A CEO will say, "this year we need to focus on getting our costs under control," and then next year the company discovers it has missed a big new opportunity while it was obsessed with slashing costs. Or a leader will demand growth and then later discover that this came at the expense of near-term earnings. So you get the pendulum effect. How does Gore avoid this? How do you decentralize the responsibility for managing tough trade-offs?

Terri: We introduce this sort of ambiguity and polarity to our associates early on. We don't protect them. If you put them in a box and feed them a simplistic model of business, they won't be able to handle these subtle trade-offs. We want to put these conflicting pressures on all associates and not just on the leaders, who often think they're supposed to protect the rest of the organization from these tensions. Our associates have a very good understanding of how complex these trade-offs really are. That's because our leaders take a lot of time to help associates understand the trade-offs. Leaders have to explain all the factors that need to be taken into account in making a decision. Rather than having a small population of individuals who are capable of making these trade-offs, we have a broad base of associates who are capable of making complex decisions.

We sometimes worry about how to scale this model. We asked that question at 50 associates; it was asked again at 500; and we'll ask it again at 10,000. But what we've found is that our management model *helps* us scale, because we're not relying on a few centralized, enterprise leaders to make all the key decisions. Instead, we push authority out to operating teams that are much better equipped to make the right decision at the right moment.

Gary: Gore is more than 50 years old and has been the subject of many case studies. Why hasn't this management model taken root in other companies? Why hasn't it been emulated more broadly?

Terri: First, I should say we're still evolving. We haven't figured it all out. But what I'd tell another CEO is this. You have to look at the values that are embedded in your company: what behaviors have been rewarded and reinforced over the decades? Is it a culture that really believes in and encourages individuals? Does it foster a collaborative spirit? Does it encourage knowledge sharing? You have to tackle this first. One of the biggest mistakes an organization can make is to articulate all these great values but then not live up to them—then people get cynical, because the values are out of synch with what they experience every day from their leaders.

Second, you have to evaluate your leadership model. It's incredibly important to look at the motivation of your leaders, how they're rewarded, what they value. If you don't tackle this, you'll be in trouble. Our model requires leaders to look at their roles differently. They're not commanders; they're not linchpins. Their job is to make the rest of the organization successful. They have to give up power and control to allow this chaotic process to happen, so you get diverse perspectives and teams coming together to make decisions.

Third, you have to be clear about the checks and balances. At Gore, it's the peer review process, but it might be something else in another organization. What is it that will reward and reinforce the values on an ongoing basis? This needs to be embedded in your management practices. This is the sequence I would follow if I were trying to foster Gore's culture in another organization.

Gary: In the past, someone might have looked at the Gore model and said, "well, that's interesting, but it's not essential—there are other ways to manage." But when I think about the core elements of your model—a collaborative decision-making process, an organization where leaders aren't appointed but emerge from below, associates that have the knowledge and authority to make the critical real-time trade-offs—it seems to me that these things are becoming competitive imperatives.

Terri: If you think about changing demographics, our young associates expect these things. They expect to have the chance to make an impact. They expect to know why they're working on something. They expect to work in a collaborative network where information is freely shared. If an organization doesn't have these things, my suspicion is that it won't be able to compete. You won't be able to attract the talent, and you certainly won't be able to retain it. This is what it's all about—getting the best brains together.

In the previous chapter I asked whether it's really possible to build a management system in which the ideology of freedom is as robustly powerful as the ideology of control. I hope you'll agree the answer is "yes." Though examples like Gore are rare, the fact they exist at all forces us to admit that there really *are* alternatives to management-as-usual. And if you think Gore is radical, wait until you meet the folks at Morning Star.

ESCAPING THE MANAGEMENT TAX

A top-heavy management structure is not only tyrannical, it's expensive, in ways both obvious and subtle. To start with, managers add overhead, and as an organization grows, this expense rises in both absolute and relative terms. To see why, imagine a small organization with ten employees and one boss. Here the ratio of managers to employees is 1:10. (Duh.) Now imagine an organization with 100,000 first-level employees and that same 1:10 span of control. This globe-spanning giant will have 11,111 managers—that's one boss for every nine employees, or 11% of total headcount. Why? Because now there are managers managing *other* managers. Assume further that each of these individuals gets paid three times the salary of a first-tier employee. In that case the costs of managing would account for 33% of the company's payroll

---

This chapter is adapted from "First, Let's Fire All the Managers" by Gary Hamel in *Harvard Business Review*, December 2011. Copyright © 2011 Harvard Business School Publishing Corporation, all rights reserved. Used by permission. http://hbr.org/product/first-let-s-fire-all-the-managers/an/R1112B-HCB-ENG

(11% × 3). In addition, of course, the colossus will have thousands of individuals in senior staff roles, in IT, finance, human resources, and planning. Their primary mission? To keep the organization from collapsing under the weight of its own complexity.

Another potential cost is the risk of a large, calamitous decision. Big decisions always carry big risks, but these risks are exacerbated in hierarchical structures. In most organizations, senior managers vet the decisions of their subordinates, but the reverse seldom happens. In theory, boards are charged with scrutinizing executive decisions, but most boards are relatively compliant—until a big decision goes wrong. Paradoxically, as decisions get bigger, the ranks of those able to challenge the decision maker get smaller. Hubris, myopia, and naiveté can corrupt decisions at any level, but that risk goes up when the decision maker's power is, for practical purposes, incontestable.

There is a related risk. The most powerful managers in most organization are the ones furthest away from frontline realities. All too often, decisions made on an Olympian peak turn out to be unworkable on the ground. Given this, it's not surprising that business magazines are filled with cautionary tales about mega-mergers, billion-dollar bets, and sweeping reorgs that failed to pay off. Give someone monarch-like authority, and sooner or later there will be a royal screw-up.

Finally, a multilayered management structure creates friction. Proposals that originate low in the ranks face an approval gauntlet as they make their way up through the hierarchy. More layers mean longer decision cycles, slower reaction times and, potentially, missed opportunities. Managers get paid to manage, but in their eagerness to demonstrate their authority, they often impede rather than expedite.

Together, these costs comprise a "management tax." The question, of course, is what a company gets in return for this levy; and can it be had more cheaply? One of the things they get is control; but as we saw with Gore, this can be acquired "duty-free," when peers, rather than superiors, are used to reinforce accountabilities. Another management value-added is coordination. Managers harmonize, synchronize, and integrate. They are the rivets that hold the organization together, by connecting activities, teams, programs, and business units. The boxes on an organization chart are, quite simply, coordination rivets. The implicit assumption, of course, is that coordination requires centralization. In other words, to effectively integrate a wide range of disparate contributions, one needs a cadre of managers, individuals who sit above the fray, who see the big picture, and have the power to compel individuals to work together when it adds value. Again, though, for all the reasons enumerated above, centralization is expensive.

MARKETS VERSUS HIERARCHIES

That's why economists have long celebrated the ability of markets to coordinate human activity with little or no top-down control. Think, for example, of the vast horde that works together every day to feed 8 million New Yorkers: the farmers, packers, wholesalers, truckers, supermarket employees, restaurateurs, and caterers. New York City doesn't have a mayor-appointed "food czar," but somehow people still get fed. The lesson? Thousands of relatively autonomous individuals making their own decisions often produce more efficient outcomes than could be achieved by a central authority. *Viva capitalism!*

Nevertheless, economists like Ronald Coase and Oliver Williamson have long recognized that markets have limits. Arms-length contracts work well when the interdependencies that must be managed are simple, stable, and easy to specify. It's straightforward, for example, to write a contract that defines the terms under which a fruit packer supplies apples to a grocery store. But when the coordination is intricate—when the inputs are highly diverse, when they must be seamlessly blended together, or when success requires the joint creation of entirely new forms of knowledge—the invisible hand drops the ball. It's hard to imagine, for example, how a group of independent contractors could succeed in melding together the kaleidoscopic array of activities that must be precisely coordinated to run a large-scale, process-intensive manufacturing operation.

Hence the need for "firms"—organizations that bring critical contributors together under one legal roof. Here, managers do what markets can't: they amalgamate thousands of highly differentiated contributions into a single, integrated product (like a Ford Focus) or an end-to-end service (like a transpacific flight on Singapore Airlines).

Managers constitute what business historian Alfred Chandler called the "visible hand." But as we've seen, the visible hand is often ham-fisted. Inflated overheads. Big blunders. Sluggish reactions. Hobbled employees. Wouldn't it be great if we could achieve high levels of coordination without a supervisory superstructure?

Peer inside an open source software project and you might think you've glimpsed this organizational nirvana. You'll find dozens or maybe hundreds of contributors and few if any managers. Yet this sort of coordination is mostly plug and play. In an open source project, tasks are modular, volunteers are able to work independently, interfaces are clearly defined, and scientific breakthroughs aren't expected. Contrast this with the coordination challenges that Boeing faces in building an all-new airliner. To succeed at this Herculean task, thousands of specialists must work shoulder-to-shoulder to solve hundreds of bleeding-edge design and manufacturing issues. As Boeing has recently learned to its sorrow, outsourcing big chunks of development doesn't make the coordination problem any less perplexing. A market can't build a Dreamliner.

So are we stuck? Is centralization the only way to coordinate complex activities? Must we pay the management tax? Economists would answer "yes." Markets are decentralized and firms are centralized, by *definition*. Most managers would also agree, because they've never come across a company that is both highly decentralized and precisely synchronized. Luckily enough, I have.

MEET MORNING STAR

If you've ever eaten a pizza, dumped ketchup on a hamburger, or poured sauce on a bowlful of spaghetti, you've probably consumed a Morning Star product. Headquartered in Woodland, California, near Sacramento, the company is the world's largest tomato processor, handling between 25 and 30% of the tomatoes processed each year in the United States. Morning Star has 400 full-time employees and generates over $700 million in annual revenues. In peak season, each of its sprawling plants can devour nearly 1,000 tons of raw material per hour. This is a complex, capital-intensive business where dozens of critical processes have to be precisely orchestrated.

Anyone who's driven through central California on Interstate 5 has probably seen Morning Star's tractor-trailers on their way from field to factory. The company was founded in 1970 as a tomato trucking operation by Chris Rufer, then an MBA student at UCLA. Forty-one years later, Rufer is still Morning Star's president.

As a young trucker, Rufer was intrigued by the challenge of making tomato processing more efficient, but frustrated that he couldn't find any industry veterans who would take his ideas seriously. Undeterred, Rufer went looking for investors and in 1983 brought his first tomato plant online.

Within a few years, Rufer was locked in a dispute with his partners over the company's direction and organizational philosophy. To end the logjam, he sold his stake in the processing plant, but kept control of the Morning Star name. Soon he was planning a new facility. Opened in 1990 near Los Banos, California, the plant spreads across more than 40 acres. Show up in mid-summer, and you'll see a long line of trucks awaiting their turn to climb a gentle gradient and unload their cargo. Water flushes the tomatoes out of the trailers and into a labyrinth of flumes. A first-stage wash cleans the tomatoes and separates out leaves, stems, and other debris. As the tomatoes cascade down toward the plant's cookers, opto-electronic sensors trigger finger-like devices that separate the fruit by color and size. Most of the tomatoes end up in paste; the rest get diced. At the end of the line, large aseptic boxes are filled with nearly 3,000 pounds of processed fruit and then loaded onto trucks and railcars.

Today, Morning Star operates three large-scale processing facilities. Within each plant there are several large, soundproof control rooms. Here, every inch of wall space is covered with plasma screens displaying real-time information on dozens of key processes. The vibe is more NASA mission control than grandma's kitchen.

Morning Star processes tomatoes according to hundreds of slightly different recipes, depending on customer needs. In addition to bulk product, the company manufactures canned tomatoes that go directly to supermarket and food service customers. The factories are just one leg of Morning Star's tomato-centric business. There's a trucking company that moves over two million tons of tomatoes each year, and another business that handles harvesting. In a typical year, Morning Star processes 80,000 acres of tomatoes, 7,000 of which are farmed directly by the company.

Over the past twenty years, Morning Star's volumes, revenues, and profits have grown at a double-digit clip; this in an industry where annual growth averages 1% per year. As a private company, Morning Star doesn't share its financial results with outsiders. I did learn, though, that the company has funded virtually all of its growth from internal sources, a feat that suggests robust profitability. Based on its own benchmarking, Morning Star believes it is the world's most efficient tomato processor. Rufer notes dryly that all five of the tomato paste companies he served as a young trucker are now out of business. Indeed, Morning Star acquired its largest factory for salvage value from the trustees of a bankrupt competitor.

UNPACKING SELF-MANAGEMENT

It's not the fruit, the factory, or the profits that make Morning Star a case study in management innovation. Rather, it's the company's fervent belief in "self-management." The goal, according to Morning Star's "organizational vision," is a company where all team members

> **will be self-managing professionals, initiating communications and the coordination of their activities with fellow colleagues, customers, suppliers and fellow industry participants, absent directives from others.**

Did you stumble on those last four words? How the heck do you run a company *absent directives from others?* How can people be "self-managing?" Here's how.

Make the Mission Boss

There are no supervisors at Morning Star. Instead, the mission is boss. Every employee (or "colleague," in Morning Star argot) is responsible for drawing up a personal mission statement that outlines how he or she will contribute to the company's goal of "producing tomato products and services which consistently achieve the quality and service expectations of our customers." For Rodney Regert at the Los Banos plant, that mission is to turn raw tomatoes into juice for downstream processing, and to do it as environmentally responsibly as possible.

Every Morning Star colleague is a member of a business unit team. Some of the company's 20 BUs are independent companies (like the trucking operation), while others are activity centers within a plant (like steam generation). Each BU has a broad mission that provides context for the mission statements of individual team members.

Rufer regards a personal mission as the cornerstone of self-management. Says Rufer, "Understanding of the mission is critical. A feedback system that lets you know how you're doing is also key. You have to feel you are primarily responsible for your mission. If someone else has an opinion on what you should be doing, they should speak up. But you are ultimately responsible for the accomplishment of your mission, and for acquiring the training, resources and cooperation with colleagues that you need to fulfill your mission." Says Paul Green Sr., an experienced plant technician, "I'm driven by my mission and my commitments, not by a manager."

Let Employees Forge Their Own Agreements

These commitments are enumerated in a "Colleague Letter of Under-standing." This document details the specific actions an employee must take to fulfill his or her mission. Each year, every employee renegotiates their CLOU (pronounced "clue") with the colleagues who are most affected by their work. That can include individuals within one's own business unit as well as downstream "customers." For example, the team member responsible for buying natural gas must negotiate with individuals from Morning Star's "steam" BU.

An employee may talk to ten or more associates in the course of negotiating a CLOU. Each of these discussions can take as little as 20 minutes or as much as an hour. A completed CLOU can cover up to thirty separate activity areas, and will also spell out relevant performance metrics.

Every CLOU gets filed centrally and can be reviewed by any employee. Taken together, the CLOUs delineate roughly 3,000 formal relationships among Morning Star's full-time employees.

As a prelude to the annual CLOU update, BU colleagues meet to discuss business challenges and share personal development goals. CLOUs also morph from year to year in ways that reflect the changing competencies and shifting interests of individual associates. Typically, experienced colleagues take on more complex assignments over time while offloading basic tasks to recently hired associates.

In explaining the logic of the CLOUs, Rufer frequently mentions the notion of "spontaneous order," the idea that a myriad of voluntary agreements among independent agents can yield highly effective forms of coordination.

"For me," says Rufer, "structure is a set of relationships that individuals freely make with other individuals. The question is not whether you have structure, but how you develop it—top down or bottom up. Our colleagues create structure: I agree to provide this report to you, or I will get these containers into a truck, or I'll operate a piece of equipment in a certain fashion. This is spontaneous order, and it gives you more fluidity. Relationships can change form more easily than if we tried to fix them from above."[1]

Rufer goes on: "There are a lot of personal nuances in how people work together, and the freer individuals are to explore those nuances, and to tailor their relationships around their own particular competencies—what they're best at and what others are good at—the better all those contributions fit together." Strikingly, Rufer doesn't see freedom as the enemy of coordination, but as its ally.

Every Morning Star colleague is a contractor in a web of multilateral commitments. As one team member put it to me: "Around here, nobody's your boss and everybody's your boss."

The CLOU has an analog at the business unit level. Each year, BUs negotiate customer-supplier agreements with one another. On average, there are fifty such agreements in force. Each BU has its own P&L, and the bargaining between units can be heated. The farming unit and processing plants, for example, will haggle over volumes, pricing, and delivery schedules. The philosophy, though, is the same as with the CLOUs: agreements reached by independent contracting entities are better at aligning incentives and reflecting market realities than centrally mandated relationships.

Empower Everyone—Really!

In most companies, the reality of empowerment falls short of the rhetoric. Not at Morning Star. On this point, Nick Kastle, a business development specialist, drew a stark comparison between Morning Star and his previous employer: "Before coming here, I worked in a company where I reported to a VP who reported to an SVP who reported to an EVP. In self-management *you* have to drive the bus. You can't ever tell someone, 'just go get this done.' You have to do whatever needs to be done." Another colleague, who had worked for two multinational food companies before coming to Morning Star, concurred: "In my other jobs, I had a boss who sat back in the office and called the shots. The operators were very dependent on a shift supervisor or a plant manager. But in a flat organization, everyone is accountable for their own area."

Among other things, this means employees are responsible for acquiring the tools and equipment they need to do their jobs. Within Morning Star, there is no central purchasing department and no senior executive who signs off on capital expenditures. Anyone can issue a purchase order. If a maintenance engineer needs an $8,000 welder, he simply orders one. The colleague's name gets noted on the PO and when the invoice arrives, he confirms that the equipment was received and sends the bill on to accounting for payment. Understandably, new vendors find the arrangement perplexing. There's no purchasing manager to schmooze and anyone can initiate an order.

Rufer explains the thinking behind the company's open requisition process: "I was signing checks one day and I recalled the famous saying, 'the buck stops here.' I thought to myself, that simply isn't true. I had in front of me a purchase order, a contract that someone in the enterprise had made with an outside party to buy a piece of equipment. And I had a note that said the stuff had been shipped, we had received it, and the price on the invoice matched the PO. And there was a check that had been prepared. Now, do I have the choice not to sign the check? Nope. So the question is not, 'where does the buck stop?,' but 'where does it start?' The buck starts with the person who needs the equipment, and they are in the best position to make that decision. I don't need to review this, and that individual shouldn't have to get a manager's approval, so we wiped that out. The person who has the talent and the information makes the decision."[2]

Doug Kirkpatrick, who joined Morning Star in 1983, underlined Rufer's point: "Our model obliterates the distinction between blue collar and white collar. My frontline colleagues have more authority than most knowledge workers in Silicon Valley."

That authority also includes hiring. Individual colleagues are responsible for initiating the hiring process when they find themselves overloaded or have identified a new role that needs to be filled.

Executives often celebrate empowerment, but it's a rare company that shares the corporate checkbook with frontline employees, or expects them to take the lead in recruiting. To Rufer, though, this is simple common sense: "I don't want anyone at Morning Star to feel they can't succeed because they haven't been given the right equipment, or don't have capable colleagues."

Don't Force People into Slots

There are no centrally defined roles at Morning Star, so employees have the opportunity to take on bigger responsibilities over time as they develop their skills. Paul Green Jr., who followed his dad into Morning Star and is responsible for the company's training and development efforts, explains: "We believe you should do what you're good at, so we don't try to fit people into a job. As a result, Morning Star colleagues tend to have broader and more complicated roles than is typical elsewhere."

One of the core tenets at Morning Star is that everyone has the right to suggest improvements in any area of the business. Individuals are encouraged to offer and solicit help from other parts of the enterprise. In doing so, there are no communication channels to navigate. Says Rufer: "The difference between Morning Star and most organizations is that if you have an idea here, you don't go to a supervisor or a boss, you go directly to the individual or the team. If they believe the idea will help them to fulfill their mission, it will get embraced."

Typically, first-level employees assume that change comes from above, but at Morning Star, there's no above, and everyone understands it is their responsibility to drive change. Paul Green Jr.: "We have a lot of spontaneous innovation and change that comes from unusual places. We have a view that you have a right to get involved anywhere you think your skills can add value, so people will often drive change outside their narrow job area."

Encourage Competition for Impact, Not Promotion

With no hierarchy and no titles at Morning Star, there's no career ladder to climb. However, that doesn't mean everyone is equal. Within any activity area, some colleagues will be recognized as being more competent than others. These differences in expertise and value-added are also reflected in compensation.

As with any organization, there's internal competition, but at Morning Star, the rivalry is around who can contribute the most rather than who gets a plum job. To get ahead, an employee must master new skills or discover new ways of serving colleagues. Ron Caoua, an IT specialist, puts it like this: "There's no such thing as a promotion here. What strengthens my résumé is more responsibility, not a bigger title."

When I asked Chris Rufer how people advance at Morning Star, he offered a golfing analogy: "How does someone move up on the pro golf tour? When Jack Nicklaus was competing, was he concerned about becoming an 'executive senior vice president golfer'? No, he enjoyed golf and knew that if he got really good at it, he would achieve what everyone longs for—a sense of accomplishment. He also knew those accomplishments would give him an income to enjoy the life he wanted. Moving up is about competency and reputation, not the office you hold."

One Morning Star colleague put it to me simply: "People who are eager to add value and grow want to work here. Our competitors get the other folks."

FREE TO SUCCEED

At the core of Morning Star's eccentric yet effective management model is a simple idea: *freedom*. Says Rufer, "An organizational philosophy has to start with people, and the conditions that allow them to be more creative and passionate about their work, and I think freedom unleashes this. Everyone does better if they are free to pursue their own path. If they are free, they will be drawn to what they *really* like, versus being pushed toward what they have been told to like. So they will personally do better; they'll be more enthused and charged up to do things."

Morning Star's employees echo this sentiment. As one operator put it, "When people tell you what to do, you're a machine." True enough, but therein lies the dilemma. To run a large-scale operation built around machines, you need people who will, at times, behave like machines. Operational efficiency requires people who are reliable, precise, and hardworking. Without a keen sense of responsibility, freedom can turn into anarchy. Yet when you walk through one of Morning Star's colossal, intricate plants, what you see is the opposite of anarchy. In most companies, supervisors and managers make sure employees keep noses to grindstones, but not at Morning Star. So how does all that freedom get channeled into drum-tight coordination?

Clear Targets, Transparent Data

People can't be self-managing without information. Visit a winter resort and you may see a blind skier being coached down the mountain. A guide follows close behind and shouts directions: "left," "right," and "stop." A sighted skier, by contrast, can navigate the same run unaided. At Morning Star, the goal is to provide employees with all the information they need to monitor their work and make wise decisions. The assumption: people *want* to do the right thing, but need a lot information to know what "right" is.

Every CLOU contains a set of "stepping-stone" measures. Employees use these metrics to track their success in meeting their colleagues' needs. In addition, a set of detailed accounts gets published twice a month for each business unit and is available to every colleague.

Efficiency is part of everyone's mission and colleagues are encouraged to hold one another accountable for results, so any unexpected uptick in expenses gets immediately noticed and queried. "Because everyone is looking at the numbers," explains Paul Green Sr., "people have no problem saying, 'why the heck are we spending money on this?'" In an environment of transparency, folly and sloth are soon exposed.

There's another reason transparency is important to Morning Star. Because the company is vertically and horizontally integrated, employees need cross-company information in order to calculate how their decisions will affect other areas of the company. Rufer wants his colleagues to think about the business holistically, and knows this will only happen if everyone has access to the same systemwide data. That's why there are no information silos at Morning Star, and why no one ever questions a colleague's "need to know."

Calculation and Consultation

Although colleagues are free to spend the company's money, they must construct a solid business case for doing so. Typically, this entails building a detailed financial model that includes ROI and NPV calculations. "Our colleagues," says Paul Green Jr., "are very aware of what constitutes a good investment versus a bad one. On average, I think they're better at doing this kind of analysis than a lot of MBA grads."

In building an investment case, Morning Star colleagues consult widely. While there's not a formal capital approval process, there's an understanding that you will be held accountable to your peers for how you've spent the company's money. An employee pushing for a $3 million investment, for example, might consult with as many as 30 colleagues before pulling the trigger. As Paul Green Jr. notes, "There's a tendency to get a lot of people involved in decisions so you don't get stranded out on a limb."

This same is true of hiring decisions. A colleague who wants to expand a BU's payroll must sell the idea to his or her peers, who will ask for a job description and a business case. If there's a consensus to move ahead, the mechanics of recruiting will get turned over to an in-house specialist.

At Morning Star, colleagues have a lot of authority, but seldom make unilateral decisions. Conversely, no individual has the power to unilaterally kill an idea. Rather than acting as jury, judge, and executioner, experienced team members serve as coaches. A young employee with a bold idea will be encouraged to seek the advice of Morning Star veterans. These experts will often provide a brief tutorial: "Here's a model you can use to analyze your idea. Go do some more homework, and when you're done, come back and let's talk further."

Virtually everyone I talked to at Morning Star acknowledged that this sort of consultation is time-consuming but was quick to praise its benefits: highly informed decisions untainted by politics, plans backed up by broad commitment, and colleagues who know they can initiate change no matter their role.

Conflict Resolution and Due Process

What happens when someone abuses their freedom, consistently underperforms, or is simply at loggerheads with colleagues? At Morning Star, there are no managers to settle disputes; no one has the authority to force a decision. In the commercial world, disagreements between contracting parties are typically settled through mediation or in front of a jury. So it is at Morning Star.

To illustrate how this process works, suppose for a moment that you and I work in different business units and you believe I've failed to meet my CLOU commitments to you. As a first step, we'd meet and you'd argue your case. I might offer an excuse, agree to do better, or toss the blame back on you. If the two of us can't resolve the matter, we pick an internal mediator, someone we both trust. The three of us meet and we present our views. Let's say the mediator sides with you but I object to the proposed remedy. At this juncture, a panel of six colleagues is assembled to help us settle our squabble. This council may endorse the mediator's recommendation or propose another solution. If I once again demur, Chris Rufer brings all the parties together, hears their arguments, and then makes a binding decision. It is highly unusual, though, for a dispute to end up on Rufer's desk.

When the concerns about a colleague's performance are serious enough, this conflict resolution process can end with termination. Nevertheless, at Morning Star, an employee's fate never rests in the hands of a single, capricious boss.

Rufer explains the benefits of Morning Star's process: "When there's a dispute and a panel of peers gets convened, the stories go back to the plant, and people can see that the process was fair and reasonable. Everyone knows they have recourse. We've taken away the power a boss might have to treat an employee as a punching bag because they have something else going on in their life."

Peer Review and the Challenge Process

Accountability is woven deeply into Morning Star's organizational DNA. First, every new employee attends a seminar on the basics of self-management. Here they learn that responsibility is freedom's twin. While they will be given a lot of discretionary authority, they will also be held accountable for their decisions. No one gets the option of handing off a tough call. Consult as widely as you like, but in the end it's *your* decision, and your colleagues will hold you accountable.

The end-of-year performance review, in which every employee receives detailed feedback from his or her CLOU colleagues, is another accountability mechanism. This process has an analog at the business unit (BU) level. In January, every BU is required to defend its performance over the previous twelve months. Because the discussion around a single BU can consume the better part of a day, this "challenge" process extends over several weeks. Each meeting brings together the relevant BU team and all those who have a stake in its performance.

Each BU presentation is, in effect, a report to shareholders. Team members have to justify their use of the company's resources, acknowledge performance shortfalls, and present plans for improvement. BUs get ranked by performance and those that come in under plan can expect a grueling interrogation. "If a business unit has made investments that aren't paying off," notes Rufer, "they'll be subject to a fair amount of ridicule, and it will be more difficult for them to get their colleagues on board for future investments." "There is a social risk," said one team member, "in doing something your colleagues think is stupid."

In February, there's a round of strategy meetings that provides another opportunity for peer review. Over the course of a few days, each BU gets 20 minutes to present its plan for the coming year before a company-wide audience. Colleagues are then given the opportunity to "invest" in the most promising strategies using a virtual currency. The competition for investment funds is intense. Any BU that fails to attract its share of fantasy bucks knows it will be under intense scrutiny.

Elected Compensation Committees

Morning Star's approach to compensation is more akin to what one would find in a professional services firm than in an industrial business. At the end of each year, every colleague assembles a self-assessment document outlining how they performed against their CLOU goals, ROI targets, and stepping-stone metrics. Colleagues then elect a local compensation committee. In a typical year, around eight such bodies will get formed across the company. Using a highly consultative process, the committees work to validate the self-assessments and uncover contributions that might not have been reported. Instances in which an associate took the initiative to help colleagues in another BU are viewed particularly favorably. Having weighed these inputs, the committee adjusts individual compensation levels in an effort to assure that value-added and pay stay closely aligned.

THE UPSIDE OF SELF-MANAGEMENT

There aren't many folks at Morning Star who've been to business school or who even have a college degree, but many have worked for other, less progressive employers—and when you ask them about the advantages of self-management, they're passionate and eloquent.

Benefit #1: More Initiative

"What is it," I inquired of a plant mechanic, "that prompts team members to be proactive in offering help to colleagues?" His answer: "Our organization is driven by reputational capital. When you have something to add to another part of the company, some valuable piece of advice, that increases your reputational capital." The logic: When roles are broadly defined and people get positive strokes for helping others, initiative flourishes.

Benefit #2: More Expertise

The self-management model also encourages operating employees to develop deep skills. At Morning Star, the experts aren't managers, senior staff members, or internal consultants; they're the people doing the work. For example, the folks filling aseptic containers on the packaging line are deeply knowledgeable about microbiology. Scott Marnoch, a quality expert, explained the incentive colleagues have to get smart: "Everyone here is responsible for the quality of their work. There's a lot of pride in this, and there's no boss to take the fall if things go wrong." Another colleague made the point even more forcefully: "Before coming here, I never knew anything but the corporate hierarchy. But looking back, I think it breeds a sense of laziness and incompetence."

Benefit #3: More Flexibility

Morning Star's management model also promotes speed and flexibility, a point Rufer makes with a cloud analogy. "Clouds form and then go away. The atmospheric conditions, the temperature and humidity, cause molecules of water to either condense or vaporize. And this happens based on the forces that surround those water molecules. Organizations should be the same. Structures need to appear and disappear based on the forces that are acting on the organization. When people are freer to act, they're more able to sense these forces and act in ways that fit best with the external reality."

Paul Green Jr. adds substance to the point by noting that in a typical year, hundreds of change projects will get initiated as employees search for ways to better serve their mission and become more valuable to colleagues. "There aren't many boundaries, so our organization is constantly morphing."

Benefit #4: More Collegiality

One of the biggest flaws of the organizational pyramid is that it's pyramidal: it tapers as it ascends. Thus, in the battle to get ahead, there are many more losers than winners. While competition for advancement can spur individual accomplishment, the zero-sum nature of the contest encourages politicking and accentuates rivalries. In a pancake-flat organization, there are no backsides to kiss and no adversaries to elbow aside. Paul Terpeluk, a Morning Star colleague with stints at two Fortune 500 companies, described the benefits of a bossless company: "There's less backstabbing here because we're not competing for that scarce commodity called a promotion. All your energy goes into doing the best job you can and helping your colleagues." In other words, when you take away the pyramid, you drain a lot of the poison out of organizational politics.

Benefit #5: More Judgment

In most organizations, key decisions are escalated to executives who've been trained in the science of business analysis. Senior managers have a wealth of data, and analytical sophistication, but what they lack is context, a subtle understanding of the "facts on the ground." That's why decisions that appear brilliant to top-level executives are often regarded as boneheaded by those on the front lines. Rather than pushing decisions up, Morning Star pushes expertise down. For example, roughly half of the company's employees have been on a course that teaches them how to negotiate with suppliers.

Morning Star's investments in colleague competence reflect a central tenet of self-management: it's easier, and more effective, to equip employees with decision-making tools than it is to equip senior executives with situational awareness. At Morning Star, the doers and the thinkers are the same people. The result: decisions that are more timely and apposite.

Benefit #6: More Loyalty

Few experienced colleagues ever leave Morning Star for a competitor, but the reverse frequently happens. One new team member gave up a 5-minute drive for a 60-minute commute when he moved to Morning Star. Why'd he make the switch? "Because here I have the chance to grow."

Each summer, as the tomatoes come off the vine, Morning Star's processing plants take on more than 800 seasonal workers. Ninety percent of these colleagues return each year, and all have been trained in the principles of self-management. It's that philosophy, Rufer believes, that explains Morning Star's industry-leading levels of employee loyalty.

Want hard evidence? A team of independent researchers recently benchmarked Morning Star's seasonal colleagues on their sense of "empowerment" and "ownership." What they found was startling. These *temporary* workers had the sort of engagement scores that are typical of *senior managers* in other companies.

Benefit #7: Less Overhead

Finally, there's the simple efficiency benefit of a manager-free payroll. Says Rufer, "In a lot of companies, you have executives telling managers what to do, managers telling supervisors what to do, and supervisors telling line guys what to do. That's a lot of overhead, but you won't find any of it here."

Some of the savings go to Morning Star's full-time employees, who earn 10–15% more than their industry peers; the rest go into funding Morning Star's above average growth.

A CHEAP LUNCH, BUT NOT A FREE ONE

Although Morning Star's organizational model dramatically reduces the costs of managing, it does have drawbacks. Experienced colleagues point to four in particular.

First, not everyone is suited to Morning Star's self-management model. This is less a matter of capability than acculturation. An individual who's spent years working in a highly stratified organization often has difficulty with the shift to self-management. This adds time and complexity to the hiring process. When his company was smaller, Rufer spent half a day interviewing every prospective employee, usually in the candidate's home and often with his or her spouse present. Much of the conversation was focused on assessing the fit between Morning Star's philosophy and the applicant's expectations. Today, every potential hire gets a two-hour introduction to self-management and is then interviewed by 10 to 12 colleagues.

Even then, mistakes get made. Paul Green Jr. estimates that as many as 50% of the company's "senior" hires leave within two years. Experienced managers, in particular, have a hard time adapting to a system where they can't "play God."

Getting colleagues to hold one another accountable is a second challenge. In a hierarchical organization, the boss is responsible for dealing with troublemakers and underperformers. At Morning Star, that responsibility is distributed. Every colleague is responsible for safeguarding quality, efficiency, and teamwork by calling out colleagues who violate policies and norms.

If colleagues shirk that responsibility, if they fail to deliver tough love when needed, then self-management can quickly become a conspiracy of mediocrity: "I'll go easy on you if you'll do the same for me." This risk gets explicitly addressed in Morning Star's training programs, and colleagues are frequently reminded that "peer regulation" doesn't work without courageous peers.

Growth is a third challenge. For years, Morning Star has outgrown its industry, and it has the financial resources to grow even faster. Nevertheless, Rufer and his senior colleagues are wary of diluting the company's distinctive culture, a concern that has kept them from acquiring a large ongoing business. Paul Green Jr. estimates that on average it takes a new associate a year or more to become fully functional within the self-management environment. Although the company has been looking for ways to accelerate this process, it has so far resisted the urge to trade away its "management advantage" for the sake of faster growth.

Tracking career progress is a fourth challenge at Morning Star. In most companies, there's a ladder to climb, and employees use the rungs to chart their personal growth: team leader, supervisor, department head, vice president, and so on. Morning Star colleagues have plenty of opportunities to enlarge their roles, and just about everyone I talked to mentioned this as one of the advantages of a meritocratic organization. At the same time, it makes it more difficult to calibrate one's progress with industry peers, and can be a handicap for an experienced colleague who wants to switch employers but can't claim to have achieved a particular organizational rank.

Rufer and his colleagues at Morning Star aren't blind to the challenges of making self-management work, but seem uniformly convinced that they are less of a burden than the management tax.

MANAGERS VERSUS MANAGING

As we sat in a simple conference room, I suggested to Chris Rufer that Morning Star had learned how to manage without managers. He immediately corrected me. "Everyone's a manager here. We are manager rich. The job of managing includes planning, organizing, directing, staffing, and control, and everyone at Morning Star is expected to do all these things. Everyone is a manager of their own mission, they are a manager of the agreements they make with colleagues, they are a manager of the resources they need to get the job done, and they are managers who can hold their colleagues accountable."

Nevertheless, Rufer knew what I was driving at. For decades there's been an assumption that the work of managing is best performed by formally designated "managers." But Morning Star's long-running experiment with self-management suggests it is both possible and profitable to distribute the work of managing to the edges of the organization. Turns out the work of managing can be done by just about *anyone* if they have the right information, incentives, tools, and accountabilities.

MARKETS *AND* HIERARCHIES

Thankfully, we *don't* have to choose between the advantages of markets and hierarchies. Morning Star isn't a loose confederation of individual contractors and it's not a stultifying bureaucracy. It is, instead, a ruthlessly efficient and highly integrated business that's a subtle blend of both market *and* hierarchy.

A Socially Dense Marketplace

On one hand, you can think of Morning Star as a *socially dense marketplace*. Colleagues are free to negotiate market-like contracts with their peers. Though it might seem this would be a contentious and complicated process, there are several factors that mitigate against this risk. First, everyone involved in the negotiations *shares the same score card*: making the company the best at what it does. In a pure market, a consumer doesn't really care whether a deal is good for the seller—"Hey! A going-out-of-business sale. Great!" By contrast, everyone at Morning Star knows they won't have a great place to work if the company doesn't do well overall. They understand it's sink or swim *together*.

Morning Star colleagues tend to be long-serving. As a team member, you know that if you take advantage of a colleague, or fail to deliver on a promise, the repercussions will catch up with you. This encourages colleagues to think in terms of relationships rather than transactions. Finally, because most folks at Morning Star have been in the tomato business for years, they have a pretty good sense of what needs to be done and who needs to do it. Not every aspect of every contract needs to be rewritten each year. Without this glue—the shared goals, long-term relationships. and deep pool of industry knowledge—Morning Star's market-like contracting system would be more fractious and less efficient.

A Naturally Dynamic Hierarchy

On the other hand, Morning Star is also a *naturally dynamic hierarchy*. Though there's not a formal hierarchy at Morning Star, there are many informal ones. On any issue, some colleagues will have a bigger share of voice than others, depending on their expertise and their willingness to pitch in and help. Critically, these are hierarchies of influence, not position, and they're built bottom-up. At Morning Star, one accumulates authority by demonstrating expertise, helping peers, and adding value. Stop doing those things, and your influence wanes, as does your pay.

In most companies, the hierarchy is neither natural nor dynamic. Leaders don't emerge from below but are appointed from above. Maddeningly, key jobs often go to the most politically astute rather than the most competent. Further, because power is vested in positions, it tends to be "sticky"; it doesn't automatically flow from individuals who are less capable to those who are more capable. All too often, underperforming managers lose their power only when they're finally demoted or fired. Until then, they can keep mucking things up. No one at Morning Star believes everyone should have an equal vote on every decision, but neither do they believe someone should have the last word simply because he or she is the "boss."

As is true at Gore, the Morning Star management model is built around the notion of natural hierarchies and natural leaders. Says Rufer, "I've brought in senior managers from other companies, and frankly, they're usually lost. They sound like leaders, they know how to dictate, but they aren't real leaders. A true leader can understand a situation, think through the complexities, come up with a solution, advocate a strategy and recruit followers. Natural leaders rise naturally, and they don't need the authority to command others or fire people."

SELF-MANAGEMENT: HOW TO GET STARTED

In Chapter 5.1 I argued that the ideology of management is seriously off-kilter, that it overweights control and underweights freedom. At Morning Star, freedom gets its due. It's not an afterthought and it's not a slogan; it's an ideological cornerstone. No one at Morning Star talks about *empowerment*, and with good reason. Embedded in the idea of empowerment is the assumption that power trickles down, that it's bestowed from above as and when the powerful see fit. But when power is distributed, when there are no managers with power to apportion, the notion of empowerment becomes nonsensical.

I'm guessing your organization wasn't built around the principles of self-management. It's not a socially dense marketplace or a naturally dynamic hierarchy. It's a bureaucracy, with a thicket of policy rules, a multilayered hierarchy, and a host of management processes that value conformance and predictability above all else. So now you stand at an ideological crossroads. You have to decide: is it going to be *boss-management* or *self-management*.

The founders of the United States didn't set out to temper the excesses of a monarchical system; they sought to supplant it. They didn't start with a program or a process, but with "self-evident" truths. You must do the same. If you don't make an unequivocal commitment to self-management, there's a risk you'll compromise where you shouldn't, or that you'll content yourself with (easily-reversed) half-measures when you should press for more.

Nevertheless, you have to start from where you are. No one's going to give you permission to blow up the old management structures, nor should they. You have to demonstrate that *self*-management doesn't mean *no*-management, and that radical decentralization isn't an invitation to anarchy.

Here are a few tips on how to get started.

First, ask everyone on your team to write down a personal mission statement. Ask them, "What's the value you want to create for your colleagues?" or "What are the problems you want to solve for other team members?" Challenge folks to think expansively and to focus on benefits delivered rather than activities performed. Once everyone has crafted a sentence or two, divide the team into dyads and triads and have them critique one another's mission statements. By doing so, you'll begin to shift the focus from rule-driven compliance to peer-negotiated accountability.

Second, look for small ways in which you can expand the scope of employee autonomy. Ask your colleagues, "What are the policies and procedures that handicap you in achieving your mission?" Once you've identified the most exasperating, sanction a limited rollback and see what happens. As we saw with the Bank of New Zealand (Chapter 4.4), it's possible to turn back the tide of control, and if you're serious about self-management, you'll do this bit by bit.

Third, work to develop a team-level P&L for everyone in your organization. The road to self-management is paved with information.

Aim to give people on the front lines the same detailed performance information that your CEO has. As we'll see in the next chapter, this was one of the first things Vineet Nayar did at HCL Technologies when he set out to flip the pyramid.

Finally, look for ways to erase the distinctions between those who manage and those who are managed. If you're a manager, you can start by enumerating your commitments to your team. Having done this, ask your colleagues to annotate the list as they see fit. Getting leaders to be more accountable to the led is a critical step in building a web of reciprocal responsibilities.

Cultivating a sense of mission, excising irksome rules, giving teams a comprehensive P&L, reinforcing the notion of mutual accountability: these are critical waypoints on the road to self-management.

I think it's time to end bureaucracy's 100-year-run run as the dominant operating system for organizations large and small. For traditionally organized companies, the road to self-management will be long and steep, but the experience of companies such as Morning Star and W. L. Gore (see Chapter 5.2) suggests that the destination is worth the effort. No longer must we choose between organizations that are highly effective and organizations that are deeply human. No longer must we pay the management tax.

CONCLUSION

Managers the world over have spent the last decade wringing inefficiencies out of their operating practices. Now they need to face the fact that management itself is a swamp of inefficiency. Some of these inefficiencies show up on the P&L, but it's the ones that don't, such as decision lags, hidden biases, and disempowerment, that may be the most costly. In a global economy, there's no place for inefficiency to hide, so companies that don't find a way to reduce the management tax will ultimately find themselves at a profound disadvantage.

While the future of management has yet to be written, the folks at Morning Star have penned a provocative prologue. Of course, questions remain. Can the company's self-management model scale?

Would it work in a company of 10,000 employees or 100,000? Can it be exported to other cultures? Can it cope with a fundamental threat to the company's business model (like a low-cost, offshore competitor)? I don't know, but these are the questions that keep Rufer and his colleagues up at night. They readily admit that self-management is a work in progress. "I think ideologically, we're about 90% of the way there," says Rufer. "But practically, maybe only 70%."

Whatever the uncertainties, two things seem certain. First, with a bit of imagination it's possible to transcend the seemingly intractable trade-offs (like freedom versus coordination) that have long bedeviled human organizations. And second, you don't have to be crazy to dream of organizations where managing is no longer the right of a vaunted few but the responsibility of all.

INVERTING
THE PYRAMID

5.4

W. L. Gore and Morning Star are positive deviants. They were *built* to be meritocratic, and have freedom woven into their DNA. The same probably can't be said for your organization. Nevertheless, with courage and vision it's possible to rebuild the ideological foundations of a tradition-bound company. Over the past few years, that's exactly what Vineet Nayar has been doing at HCL Technologies (HCLT).

HCL Enterprise is one of India's most progressive IT companies. Originally Hindustan Computers Limited, HCL today comprises two main businesses: HCL Infosystems, which focuses on hardware manufacturing and system integration, and HCL Technologies, a $3.5 billion service organization that has its roots in business process outsourcing. With 77,000 employees, HCLT operates in 26 countries. Vineet Nayar is HCLT's vice-chairman and CEO.

In a 2006 article for *Fortune* magazine, my friend David Kirkpatrick called HCLT's management model "the world's most modern."[1] A bit of hyperbole, perhaps, but in 2009, Hewitt Associates ranked HCLT as India's best employer,[2] and in 2011 the company won recognition for having one of the world's most democratic workplaces.[3]

Over the past few years, HCLT has been on a tear. Between 2009 and 2011, in the depths of the Great Recession, the company grew its top line at a compounded rate of 24% while its market capitalization nearly tripled, from $2.6 billion to $7.5 billion.

Since becoming president of HCLT in 2005, Vineet Nayar has been leading a radical management makeover. During my first conversation with Vineet, in the spring of 2008, he boldly proclaimed:

We must destroy the concept of the CEO. The notion of the "visionary," the "captain of the ship" is bankrupt. We are telling the employee, "You are more important than your manager." Value gets created between the employee and the customer, and management's job is to enable innovation at that interface. To do this, we must kill command-and-control.

Vineet's fervor was palpable, and a little weird. Revolutions don't usually start with the monarchy. I couldn't help but wonder, was he backing up his revolutionary rhetoric with action? Over the following months, I dug deeper into HCLT's transformation, and I discovered the answer was "yes." In ways large and small, Vineet and his colleagues have been working to build a company where employees have the chance to become bona fide "transformers," inspired problem solvers who work with clients to discover new ways of creating value out of technology. The guiding principle behind this effort has been the notion of "reverse accountability."

The story, of course, didn't start with a grand quest; it started with a practical problem: how do you kick growth into high gear? In 2005, HCL Technologies was a 29-year-old business with $700 million in sales and 30,000 employees. Over the previous five years, it had been growing at 30% per annum—not too shabby by most benchmarks, but not fast enough for HCLT to keep pace with its primary competitors.

In an effort to diagnose the company's subpar growth, Vineet met with thousands of employees, in groups large and small. He launched each meeting by acknowledging what many had been reluctant to admit: HCLT was slowly becoming irrelevant. With each point of lost market share, it was going out of business. Having disrobed the elephant, Vineet asked his listeners to be fearless in analyzing the company's shortcomings. The exchanges were brutally frank, and as they unfolded, two conclusions started to form in Vineet's mind.

First, HCLT was in a service business. It was frontline employees, not managers, who played the most critical role in creating value. As Vineet saw it, the world was filled with customers who had knotty business problems that could only be solved by creative and highly engaged team members. For HCLT, the "value zone" lay at the intersection of employees and customers. If employees were creating unique value for HCLT's customers, the company would prosper, and if they weren't, it wouldn't. The most important decisions for HCLT's future were the ones taken each day by first-level employees.

Second, as Vineet would later write, HCLT's top-down management model "exalted those with hierarchical power rather than those who created customer value."[4] This meant that the company's management processes were better attuned to the needs of control-obsessed executives than of customer-obsessed employees. "The archaic pyramid," Vineet wrote, "was shackling people and keeping them from contributing all they could and in ways they longed to." This was particularly true for HCLT's young, tech-savvy employees. Having grown up on the Web, they valued collaboration and mistrusted hierarchy.

In retrospect, these conclusions were hardly earth-shattering. Frontline employees are critical in *any* business that delivers a complex service, and bureaucratic processes *always* stifle imagination and initiative. Yet in most companies, these realities don't turn sober-suited executives into management heretics. Usually, CEOs opt for little tweaks: they encourage middle managers to spend more time with customers, jack up rewards for employees who exceed expectations, dump more money into training, and push for more knowledge sharing among client teams.

Vineet, on the other hand, knew this wouldn't be enough to turbocharge growth. There was only one course to follow: it led uphill and was pockmarked with unanswered questions. HCLT would have to invert the pyramid. Anything less would be quickly imitated by competitors. Although he hadn't thought through the particulars, Vineet got to work selling his vision. In setting after setting, he made the case for "employees first, customers second," or EFCS. HCLT, he argued, needed a new management philosophy. Managers needed to be accountable to those in the value zone.

At first, many wondered whether EFCS was simply a morale-boosting bromide cooked up for internal consumption. A big wedge of that skepticism disappeared when Vineet took the podium in February 2006 at a gathering of HCLT's largest clients. He laid out the logic for putting employees first, and argued that the new approach would ultimately pay big dividends for customers as well. That evening, HCLT's share price tumbled by 8%. On the other hand, thousands of employees who had heard the speech by webcast went to bed knowing that EFCS was more than a slogan.

Over the next five years, Vineet and his team would clamber up the craggy slope of management innovation. With each step they moved closer to their goal of upending the old pyramid. Some of the most important milestones:

TRANSPARENT FINANCIAL DATA

Vineet understood that it's hard to feel empowered if your manager has a lot of data you don't. With this in mind, HCLT's IT team created a simple widget that gave every employee a detailed set of financial metrics for their own team and other teams across the company. Suddenly, poorly performing teams had an incentive to improve, and high-performing teams to stay on top. Another benefit: employees now had positive proof that the company was willing to trust them with strategic information. "Need to know" became "right to know."

U&I

Early on, Vineet and his leadership team set up an online forum and encouraged employees to ask tough questions and offer honest feedback. Nothing was censored on the "U&I" site; every post, however virulent, was displayed for the entire company to see. Vineet recalls that in the beginning, "virtually 100% of the questions were 'dirty' questions. 'Why do you guys suck?' 'Why does your strategy suck?' 'Why aren't you living up to your values?'" While some managers bemoaned the fact that the company's soiled laundry was being aired online, employees lauded the forum as a symbol of HCLT's commitment to transparency and as a mechanism for holding top management accountable. Beyond that, the U&I portal had another value: it was an early warning system for critical issues facing the company.

In 2009, Vineet opened up a "My Problems" section on the U&I site where he could solicit advice on the crucial issues *he* was wrestling with. While he wanted managers to feel more accountable to the front lines, he also wanted employees to feel a sense of responsibility for helping to tackle the big, thorny issues that faced the top team.

SERVICE LEVEL AGREEMENTS

Powerful staff departments, such as HR and finance, often seem more interested in enforcing blanket policies than in making life easier for employees. Recognizing this, Vineet started querying frontline employees: "What have the enabling functions done to help you create value in the value zone?" His question was usually met with silence, and a quizzical look. When it came to interacting with these functions, most employees felt like supplicants, a situation that was hardly empowering. The solution: a web-based "Smart Service Desk" where any employee could open a "service ticket" if they had a complaint with an internal staff group.

For their part, the staff functions were charged with ensuring that open tickets were dealt with on a timely basis. Once issued, a ticket could only be closed by the concerned employee. If that didn't happen within 24 hours, the ticket got escalated up the line. In the first month, 30,000 tickets were issued, a number that came down sharply over time. Vineet believes the Service Desk system has produced three benefits: first, it has made staff departments more accountable to those in the value zone; second, it has leveled the playing field for employees—everyone's concerns now get handled quickly and efficiently, regardless of rank; and third, it has generated a raft of data that HCLT has used to improve its internal policies.

OPEN EVALUATIONS

Just about every company has its own version of a 360-degree feedback process. Nevertheless, Vineet saw several problems with HCLT's off-the-shelf approach. First, it didn't focus explicitly on how managers were impacting those in the value zone. Second, employees fearful of retaliation often pulled their punches when reviewing a supervisor. And third, the fact that feedback was solicited only from one's immediate colleagues tended to reinforce organization silos.

Over time, this would all change. Today, HCLT employees are able to rate the performance of *any* manager whose decisions affect their work lives, and to do so anonymously. These ratings are published online and can be viewed by anyone who has submitted a review. This visibility challenges managers to be more responsive and exercise their authority judiciously. The number and organizational scope of the reviews received by a manager also comprise a good indicator of that individual's zone of influence: is he or she adding value across a wide swath of the company, or only within a narrow sphere? Importantly, this "feed-forward" process isn't connected to compensation and promotion decisions; it is purely developmental. Nevertheless, there aren't many hiding places left at HCLT for mediocre managers.

MYBLUEPRINT

With HCLT's growth now accelerating again, the company's planning process started to become unwieldy. As the CEO, Vineet was being asked to weigh in on hundreds of unit-level plans each year. Recognizing the limits to his time and personal expertise, Vineet challenged his colleagues to develop an online, peer-based evaluation process. The solution: MyBlueprint. In 2009, 300 managers posted their business plans, or "blueprints," online. Each document was accompanied by an audio presentation. More than 8,000 employees were then invited to jump in and review the plans. The result was a torrent of advice and counsel. The horizontal nature of the process helped highlight opportunities for cross-unit collaboration and gave business leaders the chance to learn from interested peers throughout HCLT. At the conclusion of the exercise, nearly everyone agreed that the new process had been vastly more valuable than the old, top-down review.

EMPLOYEE FIRST COUNCILS

To move from a hierarchical organization to one that is more networked, one must strengthen the lateral relationships among employees. It was that goal that led HCLT to launch its "Employee First Councils." Supported by a web-based platform, the new initiative rapidly spawned a host of communities around cultural, recreational, and job-related issues. Each Council was asked to elect a leader, and today, more than 2,500 employees serve in that role. Vineet's team also launched 32 issue-specific councils focused on key business and technology topics, such as cloud computing. These loosely structured teams quickly demonstrated their value and have become a critical source of new strategic insights. When one of the councils reaches a consensus around a particular recommendation, it is transferred to a dedicated group that pushes the idea toward execution.

In one recent conversation, Vineet talked to me about the logic for the online communities: "We wanted to overturn the notion that there's one person who can make a key decision, who has the power to say yes or no. Instead, we wanted to gravitate towards communities of interest; these could form the basis of a parallel organization. Three years after launching this concept, 20% of HCLT's revenue is coming from initiatives launched in these communities of interest."

While EFCS is still a work in progress, the notion of reverse accountability is now firmly rooted within HCLT. There's still a hierarchy, but its role has been dramatically diminished.

Says Vineet, "We all believe that democracies are good and total-itarian systems are bad, and yet we tolerate dictatorships within our companies, even though the people at the top don't have enough information to know what needs to be done. At HCLT, we have been trying to democratize our company."

Does management innovation pay? It would seem so. In recent years HCL has significantly outperformed its Indian-based rivals.

Of course, none of this guarantees that HCLT will continue to thrive in the years ahead. There are lots of ways a successful company can come off the rails, and not even a brilliant management model can protect a corporation from all of them.

Nevertheless, if a $3.5 billion company can invert the pyramid and live to tell about it, there's hope for your company. Turns out, we don't have to content ourselves with an organizational model that was designed to serve the interests of ancient military commanders and smokestack-era CEOs.

Two concluding thoughts: first, Vineet is right that the world has become too complex for the CEO to play the role of "visionary-in-chief." Instead, the CEO must become a "management architect," someone who continually asks, "What are the principles and processes that can help us surface the best ideas and unleash the talents of everyone who works here?"

Second, it really *is* possible to change the management DNA of a large, established company. Critically, Vineet didn't start out with a master plan. Rather, he was guided by the goal of *employees first, customers second*. Nor did he start by asking HCLT's senior staff to reengineer the company's existing management processes. Such a move would have been fiercely resisted and might have risked operational chaos. Instead, Vineet asked his team to run the new processes in parallel with the old, at least for a time. As Vineet says, "The old pro-cesses were focused on running the business. We needed new processes that were focused on changing the business." Already the values of EFCS are seeping back into the old systems, but this is happening gradually, as it should.

There are some important lessons here. First, you don't need a detailed change program to get started. Bus drivers follow maps; pioneers follow polestars, and for Vineet and his colleagues, the guiding light was EFCS. Second, you don't have to blow up the existing management processes to change the management model. You can be revolutionary *and* evolutionary. So if you're a would-be management renegade, you've just run out of excuses.

AIMING
HIGHER

As managers we are too easily satisfied. If it were otherwise, we'd be working harder to counterbalance the ideology of control. While most of us aren't entirely *content* with the way our organizations work, neither are we outraged. We're not incensed by the poisonous politicking, the squandered creativity, the debilitating cynicism, the ignoble values, the ethical shortcuts, the executive egomania, and the strategic myopia that infect our organizations—or at least we're not sufficiently incensed to cry, "Enough!" and commit ourselves to creating something better.

We also seem disinclined to dream. Most of us have yet to be captivated by an alluring vision of organizations that are impassioned, meritocratic, open, boisterous, convivial, invigorating, and *fun!* In this regard, we suffer from an imagination deficit. Like a zoo-born lion that knows only its cage, we can't imagine the sweet grasses and blue vistas

---

Some material in this chapter is drawn from "Moon Shots for Management" by Gary Hamel in *Harvard Business Review*, February 2009. Copyright © 2009 Harvard Business School Publishing Corporation, all rights reserved. Used by permission. http://hbr.org/2009/02/moon-shots-for-management/ar/1

of an organizational savannah where human beings are actually free to flourish.

If this sounds like an indictment, good—it's meant to be, but I'm the first to say *mea culpa*. I've been a manager and a business school professor for 35 years, and over that span, as I've observed and endured organizational life, I have seldom been as indignant, or as hopeful, as I should have been. And that's a pity, since it's the malcontents and the idealists who ultimately change our world.

I came to that unremarkable and humbling conclusion on a treadmill. I often read the *Financial Times* while I'm exercising (even the *FT* is more interesting than a beige wall). On this particular day I had finished the paper with a mile of jogging yet to do. Casting about, I saw an abandoned copy of *People* magazine and jumped off the machine to retrieve it. Now, I'm not particularly interested in the lives of Angelina, Brad, Paris, Jen, Lindsay, Zac, Justin, Kim, and all the other estimable icons of twenty-first-century *haute culture*, but I was bored, and as there was no one else in the gym, I picked up the gossip rag. As I scanned the table of contents, one name caught my attention: Nicholas Negroponte. I've met Nick on a few occasions; he's the founder of MIT's renowned Media Lab and remains its chairman emeritus. What, I wondered, was Nick doing in *People?* As far as I knew, Nick had never been to rehab and had never been photographed getting out of a limo at two in the morning absent some crucial piece of clothing.

The story, of course, was about Nick's pioneering effort to equip the world's poorest children with computers. His nonprofit initiative, One Laptop per Child, was launched in 2005 with the goal of producing a simple, web-enabled computer that could be sold to developing countries for $100. After an arduous development process, the OLPC's first laptop model, the "XO," began shipping in late 2007. Although the $100 price target has yet to be reached (the current price is $200), XO computers have been supplied to more than thirty countries. Uruguay, for example, has purchased one for every primary school pupil.

As I read about Nick's bold project, I couldn't help but ask myself, what was *my* quest? Unlike Nick Negroponte, I'm not a digital savant or a social entrepreneur, and on most days, not all that big-hearted, either.

I'm a management professor, and I spend most of my time talking to business folks about nit-picky sorts of problems: How do you improve your planning process? How do you get more teamwork? How do you get products to market faster? Maybe these are the sorts of problems that occupy your attention as well. But what if we aimed higher? What if we dreamed bigger?

A few years back, the National Academy of Engineering convened a panel of leading technologists and asked them to create a list of the thorniest and most pressing challenges for twenty-first-century engineers. The committee included luminaries such as J. Craig Venter, the pioneering geneticist; Larry Page, co-founder of Google; and William Perry, a former U.S. Secretary of Defense. A sampling of the 14 nominated challenges: making solar energy economical, reverse engineering the human brain, and protecting cyberspace from security attacks.[1] The agenda-setting initiative was funded by the U.S. National Science Foundation with the goal of focusing attention on the engineering problems that will shape our collective future.

When I learned of this effort, I asked myself again, what are the grand challenges that should inspire those of us who aren't engineers, but are managers, executives, and leaders? What's our equivalent of carbon sequestration or creating energy from fusion? As I argued in an earlier chapter, management is the *technology of human accomplishment*. Solving the world's toughest problems or, more modestly, creating organizations that are deeply human will require more than scientific breakthroughs; it will require new ways of planning, organizing, collaborating, allocating, motivating, and yes, controlling.

As managers, we're pragmatic doers, not starry-eyed dreamers. And yet, as human beings, we are ultimately defined by the causes we serve and the problems we struggle to solve. Though big problems don't always yield big advances, small ones never do.

It was that thought that brought 36 management experts together in Half Moon Bay, California, in May 2008. Their mission: to create a roster of make-or-break management "moonshots" that would inspire business innovators everywhere. After all, even malcontents and dreamers need an agenda, something that focuses their frustrations and aspirations.

The event was organized by the Management Lab with the support of McKinsey & Company, and it brought together a diverse mix of academics, consultants, and CEOs, as well as a pair of venture capitalists. (A list of the participants can be found at the end of this chapter.) As you might imagine, the conversations were spirited and occasionally combative, but through it all no one lost sight of our objective: to define management's equivalent to eradicating malaria, unpacking the secrets of the Big Bang, or colonizing space.

The 25 moonshots that emerged are neither mutually exclusive nor collectively exhaustive. Our current management model is an integrated whole, and can't easily be broken into parts. That's why many of the challenges overlap. However, each challenge charts a critical path in the journey to Management 2.0.

In the inventory below, the moonshots have been grouped into six themes: (1) Mending the Soul; (2) Unleashing Capabilities; (3) Fostering Renewal; (4) Distributing Power; (5) Seeking Harmony; and (6) Reshaping Minds. I hope that one of these moonshots will inspire *you* to become a management innovator.

MENDING THE SOUL

Moonshot #1: Ensuring That Management Serves a Higher Purpose

Most companies strive to maximize shareholder wealth, a goal that is inadequate in many respects. As an emotional catalyst, wealth maximization lacks the power to mobilize the energies of every employee. It's an insufficient defense when people question the legitimacy of corporate power, and it's neither specific nor compelling enough to spur renewal. For these reasons, tomorrow's management practices must be focused on the achievement of socially significant and noble goals.

Moonshot #2: Embedding the Ethos of Community and Citizenship

In tomorrow's interdependent world, collaborative systems will outperform those characterized by adversarial, win-lose relationships. Traditional governance structures often exacerbate conflict by promoting the interests of some groups, such as senior executives and capital providers, at the expense of others, typically, employees and local communities. Going forward, management systems and structures will need to explicitly encompass the notions of community and citizenship. The inescapable interdependence of all stakeholder groups can no longer be ignored.

Moonshot #3: Humanizing the Language and Practice of Business

Business goals are typically described using words such as efficiency, advantage, value, superiority, focus, and differentiation. As important as these objectives are, they often lack the power to fully rouse human hearts. To create organizations that are truly human in their capacity to adapt, innovate, and engage, tomorrow's management pioneers must find ways of infusing mundane, commercial activities with deeper, soul-stirring ideals, such as honor, truth, love, justice, and beauty. These timeless virtues have often inspired extraordinary accomplishments, and must no longer be relegated to the shadowy fringes of management discourse and action.

UNLEASHING CAPABILITIES

Moonshot #4: Increasing Trust, Reducing Fear

Traditional management systems often reflect a deep mistrust of employee commitment and competence. They also tend to overemphasize sanctions as a way of forcing compliance. Yet organizational resilience depends critically on a high-trust, low-fear culture. In such an environment, risk taking is encouraged, information is broadly shared, and contentious opinions freely expressed. Mistrust demoralizes, fear paralyzes. That's why they must be wrung out of twenty-first-century organizations.

Moonshot #5: Reinventing the Means of Control

Traditional control systems ensure high levels of compliance at the expense of creativity, entrepreneurship, and engagement. Going forward, no company will be able to afford this trade-off. To overcome the discipline-versus-innovation conundrum, tomorrow's control systems will need to rely more on peer review and less on top-down monitoring. They will leverage the power of shared values and aspirations while loosening the straitjacket of rules and strictures. The goal: an organization filled with individuals who are capable of self-discipline.

Moonshot #6: Inspiring Leaps of Imagination

We know a lot about how to engender human creativity: equip people with innovation tools, set aside time for thinking, destigmatize failure, create opportunities for serendipitous learning, and so on. Yet, little of this knowledge has infiltrated our management systems. Worse, many companies have institutionalized a sort of innovation class system. They give a few individuals creative roles and the time to pursue their interests while assuming that most other employees are unimaginative and therefore undeserving of the time and space to create. Tomorrow's management processes must be built around the assumption that creativity is widely distributed and must, therefore, be systematically nurtured.

Moonshot #7: Expanding and Exploiting Diversity

Diversity is essential not just for the survival of a species but for the continued viability of any organization. Companies that don't encompass a high degree of diversity in experiences, values, and capabilities will be unable to generate the sort of unconventional ideas and experiments that fuel strategic renewal. The management systems of the future will need to value diversity, disagreement, and divergence as highly as they do conformance, consensus, and cohesion.

Moonshot #8: Enabling Communities of Passion

Passion is a significant multiplier of human effort, particularly when like-minded individuals converge around a worthy cause. Yet a wealth of data indicates that most employees are emotionally disengaged at work. They are unfulfilled, and as a result, their organizations underperform.

Companies must facilitate the emergence of communities of passion by allowing individuals to find a higher calling within their work lives, by connecting employees who share similar passions, and by better aligning the organization's objectives with the natural interests of its employees or members.

Moonshot #9: Taking the Work out of Work

Human beings are most productive when work feels like play. Enthusiasm, imagination, and resourcefulness get unleashed when people are having fun. In the future, the most successful organizations will be the ones that have learned how to blur the line between work and play. In practice, this may mean allowing individuals to choose their own work, turning repetitive tasks into the equivalent of online, multiplayer games, or creating roles that encompass a great variety of tasks. Over the past century, enormous progress has been made in engineering the inefficiencies out of work; now management innovators must engineer the drudgery out of work.

FOSTERING RENEWAL

Moonshot #10: Sharing the Work of Setting Direction

Yesterday's visionaries are unlikely to be the first to spot tomorrow's opportunities, particularly in a highly dynamic world. As the business environment becomes more complex and turbulent, it will become ever more difficult for any small group of senior executives to envision and direct the work of organizational renewal. That's why the responsibility for defining a company's future direction must be broadly shared. An added benefit to a truly participatory process is the genuine commitment it engenders. In setting direction, it is foresight and insight, rather than power and position, that should determine one's share of voice.

Moonshot #11: Harnessing the Power of Evolution

In a turbulent world, prediction is difficult and long-range planning is of limited value. Management processes that seek to surface the one best strategy through top-down, analytical methods must give way to models based on biological principles of *variety* (generate lots of options), *selection* (use low-cost experiments to rapidly test critical assumptions), and *retention* (double down on the ideas that are gaining the most traction in the marketplace). In this model, top management doesn't make strategy but works to create the conditions in which new strategies can emerge and grow.

Moonshot #12: Destructuring and Disaggregating Organizations

In an environment where opportunities come and go at lightning speed, organizations must have the ability to quickly reconfigure capabilities and infrastructure. Unfortunately, in many organizations, the rapid realignment of skills and assets is severely hampered by rigidly proscribed unit boundaries, functional silos, and political fiefdoms. In large organizational units, one way of thinking tends to predominate, thus limiting scope for experimentation. To become more adaptable, companies must "disorganize" into smaller units and create more fluid, project-based structures. A "reorg" shouldn't be a traumatic event that happens every four or five years, but something that occurs continuously and nearly effortlessly.

Moonshot #13: Creating Internal Markets for Ideas, Talent, and Resources

In the long term, markets tend to outperform hierarchies because they're better at allocating resources. While funding decisions in a corporation are usually made top-down, and are heavily influenced by political factors, resource allocation in a market-based system, such as the New York Stock Exchange, is highly decentralized and apolitical. Yes, markets can be vulnerable to short-term distortions, but in the long run, they're better at getting the right resources behind the right opportunities than big organizations. To ensure that resource allocation becomes more flexible and less political, companies must create internal markets where new initiatives and legacy programs compete on an equal footing for talent and cash.

Moonshot #14: Depoliticizing Decision Making

In most organizations, big decisions are made by people with big titles. In making those decisions, senior leaders seldom seek the advice of the rank and file. That's a problem on at least three counts. First, top-level decisions are often compromised by executive hubris, positional biases, and incomplete data. Second, it's often those on the ground who are best placed to evaluate the practical issues that will make or break a major, strategic move. And third, as the business environment becomes more complex, the number of variables that needs to be factored into key decisions will grow apace. Given all that, companies need decision-making processes that are politically neutral, exploit the organization's collective wisdom, and encompass a broad range of views and inputs.

DISTRIBUTING POWER

Moonshot #15: Building Natural, Flexible Hierarchies

While hierarchy will always be a feature of human organizations, there's a pressing need to limit the damage inflicted by top-down authority structures. Typical drawbacks include overweighting experience at the expense of new thinking; giving followers too little influence in the choice of their leaders; perpetuating power disparities that can't be justified by differences in capability; creating incentives for managers to horde authority when it should be distributed; and undermining the self-worth of those who have little formal power. To overcome these failings, formal hierarchies must give way to "natural" hierarchies, where status and influence are correlated with contribution rather than with position. Rigid hierarchies must become more dynamic, so that power flows automatically toward those who are adding value and away from those who aren't. And instead of a single hierarchy, there need to be many, with each one serving as barometer of expertise in a critical skill area.

Moonshot #16: Expanding the Scope of Autonomy

For the most part, individuals on the front lines of a large organization have little or no capacity to initiate change. A lack of self-directed time, a snarl of bureaucratic rules, and limited access to capital severely constrain their autonomy and undermine the organization's capacity to renew itself. For the sake of adaptability and engagement, the boundaries of employee freedom must be significantly enlarged. Management systems must facilitate rather than frustrate local experimentation and grassroots initiatives.

Moonshot #17: Refocusing the Work of Leadership on Mobilizing and Mentoring

Natural hierarchies require natural leaders, individuals who can mobilize others despite a lack of positional authority. Leaders must no longer be seen as grand visionaries, all-wise decision makers, and heroic deal-makers, but rather as "social architects," "constitution writers," and "entrepreneurs of meaning." They must see their primary responsibility as creating work environments that encourage their associates to collaborate, innovate, and excel.

Moonshot #18: Creating a Democracy of Information

Managerial power has traditionally depended on the control of information. When innovation is hoarded, it disempowers employees, breeds mistrust, and frustrates rapid, frontline decision making. Performance information must be broadly shared. Those on the front lines should be the best informed individuals in the organization rather than the least. In the future, companies will need "holographic" information systems that equip every employee with the data and knowledge they need to act in the organization's best interests.

Moonshot #19: Encouraging the Dissenters

Industries are typically reinvented by contrarians rather than by incumbents. Why? Because long-serving executives are often unwilling to challenge their own deeply entrenched beliefs. The solution: management systems that stimulate heretical thinking, legitimize dissent, and prevent powerful executives from killing discomforting ideas.

SEEKING HARMONY

Moonshot #20: Developing Holistic Performance Measures

Existing performance measurement systems have many flaws. First, they overweight the achievement of some outcomes, such as hitting quarterly earnings targets, while underweighting the achievement of others, such as building new growth platforms. Second, they typically ignore the environmental and social costs of executive decisions. And third, they're poorly attuned to the things that drive value in the creative economy, such as the scope and scale of customer-sourced innovation. To overcome these distortions and limitations, we need new, holistic measurement systems.

Moonshot #21: Transcending Traditional Trade-offs

Increasingly, organizational success depends on the capacity of employees at all levels to manage a set of seemingly irreconcilable trade-offs: scale versus flexibility; earnings versus growth; focus versus experimentation; and control versus freedom. Traditional management systems often rely on crude, global policies that systematically favor certain goals at the expense of others. By contrast, tomorrow's systems must facilitate healthy competition between opposing goals by giving frontline employees the information and freedom they need to optimize real-time trade-offs. The aim is to create organizations that are as flexible as distributed networks and as efficient as tightly managed hierarchies.

Moonshot #22: Stretching Management Time Frames and Perspectives

Compensation and incentive systems often truncate executives time frames and skew management priorities. For instance, research suggests that executives won't fund a viable new initiative if doing so would reduce current period earnings, even when the investment promises to yield a positive net present value. Building new incentive systems that better align CEO interests with sustained wealth creation is a critical priority for management innovators.

RESHAPING MINDS

Moonshot #23: Strengthening the Right Hemisphere

Management training has traditionally emphasized left-brain thinking. The emphasis has been on deductive reasoning, analytical problem solving, and solutions engineering. In an increasingly turbulent world, new cognitive skills will be required. These include reflective or double-loop learning; systems-based thinking; design thinking; creative problem solving; and social consciousness. Business schools and companies must redesign management training in ways that will help executives develop these new skills.

Moonshot #24: Retooling Management for an Open World

Many of today's most successful business models rely on value-creating networks and forms of social production that transcend organizational boundaries. In such environments, the usual tools of management can be ineffective, or even counterproductive. For example, in a network of volunteers and independent agents, the job of the "leader" is to energize and empower the community rather than to manage it from above. Winning in a world of open innovation and virtual collaboration will require the development of new approaches to mobilizing and coordinating human effort.

Moonshot #25: Reconstructing the Philosophical Foundations of Management

Tomorrow's organizations must be more than operationally excellent; they must also be adaptable, innovative, inspiring, and socially responsible. To imbue organizations with these capabilities, scholars and practitioners must rethink management's philosophical foundations. This will require a hunt for new management principles in fields as diverse as anthropology, biology, design, political science, urban planning, and theology. To build Management 2.0, we need more than engineers and accountants. We must also harness the ideas of artists, philosophers, designers, ecologists, anthropologists, and theologians.

GETTING BEYOND EITHER/OR

Making progress on these moonshots will help de-bureaucratize our organizations and unshackle human capabilities. The goal, though, is to overcome the limits of today's management practices without losing the benefits they confer.

For example, it would make no sense to find a cure for organizational insularity and inertia if the side effects were imprudence and inefficiency. We need organizations that are a lot more adaptable, innovative, and inspiring, but no less efficient, disciplined, or performance-oriented.

To accomplish this, we must distinguish ends from means. Executives often defend timeworn management practices because they can't imagine a less bureaucratic way of accomplishing some critical business goal. For example, many companies have detailed policies governing travel. Employees have to get permission before embarking on a trip and must abide by strict spending rules. While few would argue with the goal of keeping travel costs in check, might there be a less bureaucratic way of achieving this objective? An alternative approach might be to publish every employee's expense report on the company intranet and then rely on peer pressure to rein in profligate spenders. In practice, transparency is often as effective as a rigidly applied rulebook, and it's always more flexible and less expensive because it doesn't require an army of auditors to ensure compliance.

Let's return for a moment to where this book started: the banking crisis. Anyone who watched slack-jawed as the flames of hubris and greed consumed some of the world's leading banks can be forgiven for wondering if the problem wasn't too little bureaucracy rather than too much. After all, it's the machinery of bureaucracy—lots of rules, tight supervision, and regular reviews—that's supposed to keep employees in check. Undoubtedly, everyone would be better off today if bonus-chasing bankers had been kept on a shorter leash.

Nevertheless, in a dynamic environment, decision-making authority has to be distributed; either that or our organizations will be brittle and slow to adapt. Even in the hair-trigger world of modern finance, centralization and draconian controls may not be the best way to tackle injudicious risk taking. Those on the front lines, the "rocket scientists" who create and sell exotic financial instruments, must be held accountable for the impact of their actions on balance sheet risk and medium-term profitability. In recent years, though, many of them were responsible for little more than shoveling toxic products out the door. Like employees in every other industry, bankers need incentives that require them to take a longer-term view of success. They must see themselves as stewards, responsible for safeguarding the interests of all those who put their trust in them, rather than as mercenaries motivated only by Midas-like payouts. Risk management needs to be a distributed responsibility, backed up by transparency and peer review, rather than a centralized function. In an industry that celebrates star performers, there must be a higher-order purpose and a shared sense of community that protects organizations from excessive greed.

Control from within rather than from without, executive time frames that extend beyond the next 12 months, a passion for a higher purpose, the ethos of community; these moonshots will be essential components of any long-term solution to bankers' bulimia, the binge-and-purge cycle that has characterized the financial services industry for much of the last century.

Not all the moonshots are new. Most tackle problems that are endemic in large organizations. The goal in enumerating them is to inspire new solutions to long-simmering problems. As you probably know, the Gates Foundation has devoted itself to eradicating malaria, hardly a new goal. Yet, the people leading that charge believe that new ideas, new therapies, and new delivery systems will eventually yield historic gains. In a like vein, new minds unencumbered by old beliefs, and new tools of the sort that have powered the social revolution on the Web, may one day help us to escape the limitations of our tradition-encrusted management practices.

The challenge may seem intimidating, but take heart. Those early management pioneers had to turn free-thinking, obstreperous human beings into obedient, kowtowing employees. They were working against the grain of human nature. We, on the other hand, are working with the grain. Our goal is to make organizations more human, not less. McCallum, Taylor, and Ford and all those other early management pioneers would envy us this opportunity.

GETTING STARTED

Maybe you have an idea for how to make progress on one of the management moonshots. Perhaps you've come across an unconventional management practice that has redefined the boundaries of what's possible. Or maybe you're just curious about what other organizations are doing to escape the limits of management-as-usual. If so, you may want to visit www.hackmanagement.com, the world's first open innovation project aimed at reinventing management. There you'll find hundreds of case studies from the world's most progressive organizations, and a multitude of radical proposals for reinventing management as we know it, all of which are organized around the management moonshots.

If there's one thought I hope you take away from this book, it's this: we have the chance to make a new beginning. We don't have to live with organizations that are ethically challenged, inflexible, and inhuman. We can build organizations that are noble at their core, that honor every creative impulse, that change before they have to, stir the heart, and that are bureaucracy-free. Doing so won't be easy, but I hope you've found within these pages enough inspiration and instruction to make a start.

What matters now, more than ever, is that you question your assumptions, surrender your conceits, rethink your principles, and raise your sights—and that you challenge others to do the same. We know broadly what must be done to create organizations that are fit for the future. The only question is, "Who's going to lead and who's going to follow?" How you answer *that* question matters most of all.

APPENDIX: THE HALF MOON BAY "RENEGADE BRIGADE"

Eric Abrahamson, University of Columbia
Chris Argyris, Harvard Business School
Joanna Barsh, McKinsey & Company
Julian Birkinshaw, London Business School
Tim Brown, IDEO
Lowell Bryan, McKinsey & Company
Bhaskar Chakravorti, Harvard Business School
Yves Doz, INSEAD
Alex Ehrlich, UBS
Gary Hamel, Management Lab
Linda Hill, Harvard Business School
Jeffrey Hollender, Seventh Generation
Steve Jurvetson, Draper Fisher Jurvetson

Kevin Kelly, *Wired*
Terri Kelly, W. L. Gore
Ed Lawler, University of Southern California
John Mackey, Whole Foods
Tom Malone, MIT
Marissa Mayer, Google
Andrew McAfee, Harvard Business School
Lenny Mendonca, McKinsey & Company
Henry Mintzberg, McGill University
Vineet Nayar, HCL Technologies
Jeffrey Pfeffer, Stanford University
C. K. Prahalad, University of Michigan
Leighton Read, Seriosity
Keith Sawyer, Washington University
Eric Schmidt, Google
Peter Senge, MIT
Rajendra Sisodia, Bentley College
Tom Stewart, Booz & Company
James Surowiecki, *The New Yorker*
Hal Varian, University of California, Berkeley
Steven Weber, University of California, Berkeley
David Wolfe, Wolfe Resources Group
Shoshana Zuboff, Harvard Business School

NOTES

1.1: PUTTING FIRST THINGS FIRST

1 "Nurses Top Honesty and Ethics List for 11th Year," http://www.gallup
.com/poll/145043/Nurses-Top-Honesty-Ethics-List-11-Year.aspx.

2 "Report: Socially Responsible Investing Assets in US Top $3 Trillion;
Nearly 1 out of Every 8 Dollars Under Professional Management," https://
ussif.org/news/releases/pressrelease.cfm?id=168.

1.2: LEARNING FROM THE CRUCIBLE OF CRISIS

1 "Ex-CEO: 'Market forces' Killed Bear Stearns," http://www.msnbc.msn
.com/id/36958429/ns/business-us_business/t/ex-ceo-market-forces
-killed-bear-stearns/.

2 2009 Financial Crimes Report, Federal Bureau of Investigation, http://
www.fbi.gov/stats-services/publications/financial-crimes-report-2009
/financial-crimes-report-2009#mortgage.

3 Gary Rivlin, "The Billion-Dollar Bank Heist," *Newsweek,* July 18, 2011,
p. 10.

4 "How AIG Became Too Big to Fail," http://www.time.com/time
/magazine/article/0,9171,1886538,00.html.

5 "World of Work Report 2008 – Global Income Inequality Gap Is Vast
and Growing," http://www.ilo.org/global/about-the-ilo/press-and-media-
centre/news/WCMS_099406/lang--en/index.htm.

1.3: REDISCOVERING FARMER VALUES

1 Franklin Roosevelt's First Inaugural Address, http://en.wikisource.org/wiki/Franklin_Roosevelt%27s_First_Inaugural_Address.

1.4: RENOUNCING CAPITALISM'S DANGEROUS CONCEITS

1 Shiela M.J. Bonini, Kerrin McKillop, and Lenny T. Mendonca, "The Trust Gap Between Consumers and Corporations," *McKinsey Quarterly*, 2007, Number 2, pp. 7–10.
2 "Congress Ranks Last in Confidence in Institutions," http://www.gallup.com/poll/141512/congress-ranks-last-confidence-institutions.aspx.

2.1: DEFENDING INNOVATION

1 Data from Angus Maddison, *The World Economy: A Millennial Perspective, Organization for Economic Cooperation and Development,* Paris: Organization for Economic Cooperation & Development, 2001.
2 Mihalyi Csikszentmihalyi, *Flow: The Psychology of Optimal Experience,* New York: Harper & Row, 1990.
3 Tal-Ben Shahar, *Happier: Learn the Secrets to Joy and Lasting Fulfillment,* New York: McGraw-Hill, 2007.

2.2: CATALOGING THE WORLD'S GREATEST INNOVATORS

1 "The World's Most Innovative Companies 2010," http://www.fastcompany.com/mic/2010.
2 "The 50 Most Innovative Companies 2010," http://www.businessweek.com/interactive_reports/innovative_companies_2010.html.
3 "The Journal's Top 10," *The Wall Street Journal,* http://online.wsj.com/public/resources/documents/info-GREATEST08.html.
4 "IFI CLAIMS Announces Top Global Companies Ranked by 2010 U.S. Patents," http://www.ificlaims.com/news/top-patents.html.
5 "Will Intel Finally Crack Smartphones?" http://www.businessweek.com/magazine/content/11_25/b4233041946230.htm.
6 "IFI CLAIMS Announces Top Global Companies Ranked by 2010 U.S. Patents," http://www.ificlaims.com/news/top-patents.html.
7 For more on IDEO's approach to creative thinking, see Tom Kelly's book, *The Art of Innovation,* Random House, 2001.
8 Phone conversation with Nancy Tennant Snyder, July 1, 2010.

2.3: INSPIRING GREAT DESIGN

1 Personal conversation with Tim Brown, CEO of IDEO, October 5, 2009.

2.4: TURNING INNOVATION DUFFERS INTO PROS

1 Ben Hogan, *Five Lessons: The Modern Fundamentals of Golf,* New York: Simon & Schuster, 1957.

2 "Your Guide to Cutting the Cord to Cable TV," http://www.pbs.org /mediashift/2010/01/your-guide-to-cutting-the-cord-to-cable-tv008.html.

3 "Some Chinese Kids' First English Word: Mickey," http://www .businessweek.com/magazine/content/11_25/b4233024744691.htm.

2.5: DECONSTRUCTING APPLE

1 Corporate Financials Online, http://www.cfonews.com/atxa/d092898z.txt .html.

2 "Nine out of 10 Premium-Priced PCs Sold at U.S. Retail Is a Mac," http:// www.betanews.com/joewilcox/article/Nine-out-of-10-premiumpriced -PCs-sold-at-US-retail-is-a-Mac/1265047893.

3 "Apple iTunes: 10 Billion Songs Later," http://tech.fortune.cnn.com/2010 /02/24/apple-itunes-10-billion-songs-later/.

4 Author analysis.

5 "Android's Pursuit of the Biggest Losers," http://www.asymco.com/2010 /08/17/androids-pursuit-of-the-biggest-losers/.

6 "Financial History of the Apple Retail Store," http://www.macworld.com /article/159499/2011/05/applestoresinancials.html.

7 "Apples for Sale on New York City's Upper West Side," http://abcnews .go.com/Technology/AheadoftheCurve/apple-store-opens-york-citys -upper-west-side/story?id=9074803.

8 http://en.wikipedia.org/wiki/App_Store_(iOS).

9 Apple Events, January 2010, http://www.apple.com/apple-events/january -2010/.

3.2: BECOMING AN ENEMY OF ENTROPY

1 Alexis de Tocqueville (trans. by Arthur Goldhammer), *Tocqueville: Democracy in America,* New York: Library of America, 2004, p. 12.

2 Dinesh D'Souza marshals the evidence for this assertion in *What's So Great About Christianity?* Washington, D.C.: Regnery, 2007.

3 John Meacham, "The End of Christian America," *Newsweek,* April 4, 2009. See also chapter 13, "Religion and Good Neighborliness," in Robert D. Putnam and David E. Campbell, *American Grace: How Religion Divides and Unites Us,* New York: Simon & Schuster, 2010.

4 John Meacham, "The End of Christian America."

5 Ibid.

6 David T. Olson, *The American Church in Crisis,* Grand Rapids, MI: Zondervan, 2008, p 36.

7 Ibid., pp. 35–36.

8 David Kinnaman and Gabe Lyons, *Unchristian,* Grand Rapids, MI: Baker Books, 2009, p. 25.

9 ARIS (American Religious Identification Survey) 2008, http://www
   .americanreligionsurvey-aris.org/reports/ARIS_Report_2008.pdf.

10 Thomas S. Rainer and Sam S. Rainer III, "Surprising Insights," *Outreach,*
   January-February 2007.

11 ARIS (American Religious Identification Survey) 2008, http://www
   .americanreligionsurvey-aris.org/reports/ARIS_Report_2008.pdf.

12 "Making Sight Affordable," http://www.mitpressjournals.org/doi/pdf
   /10.1162/itgg.2007.2.4.35.

3.5: FUTURE-PROOFING YOUR COMPANY

1 "Can Google Stay on Top of the Web?" http://http://www.businessweek
   .com/magazine/content/09_41/b4150044749206.htm.

2 "Toyota Adopts New Flexible Assembly System," http://wardsautoworld
   .com/ar/auto_toyota_adopts_new/, and "Toyota's Global Body Shop,"
   http://money.cnn.com/magazines/fortune/fortune_archive/2004/02/09
   /360102/index.htm.

4.1: EXPOSING MANAGEMENT'S DIRTY LITTLE SECRET

1 "Towers Perrin Global Workforce—Global Report, 2007–2008," pp. 4,
   http://www.towersperrin.com/tp/getwebcachedoc?webc=HRS/USA
   /2008/200803/GWS_Global_Report20072008_31208.pdf.

2 Ibid., p. 5.

3 For a deep dive into the relationship between engagement and performance,
   read *Firms of Endearment,* by Raj Sisodia, David Wolfe, and Jagdish Sheth,
   Wharton School Publishing, 2007.

4 "Apple Now Bigger Than Nokia in Mobile Biz," http://blogs.computer
   -world.com/18171/apple_now_bigger_than_nokia_in_mobile_biz.

4.2: PUTTING INDIVIDUALS AHEAD OF INSTITUTIONS

1 "Nurses Top Honesty Ethics List for 11th Year," http://www.gallup.com
   /poll/145043/nurses-top-honesty-ethics-list-11-year.aspx.

2 "Trust in Business Rises Globally, Driven by Western Economies," http://
   www.scribd.com/full/26268655?access_key=key-1ovbgbpawooot3hnsz3u.

3 "Kraft Rebuked for Broken Pledge on Cadbury Factory," http://www
   .guardian.co.uk/business/2010/may/26/kraft-censured-over-cadbury
   -takeover-pledge.

4 "Congressional Performance," http://www.rasmussenreports.com/public
   _content/politics/mood_of_america/congressional_performance.

5 "The Shape of the Emerging 'Deal': Insights from Towers Watson's
   2010 Global Workforce Study," http://www.towerswatson.com/assets/pdf
   /global-workforce-study/TWGWS_Exec_Summary.pdf.

6 "Challenging Work and Corporate Responsibility Will Lure MBA Grads," http://www.gsb.stanford.edu/NEWS/research/montgomery_mba.html.

7 "Jobless Recovery in the U.S. Leaving Trail of Recession-Weary Employees in Its Wake, According to New Study," http://www.towerswatson.com /press/1365.

4.3: BUILDING COMMUNITIES OF PASSION

1 "Church of England Sees Greater Decline in Church Attendance," http:// www.ekklesia.co.uk/node/11080.

2 "Attendance," http://www.churchsociety.org/issues_new/church/stats /iss_church_stats_attendance.asp.

3 "Churchgoing in the UK," http://news.bbc.co.uk/2/shared/bsp/hi/pdfs /03_04_07_tearfundchurch.pdf.

4 "WhyChurch: Belonging and Believing," http://www.whychurch.org.uk /trends.php.

5.1: CHALLENGING THE IDEOLOGY OF MANAGEMENT

1 W. Carus, ed., *Memoirs of the Life of the Reverend Charles Simeon,* London: Hatchard and Son, 1847, p. 47.

2 Max Weber, *The Theory of Social and Economic Organization,* ed. and trans. A. M. Henderson and Talcott Parsons, New York: Free Press, 1947, p. 337.

3 Max Weber, speech to the Verein fur Sozialpolitik (Association for Social Policy) in 1909. From J. P. Mayer, *Max Weber and German Politics,* Appendix I, London: Faber & Faber, 1944, pp. 125–131. Quoted selection excerpted from: http://www.faculty.rsu.edu/users/f/felwell/www /Theorists/Weber/Max1909.html#Max.

5.3: ESCAPING THE MANAGEMENT TAX

1 Morning Star's "purchasing councils" are one example of a bottom-up structure. Although purchasing is decentralized at Morning Star, colleagues who buy similar items in large quantities, or from the same vendor, realized they could save money by consolidating their buying power, so they established councils, which meet periodically to coordinate purchasing.

2 What happens, you may wonder, when Morning Star runs out of capital? Thanks to the company's strong cash flow, it is able to make significant capital investments each year, and although it eschews long-term debt, it will borrow short-term when the returns are attractive enough. Occasionally, though, there are more projects than cash and when this happens, investments get postponed. Nevertheless, the role of Morning Star's finance staff is to find capital rather than to allocate it.

5.4: INVERTING THE PYRAMID

1 "The World's Most Modern Management – in India," http://money.cnn .com/2006/04/13/magazines/fortune/fastforward_fortune/index.htm.

2 "HCL Best Employer in India, Says Hewitt Study," http://www.financial -express.com/news/hcl-best-employer-in-india-says-hewitt-study/442332/.

3 "The WorldBlu List," http://www.worldblu.com/awardee-profiles/2011 .php.

4 Vineet Nayar tells the story of HCLT's transformation in *Employees First, Customers Second,* Boston: Harvard Business School Publishing, 2010.

5.5: AIMING HIGHER

1 You can find the full list here: "Grand Challenges for Engineering," http:// www.engineeringchallenges.org.

ACKNOWLEDGMENTS

No matter what it says on the jacket, a book is never a solo project. Many of the chapters in this volume had their first airing in my blog for the *Wall Street Journal*. I am deeply indebted to the *Journal*'s Erin White and Francesca Donner for their encouragement and editorial guidance. Over the years I've also had a very fruitful partnership with Anand Raman, Senior Editor at *Harvard Business Review*. Two of the chapters in this book started life as *HBR* articles and benefited greatly from Anand's wise counsel.

Polly LaBarre and Michele Zanini, my colleagues at the Management Lab, have been wonderful thought partners in recent years and their insights are sprinkled throughout this book. Umair Haque, author of the *The New Capitalist Manifesto* and my former student at the London Business School, was also generous with his ideas and proved to be a lively intellectual sparring partner.

I am also grateful for the generous contributions of the management innovators whose stories I tell in this book. Chris Bayliss, Drew Williams, Chris Rufer, Paul Green, Jr., Terri Kelly, Vineet Nayar, and Tim Brown deserve particular thanks.

Kudos as well to Susan Williams, Executive Editor of the Jossey-Bass Business division at John Wiley and Sons. She and her team exceeded every expectation. Without their passion and dedication, this book would not exist.

Finally, to my personal assistant, Grace Reim, also a hearty thanks. Luckily, she has all the project management skills I lack and was an indispensable partner at every stage.

ABOUT THE AUTHOR

The *Wall Street Journal* recently ranked Gary Hamel as the world's most influential business thinker, and *Fortune* magazine has called him "the world's leading expert on business strategy."

Hamel's landmark books, *Leading the Revolution* and *Competing for the Future* (coauthored with CK Prahalad), have appeared on every management bestseller list and have been translated into more than 20 languages. His last book, *The Future of Management*, was selected by Amazon.com as the best business book of the year.

Over the past twenty years, Hamel has authored 17 articles for the *Harvard Business Review* and is the most reprinted author in the *Review*'s history. He has also written for the *Wall Street Journal*, *Fortune*, *The Financial Times*, and many other leading publications around the world.

Hamel is on the faculty of the London Business School, where he is currently Visiting Professor of Strategic and International Management.

As a consultant and management educator, Hamel has worked with many of the world's leading corporations. His pioneering concepts such as "strategic intent," "core competence," "industry revolution," and "management innovation" have changed the practice of management in companies around the world.

Hamel speaks frequently at the world's most prestigious management conferences and is a regular contributor to CNBC, CNN, and other major media outlets. He has also advised government leaders on matters of innovation policy, entrepreneurship, and industrial competitiveness.

At present, Hamel is leading the world's first open innovation project aimed at reinventing management. The Management Innovation Exchange (www.managementexchange.com) has been designed to radically accelerate the evolution of management knowledge and practice.

Hamel is a Fellow of the World Economic Forum and the Strategic Management Society. He lives in Northern California and can be reached at ghamel@managementlab.org.

INDEX

Control (*Continued*)
accountability and low, 158–159;
reinventing means of, 247–248;
stifling creativity with, 235;
tension between freedom and,
189–191
Cooperation within communities,
160–161
Cox, Christopher, 17, 18
Creativity: inspiring, 248; spotting
trends in, 121–122; substituting
resources for, 108
Crosby, Sidney, 46
CrossPad, 73
Csikzentmihalyi, Mihaly, 43
Customers: Apple's attraction to, 76;
benefits of "employees first,
customers second", 236;
exceeding expectations of, 78,
80; product value and price
matched to, 80–81; providing
good design for, 56–59;
responses to bad and good
design, 55–57; solving unspoken
needs of, 68–72; toxic business
assumptions about, 32
Cyborgs of innovation, 50–51

D

Dawkins, Richard, 92, 93
de Klerk, F.W., 24
De Tocqueville, Alexis, 92
Decentralizing: control, 163–169;
management, 203. *See also*
Collaborative decision-making
Defensive thinking, 107
Dell, 125
Denial: guarding against, 98–100;
seen in U.S. banking crisis,
16–18
Depoliticizing decision making, 251
Design: aligning with stewardship, 57;
impact of bad and good, 55–56;
indicators of good, 56–57
Diagnosing decline: companies in
decline, 103–104; death of
business strategies, 105–106;

physical laws applicable to
decline, 104–105
Dialectic thinking, 123–124
Disney, 67–68
Dissent: allowing right to, 196; building
foundation of trust, 198;
encouraging, 252; finding
like-minded individuals for, 175
Distributed leadership model, 195–197,
198–199
Diversity, 123, 248
Dodd-Frank Act, 6

E

Economic downturn: complexity of
mortgages in, 12; costs of
corporate failures in, 113–116;
declining customer service in,
80–81; HCLT's growth in,
234–235; lack of values
culminating in, 13–15; U.S.
banking crisis and, 9–11,
255–256. *See also* U.S. banking
crisis
Edelman Trust Barometer, 146
Eden, Sue, 164–165
Education models, 101–102
EMI, 103
Employees: advantages of
self-management, 222–225;
allowing right to dissent, 175,
196, 198, 252; Colleague Letter
of Understanding for, 213–215,
219; creating value to customers,
235–236; cultivating passion for
customers, 168; encouraging
team initiative, 223; engagement
of, 36, 138–139; expanding
autonomy of, 163–169,
216–217, 230; financial
transparency with, 236; growth
in self-management
organizations, 226; hierarchy of
human capabilities in, 150–151;
innovation processes lacking for,
52; investing in innovation skills
for, 63–64; loyalty of Morning
Star, 225; making mission boss,